Jean Piaget and Neuchâtel

Jean Piaget is widely acknowledged as one of the most important scholars of the twentieth century. His passionate philosophical search for an understanding of the nature of knowledge led him to make major contributions to the study of child development and epistemology. But how did his early life in Neuchâtel inspire him to embark on this search?

Taking a socio-historical and cultural perspective, this book outlines the development of Piaget's understanding of major issues regarding mind, faith, science, logic, peace, and social rights in a time of anxiety and world wars. The international and multidisciplinary contributors investigate Piaget the adolescent as he begins his quest for autonomy of reason and sets out to create his own explanatory system for cognitive growth. The latter part of the book goes on to consider the early reception of Piaget's work in different cultural contexts and his impact on issues of psychology and educational reform.

Piaget's theoretical system can be seen as an expression of the values he developed during his childhood and adolescence as he searched for the conditions of reciprocal relationships and rational dialogues. *Jean Piaget and Neuchâtel* demonstrates that in today's climate, the questions Piaget addressed remain very relevant and invite new enquiries from different standpoints. This book will therefore be of interest to psychologists, educators, and philosophers.

Anne-Nelly Perret-Clermont is Professor at the University of Neuchâtel. Her main areas of interest are the social psychology of cognitive development, the transmission of knowledge, and the transition from youth to adulthood. She has also been awarded the National Latsis Prize by the Swiss National Science Foundation.

Jean-Marc Barrelet is a specialist in history of economy and social history of the nineteenth century. He was Archivist at the Record Office of Neuchâtel between 1988 and 2003. He has also edited many publications of the Canton of Neuchâtel.

Jean Piaget and Neuchâtel
The learner and the scholar

Edited by Anne-Nelly Perret-Clermont
and Jean-Marc Barrelet

Psychology Press
Taylor & Francis Group
HOVE AND NEW YORK

swiss arts council
prohelvetia

First published in French as *Jean Piaget et Neuchâtel: l'apprenti et le savant*
by les Editions Payot Lausanne

French language edition © 1996 Editions Payot Lausanne

First published 2008
by Psychology Press
27 Church Road, Hove, East Sussex BN3 2FA

Simultaneously published in the USA and Canada
by Psychology Press
270 Madison Avenue, New York NY 10016

*Psychology Press is an imprint of the Taylor & Francis Group,
an Informa business*

© 2008 Psychology Press

Typeset in Times by RefineCatch Limited, Bungay, Suffolk
Printed and bound in Great Britain by
TJ International Ltd, Padstow, Cornwall
Cover design by Lisa Dynan

The publication has been produced with paper manufactured to strict
environmental standards and with pulp derived from sustainable
forests.

British Library Cataloguing in Publication Data
A catalogue record for this book is available from the British Library

Library of Congress Cataloging-in-Publication Data
Jean Piaget et Neuchâtel. English
    Jean Piaget and Neuchâtel : the learner and the scholar / edited by
Anne-Nelly Perret-Clermont & Jean-Marc Barrelet.
        p. cm.
    Includes bibliographical references.
    ISBN 978-1-84169-657-7 (hardback)
    1. Piaget, Jean, 1896-1980. 2. Neuchâtel (Switzerland : Canton) –
Intellectual life – 20th century. I. Perret-Clermont, Anne Nelly. II.
Barrelet, Jean-Marc. III. Title.
    BF109.P5J4313 2007
    155.4′13092 – dc22
                                                            2007021226

ISBN: 978-1-84169-657-7

Contents

Contributors

Jean-Marc Barrelet is Archivist at the Archives of the State of Neuchâtel, Neuchâtel, Switzerland.

Sylvie Béguelin is Manuscripts Curator at the Bibliothèque de la Ville de La Chaux-de-Fonds, Neuchâtel.

Jean-Jacques Ducret is Scientific Researcher at the Service de la Recherche en Education du Canton de Genève, Switzerland.

Daniel Hameline is Honorary Professor at the Faculté de Psychologie et des Sciences de l'Education, University of Geneva, Switzerland.

Jean-Pierre Jelmini is a historian and Director of the Institut Neuchâtelois, Neuchâtel.

Marie-Jeanne Liengme Bessire is Research Associate at the Institute of Psychology and Education, University of Neuchâtel.

Jürgen Oelkers is Professor at the Pädagogisches Institut, University of Zurich, Switzerland.

Anne-Nelly Perret-Clermont is Professor at the Institute of Psychology and Education, University of Neuchâtel.

John Rijsman is Professor at the Faculty of Social Sciences, Tilburg University, The Netherlands.

Carlo Robert-Grandpierre is Philosopher at the Haute Ecole Pédagogique, Porrentruy, Switzerland.

Jean-Paul Schaer is Honorary Professor at the Institute of Geology and Hydrogeology, University of Neuchâtel.

Anne-Françoise Schaller-Jeanneret is a historian at the University of Neuchâtel.

Charles Thomann is Honorary Professor at the Ecole supérieure de commerce, La Chaux-de-Fonds.

Maurice de Tribolet is Cantonal Archivist, Archives of the State of Neuchâtel.

René van der Veer is Professor, Social and Behavioural Sciences, University of Leiden, The Netherlands.

Fernando Vidal is Senior Research Scholar at the Max Planck Institute for the History of Science, Berlin, Germany.

Tania Zittoun is Junior Associate Professor at the Faculty of Psychology, University of Lausanne, Switzerland.

Acknowledgements

We would like to thank Claude Béguin, Vanessa Bille, Sandra Geiser, Olivier Girardbille, Janine Gremaud, Mireille Nardo, Laurent Piaget, Patricia Rey, Maryse Schmidt-Surdez, the Jean Piaget Archives, Alexandra Bugnon and Yannick D'Ascoli for their help.

We thank David Jemielitly for his translation of Chapter 6. We are grateful to Martha Ritchie for her work with most of the translation, and Kate Schrago for her contribution. Our gratitude goes also to Athena Sargent for her patience in proofreading. But as editors we have taken responsibility for the ultimate form of the translation of this book, as we wanted to privilege the scientific aspects over the literary ones.

Our sincere gratitude to the institutions that provided financial support:

Pro Helvetia, Swiss Arts Council

The State of Neuchâtel

Faculté des Lettres et Sciences Humaines de l'Université de Neuchâtel

Preface

The first edition of this work appreared in French in 1996 while we were celebrating the centenary of Jean Piaget's birth in Neuchâtel, his native city, and at whose university he took up his first professorial position. This book is neither a laudatory description nor a biography that relates the actions and the intellectual course of the savant. The latter has already been skilfully done, and Piaget's scientific contribution is still being translated, evaluated, analysed, and reconsidered.[1] The intention is not to 'explain' Piaget, even less to discern his career as determined by social or personal destiny.

Our aim is otherwise: we hope, above all, to reconstruct the historical context, in the broad sense of the term, that gave birth to Jean Piaget's thinking. We have tried to recreate the 'climate' that favoured his learning and intellectual curiosity about everything relating to knowledge. Certainly there is a great part of personal genius involved, but his work is also very much the result of a process, that of growing up in a particular social and cultural milieu – in a culture medium, to borrow a biological metaphor. Certainly Piaget would have enjoyed such a metaphor taken from biology, the discipline in which he prepared his doctoral thesis. Yet our perspective here is another one. We want to borrow a historical cultural perspective from another psychologist, born in Russia on the same year – Lev Vygotsky. We will consider Piaget's activities as an adolescent, growing up to become a man of his time in close interaction with younger and older people within precise cultural and institutional settings marked by habits, values, goals, and legacies of identifiable conflicts and stakes.

Who crafted this socio-cultural milieu; who are the co-authors, the partners, the questioners at the source of Jean Piaget's early career? What events, what ideas confronted him? Against the background of the specific historical–cultural setting of Neuchâtel we will look at his family, their social life, his education and schooling, his interests as a student at university, his friendships, and his participation in groups such as the Society of the Young Friends of Nature (Amici Naturae), in Christian circles, and at scientific gatherings. The first part of this book is given to his years in Neuchâtel in the first quarter of the twentieth century – decisive years for Piaget's future. If we focus on the roots of his socialization, it is to understand how much of Piaget's endeavours stemmed from his first questions as an adolescent and how much is owed to the richness of the intellectual and emotional interactions he experienced in his native country at a time of vivid religious, scientific, and political debates.

In the second part of the book we will try to 'zoom out' of Neuchâtel and see how Piaget succeeded in placing himself on the international scene at the centre of a stream of questions that sprang to life in the second half of the nineteenth century, particularly in the social sciences. Piaget was very quickly recognized as a valid interlocutor in a great number of disciplines – pedagogy, logic, philosophy, and sociology, as well as child psychology. From his first writings in the second decade of the twentieth century, Piaget was present in the debates. Notably, as early as the 1920s Vygotsky published a translation into Russian of one of Piaget's early books.

The authors of the second part show us how Piaget figures in the intellectual network of his day. Behind the birth of psychology as a science lies the work of the Russian physiologist Ivan Pavlov and that of Wilhelm Wundt, who founded the first laboratory of experimental psychology in Germany. Psychology also has its roots in the new approach to madness – or, rather, the unconscious – in psychiatry with Sigmund Freud in Vienna and Carl Jung in Zurich. Finding part of their inspiration in theories coming from North America, the newly born paediatrics 'reinvented' the role of infancy and turned towards psychological conditions in education: Maria Montessori in Rome, Ovide Decroly in Brussels, Edouard Claparède in Geneva, where he founded the Jean-Jacques Rousseau Institute with Pierre Bovet as co-director, and then Jean Piaget. Public education, now compulsory, faced administrative problems that left their mark on the new psychology, notably via Alfred Binet's efforts to build a test to assess intelligence in order to detect children with severe difficulties. It was in Binet's laboratory that Jean Piaget carried out his first studies in child psychology, at the instigation of Theodore Simon. Back in Switzerland, Piaget no doubt remembered the psychoanalytic debates he engaged in as a student in Zurich and pursued for a while with Sabina Spielrein in Geneva, pondering upon the young child's pseudo-autistic behaviour and early egocentrism. Invited by Claparède to organize research on matters relevant for education, Piaget recalled the connections between logic and the development of knowledge proposed by his Neuchâtel professor, the philosopher Arnold Reymond, and his own experiences in the youth movement founded in Neuchâtel by Pierre Bovet, a fervent Christian and a reader, like himself, of William James.

Scientific minds of the time were interested in the relationship of the individual to society, the evolution of the species and the growth of knowledge, and the respective roles of nature and nurture. Europe was in contact with its colonies and fascinated by the diversity of humankind. It had also been at the centre of the First World War. Piaget was a child of a complex era, in a deep quest to find meaning to life and society. He tried out his own answers. The reception of his work was quite diverse: As shown here by Daniel Hameline, there are many avatars of our hero.

Jean Piaget's intellectual itinerary

Jean Piaget was born on 9 August 1896 in Neuchâtel, the small capital city of a republic and Swiss canton that lies at the foot of the Jura mountain range. He was raised in a milieu of cultural and religious values that were often in conflict.[2] School was easy for Jean and left him time for outside activities. His early passion for the natural sciences was soon noticed and cultivated by attentive and supportive researchers and professors. Piaget made a number of friends among like-minded students; he was also interested in the social Christianity preached by the pastor Paul Pettavel from La Chaux-de-Fonds, another intellectual, economic, and artistic city in the Canton of Neuchâtel marked by union activities. Piaget's early publications bear witness to this double passion for scientific matters and for philosophical and religious ideas.

Piaget seems to have carried out his studies at the Faculty of Sciences at the University of Neuchâtel with the attitude of a dilettante, while at the same time following subjects taught in other faculties. His delicate health required him to make frequent visits to the Alps, where he took the opportunity to collect molluscs, which provided the primary material for his doctoral thesis. It was somewhat short, but the number of works that he had already published had given him a solid reputation among specialists.

Trained as a biologist, Piaget was preoccupied with the philosophy of science and the relationship between knowledge and belief. He often spoke of himself as having made a detour via psychology and its new methods to address the central question of epistemology. Thus, it is perhaps in spite of himself that he is known today above all as a psychologist and a pedagogist.

After his solid education at Neuchâtel, Piaget went on to study in Zurich and in Paris. He found himself at the crossroads of French and German culture, as epitomized by Immanuel Kant and Henri Bergson, and also Sigmund Freud and Léon Brunschvicg. As Jean-Jacques Ducret suggests, Piaget got involved in child psychology research not only because it offered him the possibility to investigate his philosophical questions empirically, but also, to some extent, in order to verify the hypotheses of his master, Arnold Reymond.

Geneva, where Piaget settled in 1921, was to become the place where he did most of his work, with temporary appointments in Neuchâtel, Lausanne, and Paris. He returned to his native city to teach philosophy, history of science, psychology, and sociology from 1925 to 1929. In the French capital, from where his maternal ancestors had come, he first worked in Binet's laboratory. Much later, in 1942, he returned to Paris to teach at the Collège de France, and in 1952 he replaced Maurice Merleau-Ponty as the chair of philosophy at the Sorbonne.

But Geneva remained Piaget's operating base. After Edouard Claparède and Pierre Bovet, founders of the Jean-Jacques Rousseau Institute, he became head of the institute, a role he fulfilled thanks to the help of his co-directors, the eminent pedagogues and compatriots Samuel Roller and Laurent Pauli, from La Chaux-de-Fonds in Canton Neuchâtel. As of 1929, Piaget held the chair of history of scientific thought at the University of Geneva, where he also taught experimental psychology, and from 1939 to 1952 he assumed the chair of sociology. In 1929 he became president of the International Office of Education. In 1936 he also taught experimental psychology and sociology in Lausanne. In Geneva he founded an International Centre for Genetic Epistemology in 1955. The creation of this original and multidisciplinary laboratory marked a new start in his impressive scientific career that would last 25 more years and would produce a large number of publications. It is important to note how his work was sustained internationally. He received crucial research funding from the Rockefeller Foundation; with discretion and efficiency, Jerome Bruner[3] participated in making it possible for Piaget to pursue his work.[4]

Given the abundance and diversity of Piaget's work, it cannot be summarized. Yet it is rooted in one major question that prevails throughout, a question that Piaget takes over from Kant: 'How is knowledge possible?' Piaget tries to answer it via an empirical observation of how knowledge develops.[5] His writings, covering some 70 years of work, have been widely disseminated and have had a considerable impact, with numerous translations in all major languages; they are used as reference works in universities and laboratories worldwide.[6] Controversial at times, yet for the most part admired, Piaget received more that 30 titles of doctor *honoris causa* and was awarded many prizes, among which were the Erasmus Prize in 1972 and the Balzan Prize in 1980. The Foundation of the Jean Piaget Archives[7] in Geneva still receives books and articles related to his work.

The promoter of a system

Jean Piaget appears clearly as a man of continuity, faithful to a coherent system, who patiently and laboriously stays within a groove, which he follows in earnest while making use of collaborators to construct a clearly specified work. From his first essays on molluscs to his most brilliant and fully elaborated works on the development of human intelligence, Piaget remained dominated by a single idea, expressed in multiple ways; he was faithful in that respect to the lessons of Bergson.

Piaget could, however, appear disconcerting, for there were so many paths he explored. As it was for Piaget himself, it is necessary for his readers to look for the *system* that underlay the abundance. He described his epistemology as structuralist. One would like to call him a philosopher, but he had a major conflict with treating philosophers as 'wise men', refusing to grant any scientific credibility to writings that were not based on experimentation. Only the logicians among them stayed in contact with Piaget, although it was a somewhat tense contact.

Is Piaget a psychologist, then? Yes, but psychology for him was only a way to approach epistemological questions. As René Van der Veer tells it, Russian psychologists were attentive to his work, yet they reproached him for not giving greater importance to social factors. Indeed, Piaget did not show much concern with social realities (even while teaching sociology), and he left the field of psychoanalysis early in his career.

Nor is Piaget really a pedagogue. He maintained an ambiguous attitude towards education. Working for the International Bureau of Education and often referred to as a theorist of the New Education, he wished – paradoxically? – to study the child's thinking free of all external influences, in particular that of school, as Jürgen Oelkers writes here. Nevertheless, Piaget contributed greatly to progress in pedagogy: His theories and stages of development of the child's intelligence have been used by others to modernize schools and teaching practices for the benefit of children's pleasure to learn and of mutual understanding between adult and child.

Twenty-five years after his death, it is still difficult to make a precise assessment of the multifaceted impact that Piaget has had on our scientific culture: 'Piaget's work continues to be well regarded. Beilin[8] reckoned that his influence on Developmental Psychology was comparable to that of Shakespeare on English.'[9]

Jean-Marc Barrelet
Anne-Nelly Perret-Clermont

Notes

1 See, for instance, the latest translation: J. Piaget (2006) Reason [translated and commentary by Leslie Smith]. *New Ideas in Psychology*, *24*, 1–29. Of interest also for an appraisal of the present debates around Jean Piaget in English: L. Smith (1992) *Jean Piaget: Critical assessments*. London: Routledge.

2 N. L. Perret (2006) *Croyant et citoyen dans un Etat moderne. La douloureuse négociation du statut des églises issues de la Réforme à Neuchâtel, 1848–1943*. Neuchâtel, Ed. Messeiller.

3 It is interesting to note the key role played by the same J. S. Bruner in the 'rediscovery' of Vygotsky's major contribution to psychology.

4 The story of Piaget's relationships with Geneva and Switzerland is still to be written. He made himself *persona non grata* in some academic circles after the publication of his polemical book *Insights and Illusions of Philosophy* (New York: The World Publishing Company, 1971). He disappointed Pierre Bovet's expectations to see him expand educational research in concrete ways. He might have felt a lonely prophet in his country as we remember his joy and his words when he announced to his students in 1970 that an international organization named the Jean Piaget Society had been established to explore the nature of the developmental construction of human knowledge.

5 L. Smith (1993) *Necessary knowledge* (pp. 35ff.). Hove, UK: Lawrence Erlbaum Associates.

6 M. Cole, S. Cole, & C. Lightfoot (2005) *The development of children* (5th ed.).

New York: Worth Publishing. H. Beilin (1992) Piaget's enduring contribution to developmental psychology. *Developmental Psychology, 28,* 191–204. E. Scholnick (1999) *Piaget's legacy: Heirs to the house that Jean built.* In E. Scholnick, K. Nelson, S. Gelman, & P. Miller (Eds.), *Conceptual development: Piaget's legacy.* Mahwah, NJ: Lawrence Erlbaum Associates, Inc. L. Smith (2002) Piaget's model. In U. Goswami (Ed.), *Blackwell Handbook of Childhood Cognitive Development:* Oxford: Blackwell. For further updated references, see the website of the Jean Piaget Society: www.piaget.org.
7 The Jean Piaget Archives, Uni-Mail, 40 Blvd du Pont d'Arve, 1205 Geneva, Switzerland. Website: www.unige.ch/piaget.
8 Beilin, op. cit.
9 L. Smith, personal communication.

Part I
Growing up in Neuchâtel

1 Neuchâtel

Jean-Marc Barrelet

Neuchâtel, a stimulating microcosm

It would perhaps be too bold to speak of a sense of a Neuchâtel identity to evoke the origins of Jean Piaget's body of work, because he always declared the universality of science. However, it was he who would often lay claim to his origins and the importance of one's roots. In effect, the canton of Neuchâtel did not constitute a unique cultural entity with well-defined contours even though, in the French-speaking part of Switzerland, it was a region that was well distinguished from the others. Its history, for example, places it outside all known situations in Switzerland as well as in Europe. Neuchâtel had already been spared from wars, and its geographical placement made it a transitional place between France and the Swiss plateau, as well as between the Swiss Germans and the Swiss Romands (French speakers).

Although Neuchâtel was situated at a distance from the main centres of communication, it had always depended on other regions, either politically (at least until the revolution of 1848) or economically. Even at an early point in its history, Neuchâtel had been dominated by French families during the Renaissance, followed by the Hohenzollern of Prussia from 1707 to 1848 (with the exception of the Napoleonic interlude). Neuchâtel saw early that its destiny lay with the bigger European nations. As of the eighteenth century, the economic prosperity of the population depended on the export of manufactured goods, such as painted canvases, lace, and watches and clocks.

If not by nature, it was at least by necessity that the people of Neuchâtel were avid for exchanges with the outside world. They had a keen understanding of the importance of fine craftsmanship and technical expertise in the value of goods. It was not long before watchmakers demanded high-quality schools and teachers. Used to international trade and travel, the people of Neuchâtel would return home from their journeys with a wealth of knowledge of foreign civilizations, and contemporaries of Piaget, such as Blaise Cendrars and Le Corbusier, were not exempt from wanderlust.

This openness to the outside world, however, did not necessarily lead to an openness of the mind. On the contrary, a narrow conservatism and a desire to turn inwards would remain a part of the Neuchâtel mentality. The people of this region would continue to possess a provincial character and fervently adhere to the cultural particularities of the region. But was not that true elsewhere in Switzerland?

At the beginning of the twentieth century, Neuchâtel was a microcosm that, despite its small size, sheltered extraordinarily rich cultural and scientific activity, the mystery of which we are incapable of elucidating in this work. How could we explain this generation, which, over such a brief period of time, generated so much talent and originality? Along with Jean Piaget and the above-mentioned Cendrars and Le Corbusier, there were the Nobel physicist, Charles-Edouard Guillaume, the writer Denis de Rougemont, and the literary critic and editor Albert Béguin. While Neuchâtel was not large enough to contain men of such stature, the area was no stranger to their flowering.

It would perhaps be pretentious to assume an exemplary spirit on the part of the people of Neuchâtel when, during the same period, the whole of French-speaking Switzerland was producing exceptional innovators. In fact, the Neuchâtel 'exception' flowed into other areas of French-speaking Switzerland, as described so well by Alfred Berchtold.[1] How can such effervescence be explained if not by the tensions that existed throughout all of Swiss society? At the beginning of the twentieth century, as Victor Hugo commented, Switzerland had definitely put an end to 'milking their cows and living in peace'.

In spite of its relative isolation, Neuchâtel had a thirst for great, and sometimes passionate, debates that animated political, social, and cultural life at the beginning of the century. Living in Neuchâtel since the middle of the 1890s, the Piaget family's life was centred on conflicts between religious and ideological order, which created strong spirits.

Youth in Neuchâtel

Amid a rich and active circle of relations, young Jean Piaget quickly demonstrated his unique qualities as a brilliant student, dominating his class with his exceptionally knowledgeable and creative intellect. He thus distinguished himself as someone out of the ordinary whose keen interests in the natural sciences, his curiosity, even his rebelliousness, set him apart as a leader. There were, of course, other young people from similar backgrounds, such as the future theologian Maurice Zundel and the mathematician Gustave Juvet. These young people met and confronted one another in epic oratorical contests at the Club of the Friends of Nature.

Piaget completed flawless, if not brilliant, studies, while at the same time pursuing interests outside the normal course of study. He entered university with an already impressive number of publications and scientific discoveries. His thesis, a minor work compared to the totality of the publications from his youth, was accepted upon simple request without having to be defended; it was as if the university authorities had tacitly admitted that Piaget's scientific interests placed him outside the normal academic sphere.

Piaget, the fervent young Christian, followed an unusual path marked by his ardent writings, which were later lost in his scientific psychology works. His adolescent faith was one of a tormented soul seeking truth by frantically searching throughout philosophical and religious texts. Young Piaget was not indifferent to his immediate surroundings or to the world, and he left a strong mark wherever he went. He vacillated between science and philosophy and never ceased trying to deepen their relationship; he was divided between faith and reason, and in fact he bore a resemblance to many adolescents. What distinguishes him, perhaps, is the quality of his thought and his desire to embrace all acquired knowledge and to express his ideas over hundreds of pages that would never be published. It was already evident at the time that this young man's goal was to create a system.

The image that we traditionally hold of Jean Piaget as an austere and rigorous scholar does not fit with that of an adolescent impassioned by social and humanitarian causes. He was, indeed, an original figure in a town characterized by conformism.

Certainly, the life of Jean Piaget and his contemporaries in Neuchâtel cannot be compared to that of Sigmund Freud in Vienna, who said that he launched himself into a scientific career as a result of exclusion caused by anti-Semitism.

The family of Jean Piaget, whose father was a brilliant and esteemed intellectual and the first rector of the university as well as the first State Archivist, was not banished by society. However, like many original thinkers, could the Piagets be considered victims of a certain ostracism and miscomprehension on the part of the bourgeois society, who rejected any sort of self-questioning and critical thinking?

The scientific works of Arthur Piaget were looked down upon when he called a certain intellectual comfort into question and upset local myths. Rebecca Piaget's religious involvement in evangelical circles did not prevent her from taking a militant position on women's suffrage or sitting on the town's school committee for the Socialist Party. These activities are what makes one stand out in a provincial society comprising numerous distinct and closed circles, but paradoxically rich with its 'margins', with its intellectual fermentation, and with its presence of immigrants. The canton knew how to welcome political refugees such as the Fribourgeois, Alexander Daguet, a Republican from a Catholic canton, or adversaries of Napoleon III such as Ferdinand Buisson, and later the fleeing Communards.

Neuchâtel at the turn of the twentieth century

A small town of 20,000 inhabitants in 1900, Neuchâtel was often described as a bourgeois university town and was contrasted with La Chaux-de-Fonds, the watchmaking town situated in the mountains of Neuchâtel which had a population of 33,000 people. In the 1940s the writer Guy de Pourtalès described the town during the period of Piaget's youth with tender irony:

Neuchâtel is not an important Swiss town. It is located at a distance from the main thoroughfares of the country. Furthermore, its once flourishing wine producing and watch making activities have been severely weakened by economic crises and wars. Depleted and consequently excluded from the trade and commerce circuit, the little principality slowly went to sleep. It is a city of students and retired folk, of those who never took flight and those who did, but who return only to die in a calm place.[2]

What else could one do in the canton of Neuchâtel but delve into the study of science or make watches? Although it can be said that this member of the Swiss Confederation cultivated its differences, it was not completely separate from the rest of the world. It was subjected to the ideological, cultural, and scientific influences that spread across Europe prior to the Great War of 1914–1918. In fact, Neuchâtel formed a microcosm representing all currents stirring the Western world at the turn of the twentieth century; from the most conservative to the most revolutionary, from the most conformist to the most modernist in political, artistic, and cultural areas.

The monumental caricature in the stairwell of the Fine Arts Museum of Neuchâtel, painted by Léo-Paul Robert, depicts the canton of Neuchâtel divided into two distinct worlds: the world of work in the hills, where the commercial and industrial towns of Le Locle and La Chaux-de-Fonds were situated, and the world of the lakeside, where the intellectuals, the wine-growers, and the retired could be found. Even today, the region is divided in this way and offers a great diversity of landscape, activities, and mentalities.

Dominated by the watchmaking industry since the middle of the nineteenth century, the economy underwent several profound mutations beginning in the 1880s. It evolved from being spread out and artisanal to becoming industrial with the development of small factories that brought in a concentration of the population. This led to an urbanization that had been unknown up to then. If Neuchâtel saw rapid transformation and development, La Chaux-de-Fonds soon began to appear as a town of the future with an original and modernist urbanization resembling an American city more than a medieval village.

The industrialization and modernization of the economic structures led to tensions and new social divisions. According to an expression coined by François Walter,[3] pre-ecological sentiments were born at the beginning of the century. The Heimatschutz (the Swiss League for the Protection of a Picturesque Switzerland) was founded in 1905; the Naturschutz (the Swiss League for the Protection of Nature) in 1909. The Alps – where Piaget loved working and hiking – became the symbol of an environment to be preserved from the ravages of modernization, and of tourism in particular.

In opposition to those who rejected progress and who sought refuge in an often mythologized past were the partisans of development, economically as well as culturally. There were those who feared the disappearance of old customs and the beginning of moral degradation, the destruction of the countryside and the reign of business and money, while others welcomed a new mode of urban life based on materialism. In fact, these new contradictions spread throughout Switzerland, partly explaining the activities of the intellectuals and the emergence of new aesthetics.

Political life

In 1896, the year in which Jean Piaget was born, the political life of Neuchâtel was calm compared to the tumultuous years preceding and following the Revolution of 1848. The Republican regime was no longer questioned, and the political parties confronted one another only during electoral periods. A certain consensus was established between the two large rival bourgeois political factions.

The Radical Party, originating from revolutionary republican movements, often joined forces with the more traditional and conservative Liberal Party. Basically, the only issues dividing them were those concerning the Confederation and the politics of centralization: The Radical Party wanted a strong centralized Swiss government, whereas the liberals, who were more federalist, wanted to protect the autonomy of the cantons and preserve regional differences.

In fact, this alliance between the two parties was consolidated out of fear of the rising Socialist movement, which could be observed especially in the watchmaking towns of the Neuchâtel Mountains. It was thus more of a marriage of reason than of love that united the ruling classes of the canton, who did not necessarily share the same vision of society but who preferred to work together in order to avoid stirring up conflicts from the not too distant past.

Political writings that contributed to a spirit of unity were preferred over scientific debates and ideological discussions. At least, that is what Jean Piaget's father learned when the Radicals chose the eminent liberal, Philippe Godet, over a history critic to write a piece entitled *Neuchâtel-Suisse* for the 50th anniversary of the revolution.

The politics of unity remained more of a façade than anything representative of profound convictions. The Radical Party found its support in the *petit bourgeois* merchants, in the middle-class bureaucrats, in certain business circles, and among small industrialists and the liberal professions. It continued to refer to the revolution of 1848 and to a certain republican and democratic spirit. Secular and often Freemason, the Radical Party willingly affirmed patriotism and nationalistic values when defending the interests of the new Swiss Confederation and its institutions. This party provided Switzerland with prestigious ministers such as Numa Droz and Robert Comtesse.

Geographically, the Radical Party had its roots in the towns and the industrial areas of the state. It exerted its unilateral power until 1892, when proportional representation was introduced and the conservatives received a share of control. The Radicals were present in all the various sectors of society: the sharp-shooting clubs, the choirs, and the gymnastic organizations. They organized patriotic festivals, such as the 50th anniversary of the Republic in 1898, because their political rivals had little esteem for such ceremonies.

The Liberal Party recruited its members among the *haute bourgeoisie*, in the liberal professions, of course, but also among the farmers, the wine growers, and the retired. Founded in 1873, the Liberal Democratic Association was essentially rooted in the lower part of the canton, although it counted on numerous supporters in the upper towns and in certain localities where the population remained attached to traditional values that the Radical Republic had eliminated in 1888, namely the old-moneyed classes. Before 1848, being bourgeois meant belonging to a privileged part of the population who benefited from additional rights recognized by the prince. Because the Liberal Party was a movement of moderate and conservative republicans, it also welcomed partisans of the *Ancien Régime*.

In fact, the patricians of Neuchâtel joined ranks with the moderate republicans only after the unsuccessful Royalist counterrevolution of 1856, which ended with the Treaty of Paris in which the King of Prussia definitively renounced his rights to his former principality. This aristocratic circle merits more study, because it had a significant influence on the social and cultural life of the town of Neuchâtel, where the Piaget family lived.

Having lost their political power, the patricians initially isolated themselves and then went on to exert their leadership role in charity, art, and cultural patronage. They cultivated their separateness and stayed in their closed circle, the Garden Society (also called 'the Chamber'), which was founded in 1759. It included all the Neuchâtel nobility and certain industrial families they had chosen. These noble families, who had titles, residences in the city, and beautiful properties in the country, were of independent means for the most part. Their most illustrious members had diplomatic careers or served abroad; many others were gentlemen farmers. As Guy de Pourtalès, a privileged observer, noted:

> The residences of Neuchâtel's high society could be found, for the most part, grouped together next to one another along the Faubourg. I had relatives and cousins residing there and was often invited to a formal luncheon or a lavish Sunday dinner. The feasts were usually followed by a game of skittles at the noble circle of *The Chamber* where retired military officers laid aside their frock-coats and with great seriousness, tossed balls and recounted their military stories. The older ones among them would recall their exploits during the thwarted Royalist revolution of 1856.[4]

For a family like the Piagets, entry into this exclusive circle was impossible, despite their frequent contact with professors, doctors, and theologians. This aristocracy remained valuable to the city as it contributed greatly to maintaining charitable institutions, hospitals, museums, works of art, libraries, and even religious institutions such as the Independent Church, which was financed entirely by private donations. Thus, political unity masked deep social divisions between the 'old people of Neuchâtel' and a whole other part of the population that did not necessarily take part in cultivating local roots and felt they belonged more to Switzerland than to the old country.

At the other extreme there emerged a frightening pacifist and internationalist socialist movement. The Socialist Party of Neuchâtel originated in the 1880s and developed mainly in La Chaux-de-Fonds among the watch industry workers, some of whom had been involved in the anarchist movement led by James Guillaume. The gap between the left and the right began to widen, and a major strike broke out among masons in La Chaux-de-Fonds in 1904. The government mobilized troops and occupied the town. The Socialist Party, however, remained relatively marginal until the war of 1914–1918, despite electoral successes in the working-class mountain towns of Neuchâtel. Its policies, namely its pacifist position and its leaders' campaign against alcoholism, drew it close to the Social Christians in whom Jean Piaget showed an interest. The Protestant Church was also divided, but it had nourished the socialist movement, especially through the emblematic figure of Jules Humbert-Droz, a pastor who left Neuchâtel in the 1920s in order to join the Third International in Moscow.

The strength of the state's three principal political movements was reflected in the Grand Council's (cantonal legislative assembly) 1904 election results. The Radicals dominated with 62 candidates elected, followed by the Liberals with 32 deputies, and, lastly, the Socialists, who obtained 15 seats.

Religious life

Reformed since the sixteenth century, the Protestant church of Neuchâtel participated fully in power until 1848. The Reform had been introduced as of 1530 by Guillaume Farel, a pastor who came from Gap in Dauphiné. Supported by the powerful state of Bern, it gained enough momentum to impose itself throughout the principality with the exception of three small communes in the western part of the state.

In the sixteenth century Neuchâtel even became an important centre for the distribution of Reform literature due to the presence of Pierre de Vingle, a French printer established in Neuchâtel since 1533. From that period, the Venerable Class – which meant the society of pastors – had a monopoly on education and exerted a very strong influence on the social and cultural life of the principality, even though it remained in the hands of a Catholic family, the Orléans-Longuevilles. In 1707 the ministers welcomed the passage of power to a Protestant prince and showed themselves to be the strongest guarantors against any change.

As of 1848 'the Class' was also confronted with conflicts and contradictions, such as those of pietist or rationalist pastors, who even went so far as to question certain dogma.

With the revolution of 1848 the ecclesiastical administration passed into the hands of the state and the Church was 'nationalized' and democratized. Its pastors were henceforth elected by the parishes. Twenty-five years later, this secularized Church split apart.

In the domain of religious institutions, Neuchâtel was comparable to other Reformed cantons of the French-speaking part of Switzerland. This was primarily due to ruptures that occurred in the Protestant Church during the second half of the nineteenth century with the appearance of the Awakening and the creation of the Free Evangelical Church.

According to Philippe H. Menoud,[5] in the nineteenth century the Church of Neuchâtel possessed three characteristics: It was national and autonomous because it wanted to have hegemony over the whole of the population while at the same time remaining entirely independent; it was clerical, governed by a group of pastors; it was evangelical, preaching unity of doctrine that limited any liberal tendencies.

Introduced through the teachings of Ferdinand Buisson (1841–1932), from the 1860s liberal thinking progressed rapidly within the parishes of the region and profoundly divided the Church of Neuchâtel. Buisson, aggregate professor of philosophy, refused to give allegiance to Napoleon III and took refuge in Neuchâtel, where he was named professor at the Academy. It was there that he intervened in the debates that animated Protestantism at the time, taking a position against the profession of faith and for freedom of conscience. He also demanded that biblical history no longer be a part of the school programmes but be replaced by the history of the humanities. Having returned to France after the fall of the Empire, Buisson performed high functions alongside Jules Ferry. He left a strong mark on Neuchâtel and the French-speaking part of Switzerland, obliging men like Félix Bovet to place themselves somewhere between dogmatism and liberal ideas.

Two concepts of religion opposed one another and were at the root of the problem of separation of church and state advocated by the liberal wing. The ecclesiastic law of 1873 guaranteed pastors' freedom of conscience and, from that date on, their training was assured by the Academy and overseen by the state. However, the refusal of separation by the people led to the creation of the Evangelical Church of Neuchâtel, independent from the state. This was the church that Jean Piaget's mother attended.

In fact, this religious split was less absolute than it appeared; the two churches cooperated with one another, and both contained elements of liberal and social Christianity, for example, but the Independent Church wished to remain faithful to the traditions of the old church of Neuchâtel and to the dogma of 'the Holy Scriptures of the Old and the New Testament'.

The idea of separation resurfaced in 1907 on the occasion of a new popular vote. A sizeable heteroclite league pleaded for the cause of separation. Directed against the Radical Party, which was still hegemonic, and believing that the church should be serving the state, it regrouped all the extreme tendencies of the Political Exchequer: the socialist Charles Naine and the conservative Otto de Dardel; the agnostic Arthur Piaget; the social Christian, Pettavel; and even Pierre Bovet, who was a member of the National Church.

This episode shows the vigour of religious debate in the canton of Neuchâtel, a vigour from which the Piaget family did not escape. This form of active Protestantism, combined with Anglo-Saxon pragmatism, which gave primary importance to action, was present in the education of the future intellectual. The theories of William James, which were introduced to the French-speaking part of Switzerland by the Geneva-born psychologist Théodore Flournoy, were one of the references of Grandchamp and of Pierre Bovet.

The cultural circles

Young Piaget most certainly frequented the university, the library, and the Friends of Nature meetings more that the art museums, the literary circles, and the concert halls. He could not, however, completely escape these cultural groups, where many contradictory ideas and influences, some extremely conservative and others highly innovative, coexisted. These debates were sometimes confusing, as can be seen by examining the minutes of the Friends of Nature meetings; they must have attracted Piaget more than the art and literary discussions. In any case, at the university as well as in the street, art and literary discussions would not leave anyone completely indifferent, because within them many important social and political directions were at stake.

At the end of the nineteenth century, the arts in Neuchâtel were dominated by the figure of Philippe Godet (1850–1922), who was a literary critic and a professor at the Academy. He was especially known for his *Literary History of the French Speaking Part of Switzerland*, which appeared in 1890. A 'formidable polemicist' according to Alain Clavien,[6] Godet perfectly typified the liberal intellectual, haughty and suspicious, and an adversary of radicalism, which he considered ignobly utilitarian and materialistic.

In fact, Godet rose up against modernism and the mutations of an urban and industrial society. Thus, as Michel Schlup[7] noted, Godet did not hesitate to defend a moral and national art in order to denigrate 'systematically the avant-garde essays of the young writers attracted by foreign literary fashions'. Godet, founding member of the Heimatschutz, was fully part of this current of fear of modernity, as he would demonstrate in his combat against tourism, which was invading the Alpine valleys. Jean Piaget, who travelled the regions in search of molluscs for his collection, shared the same admiration of nature.

According to Schlup, 'The call for adventure become an obsession for many of those dreaming of wider horizons, impatient to escape the intellectual torpor of the region and desiring to measure their talents against those of the Parisians and even the Europeans.'[8] As we have seen, that call would be heard.

Numerous artists from Neuchâtel yearned for exile, often as a reaction to the existing climate of conformism and the narrow observance of academic traditions. It was in this atmosphere that Charles Edouard Jeanneret, alias Le Corbusier, left there definitively in 1917 (like Cendrars, who, had been born and raised in La Chaux-de-Fonds). Le Corbusier, however, learned a great deal in his hometown art school under the guidance of his art professor, Charles L'Eplattenier, who advocated a new style of art adapted to the spirit and the landscape of the Jura region. But it was in Paris that Le Corbusier discovered his creative talent.

Previously, art in Neuchâtel was part of the whole Swiss Romantic movement and one could hardly speak of a uniquely Neuchâtel school. The Fine Arts Museum, inaugurated in 1885, permitted the population of the capital to view the works of Maximilien de Meuron (1785–1868) and Léopold Robert (1794–1835). Meuron – who presided over the Society of Friends of Art, founded in 1882 – was one of the most remarkable figures of Swiss landscape art. He was famous for his portrayal of the Alps, whereas Léopold Robert no longer felt at ease in describing the romantic views and scenes of southern Italy. By the end of the nineteenth century, Neuchâtel artists had discovered the richness of the Jura landscapes and the local daily life of the region, while other artists, such as Théophile Robert, borrowed styles from the Parisian schools.

The omnipresence of nature in the Neuchâtel picture mouldings probably partly explains their attraction for scientists.

The scientific circles

In fact, the discovery of the Alps and their sublimation by the Romantic Movement was paralleled in the scientific sphere, as was demonstrated by François Walter.[9] In Neuchâtel, the professor Louis Agassiz (1807–1873) contributed to the definition of glaciations. A fixed theoretician, Agassiz assisted the establishment of a naturalist school in Neuchâtel by founding the Neuchâtel Society of Natural Sciences in 1832. After leaving for the United States, Agassiz had several very worthy successors such as the naturalist Paul Godet (1836–1911), who initiated Jean Piaget, and before him, the geologist Edouard Desor (1811–1882), who had been Agassiz's secretary.

A scientific community grew out of those pioneers in the second half of the nineteenth century. The community had its scholarly societies, its bulletins, and its reviews, which were clearly inspired by a spirit of universality and an obvious pedagogical purpose.

Historians and ethnologists, zoologists and geologists, geographers and archaeologists were all interested in the array of scientific activities and the philosophies behind them, and everyone seemed to have a strong interest in their popularization. We can understand, therefore, why someone like Paul

Godet looked after the works of young Piaget and published them in a review written for the general public entitled *Le Rameau de Sapin* (The Fir Branch), which was the voice of the Club Jurassien (Jura Club). In this scientific climate, explored in more detail elsewhere in this work, Jean Piaget received a quality education, a taste for research and verification, and a warm welcome and dialogue that strengthened him in his work.

Neuchâtel was certainly not the land of great thinkers and visionaries but, rather, the home to pragmatists and experimenters. The Enlightenment failed to find fertile ground there after Rousseau was chased away in 1765. Instead of abstract knowledge and ideas, a preference for a practical culture and a solid pragmatic education prevailed.

Jean-Jacques Rousseau spent three years in the Principality of Neuchâtel, from 1762 to 1765, because he was persecuted for his publication of *Emile, or on Education* and *The Social Contract*.[10] He took refuge in the mountain village of Môtiers thanks to the protection of the King of Prussia (and Prince of Neuchâtel), Frederic II, and his governor George Keith, Marshal of Scotland (nicknamed 'Milord Marshal'). He struck up a relationship with several key figures, in particular the very wealthy Alexandre DuPeyrou, a dedicated supporter of the philosophies of the Enlightenment. At this time he was initiated to botany by Jean-Antoine d'Ivernois, a medical doctor, and Abraham Gagnebin, a naturalist. In Môtiers Rousseau wrote his *Letters Written from the Mountain* (1764) in response to his detractors, a plea for the natural religion that provoked the ire of the Venerable Class (the Protestant clergy). Hence he had to escape to the nearby canton of Bern on the Ile Saint-Pierre (Saint Peter's Island).[11] Only a small minority of disciples of the Enlightenment had welcomed Rousseau during his brief stay. Nevertheless he made a lasting impression on the memories and debates of the Neuchâtelois, and the publication of his books was continued by the publishers of the Principality.

Notes

1 A. Berchtold (1963). *La Suisse romande au cap du XXe siècle. Portrait littéraire et moral.* Lausanne: Payot.
2 G. de Pourtalès (1881–1919). *Chaque mouche a son ombre* (Vol.1, pp. 70–71). Paris: Gallimard.
3 F. Walter (1990). *Les Suisses et l'environnement. Une histoire du rapport à la nature du 18ᵉ siècle à nos jours.* Carouge-Genève: Ed. Zoé.
4 De Pourtalès, op. cit., pp. 81–82.
5 Ph. H. Menoud (1973). L'Eglise réformée neuchâteloise il y a cent ans. *Musée neuchâtelois*, no. 1, 51–76.
6 A. Clavien (1993). *Les Helvétistes. Intellectuels et politique en Suisse romande au début du siècle.* Lausanne: Ed. d'en Bas.
7 M. Schlup (1993). La littérature. In *Histoire du Pays de Neuchâtel* (Vol. III, pp. 283–294). Hauterive: G. Attinger.
8 Ibid, p. 289.
9 Walter, op. cit.

10 *Emile, or on Education* (trans. A. Bloom), New York: Basic Books, 1979; *The Social Contract or Other Political Writings* (trans. V. Gourevitch), Cambridge, UK: Cambridge University Press, 1997.
11 Interested visitors can read in the museum located in the same building as Piaget's school a letter from the King of Prussia admonishing the Protestant clergy to behave more tolerantly and in a more Evangelical spirit.

2   Neuchâtel, Jean Piaget's home town

Jean-Pierre Jelmini

Conceived during the time of gas-lit streets and apartments, Jean Piaget was born on 9 August 1896 when the city was already basking in the early throes of electricity. On the preceding 1 January, the Municipality of Neuchâtel had announced that electrical current was available for public, domestic, and industrial use. While some may see this coincidence as an obvious omen, others may settle for pointing out the extent of the technological changes that were revolutionizing the world at that time, making the five decades that led up to the First World War one of the most dynamic times in modern Western history.

It seems both useful and interesting at the beginning of this study to evoke the world in which Jean Piaget grew up: Neuchâtel, a small Swiss city that serves as the capital of the canton of the same name, lies in the eastern foothills of the Jura and offers a view of the Alps that festoon its distant horizon.

At the time of Jean Piaget's birth, both the city and the canton were about to celebrate feverishly the 50th anniversary of the republican regime that, like many others in Europe, came out of the revolutionary havoc of 1848. Does that mean that a member of the Swiss Confederation – which is often cavalierly called the world's oldest democracy – maintained its feudal system well into the nineteenth century? That was exactly what happened, and the exceptional fate of this canton merits a moment's reflection, if only to understand better the impact on the young Piaget of having been born in an open-minded society. Neuchâtel has a long history of international contacts and an old tradition of staying in touch with the outside world.

Neuchâtel, from medieval town to cantonal capital

The original small town gave its name to the surrounding lands when the first landlords took up residence in the country and borrowed the name for their feudal houses. From the eleventh century (time of the first use of the name *novum castellum, regalissimam sedem,*[1] a gift from the king of Burgundy to his spouse in 1011[2]) to the nineteenth century, Neuchâtel was not unlike any other medium-sized feudal city: festive moments (Pope Felix V's visit in 1446;

the arrival of Philippe the Good, Duke of Burgundy, for the baptism of his godson Philippe de Hochberg in 1454; etc.) and devastating catastrophes (fire in 1450 and flooding in 1579). The city had established neighbourly relations since the Middle Ages with surrounding cities: Besançon in Franche-Comté; Fribourg, Bienne, Berne, Soleure, and Lucerne on the side of the Swiss leagues. However, during all this time neither the city nor the principality became Swiss.

Having belonged to the French family Orléans-Longueville since the beginning of the sixteenth century, the small medieval county was made a principality in 1648 by Henri II of Orléans, Duke of Longueville. Upon the death of its last French princess, the Duchess of Nemour, who left no heirs, the principality passed into the hands of the ruling Prussian House of Hohenzollern. The gift was made during a big trial in Neuchâtel in 1707. The Prussian kings ruled over Neuchâtel until 1848, with the exception of a brief period between 1806 and 1814, when the marshal of the Empire Alexandre Berthier ruled over it.

In 1815, profiting from the reorganization of Europe by the Congress of Vienna, Neuchâtel became partially integrated into the Swiss Confederation at the same time as it was returned to the House of Hohenzollern because of the legitimate claim of the Prussian king on his former principality. This exceptional situation of becoming the 21st canton in the Swiss Confederation while still belonging to a foreign monarch put Neuchâtel in a delicate position.

Tensions quickly sprang up, and republican groups aimed at overthrowing the old regime. A failure to do so in 1831 was followed by a successful attempt on 1 March 1848, and the Republic was proclaimed the next day, making Neuchâtel a democratic state and a fully fledged Swiss canton. A constitution was drawn up and institutions founded, free of any restraints outside those laid down by the democratic Swiss Constitution.

An attempted royalist counter-revolution was rebuffed before it was hatched in 1856, and Napoleon III convoked an International Congress in Paris to solve 'the question of Neuchâtel'. On 26 May 1857 the European powers signed the Treaty of Paris, which released Neuchâtel of all feudal and foreign ties. This event put the final touch to the break-up of 1848 and drove several Neuchâtel families into 'exile'. Among them were Jean Piaget's paternal grandparents, who took refuge in Yverdon in the nearby Canton of Vaud.

As one can see, the fate of both the country and the small city of Neuchâtel, where Jean Piaget was born, was far from being banal. The memory of the old regime remained ever present throughout the second half of the nineteenth century. Half despised it while the other half longed for it; this fuelled public opinion and political debate. Under the distant gaze of the ultra-royalists, the winners of 1848 and 1856 hammered away at setting up the promised new society. The conservatives populated the lower regions of the canton (the wealthier and the more privileged areas during the *Ancien Régime*), but there were also pockets of resistance to new ideas in some of the country villages. The conservatives were a divided group. Extremists and moderates, among whom were numbered honest supporters of the Swiss cause, took up divergent stances. The fiercest partisans of the princely regime obstinately adopted a stand-off policy on all public matters, while the more conciliatory among them tried to organize themselves into a political party that would carry some weight in laying the foundations of the new canton. At the moment when the young Republic had finally come *sous le soleil de la liberté* (under the sun of liberty),[3] it faced the task of reconciling these warring sides that had been destroying each other for over half a century.

Fifty years later, agreement was still a long way off between the 'radicals', heirs to the 1848 revolution, and the 'liberals', the constructive wing of the old conservatives; yet they managed to share power on both cantonal and local levels. As of 1888, when a law was passed on local governments, Neuchâtel rather undemocratically allotted the 40 seats between the Radical and the Liberal Parties in the General Council. Two lists of candidates (25 for the Radicals and 15 for the Liberals) were put forward for a three-year term of office (three-eighths of the votes sufficed to be elected). The ballot was such that the electorate could randomly tick off names in a sort of popularity contest. About 60 per cent of the population voted in local elections, and the least popular of the Radicals was able to out-poll the most popular of the Liberals by some 100 votes. These figures give us an idea of the Radical Party's dominance. Democratic principles were still only very cautiously applied, and the time when they would be strictly enforced was still a long way off: Only two parties held and shared power.

The local political scene was not changed by the submission of a list of 'labour candidates' for election in 1891. The best candidate on the list received 122 out of 3000 votes cast. Let it be noted, however, that in the same year the Neuchâtel political authorities made two decisions that were socially progressive: On the one hand, communal contracts would be awarded only to firms that were ready to guarantee the agreed minimum daily wages to their workers; on the other hand, burial – a source of expense and concern for the poor – would be assured freely by the government for all city residents. On the purely political level, a new balance of power came about only in 1912, in the wake of the arrival of the proportional system in 1894. The ballots sent 15 Liberals, 14 Radicals, and 11 Socialists to the Council. In the cantonal highlands, where the revolution of 1848 got its start, the Radical Party was turned upside down and the largest city of the Canton, La Chaux-de-Fonds, became a leftist bastion for the rest of the nineteenth century.[4]

Benefiting from the breach made in La Chaux-de-Fonds in 1888, three major parties (Radical, Liberal, and Socialist), which even today represent the political skeleton of the State of Neuchâtel, were represented in the cantonal legislature as of 1889. Five years later, proportional representation was adopted for elections to the cantonal legislature. These were major ground-breaking steps in the slow and difficult process of making the principality of Neuchâtel a democratic and modern state throughout the course of the nineteenth century.

The city of Neuchâtel

The city of Neuchâtel, where Jean Piaget was born, grew up, and studied, deserves a detailed description. In fact, even if its development is closely tied to that of the new canton, the city is quite different from the rest of the canton – especially La Chaux-de-Fonds – owing to its resistance to change, which caused internal divisions as well as numerous positive achievements.

In this eponymous city of the principality which was to become the capital city of the canton, the combat between those who held new ideas and the grand families who profited from the feudal system – with favours and fortunes varying according to the regimes and dynasties – was more complex than elsewhere in the Canton. Heirs of the tradition and the fortune of the bourgeoisie of Neuchâtel – the members of the 'bourgeois community' – refused at first to hand over to the Municipality, instituted by the Republic, the colleges, the hospital, and the town hall they had built with the money inherited from David de Pury. This wealthy Neuchâtel merchant, who died without heirs in Lisbon in 1786, had generously endowed the city with his fortune: 'all the inheritance of his remaining goods, present as well as future, to the city and the bourgeoisie of Neuchâtel in Switzerland'. However, the Republic pondered the serious question of how to manage and use the revenues of Baron Pury's fortune, still sizeable in spite of the major works that had been undertaken: a hospital, the town hall, a grammar school (called a *gymnase* under the reign of the last Hohenzollern prince of Neuchâtel, before becoming the famous *Collège latin*, a venerable institution where Jean Piaget, like so many others, completed his secondary education), a girls' school, and the turning aside of the River Seyon, a small waterway that flowed through Neuchâtel wreaking damage on the city for centuries. Now the bourgeoisie of Neuchâtel felt – rightly, according to the Federal Court[5] – that they were the owners of the various buildings, and they had no intention of handing over the control of David de Pury's fortune to the Municipality by giving it outright what had been accomplished under the *Ancien Régime*. By suppressing the bourgeoisie with the new law of the communities of 1888, the Republic placated the situation without resolving the conflict that weighed on relations between the Municipality and some of the old bourgeoisie families into the middle of the twentieth century.

All the mishaps stirred up by the local quarrels would be of little interest in the present study had they not had a marked effect on the Neuchâtel mentality. In fact, the bourgeoisie of Neuchâtel who had held the seat of political and economic power (the most powerful public corporation of the country) – men accustomed to power and security – had to sit by and impotently watch the undoing of a way of life in which they had been brought up and had acquired position, a way of life that would never be restored. Little by little, everything would be taken away from them: the *Ancien Régime*, their prestige, and even – thanks to Arthur Piaget, Jean's father, in 1895 – that which they considered to be the most authentic source of their history: the apocryphal *Chronique des chanoines* (Chronicle of the Canons).[6]

Events had rendered the old bourgeoisie into a powerless and silent stupor. They had considered themselves – and not without reason – the heirs of the moral and material inheritance of a city that belonged to the *Ancien Régime* as well as to its magistrates for having overseen its beautiful construction in the first half of the nineteenth century. Yet the new men who were on the rise proved themselves to be no less capable than their predecessors in running the show. All of Neuchâtel was to benefit from this lively rivalry.

The demographic explosion (1850–1920) and its consequences

One of the most concrete signs – without being necessarily conclusive – of the successful development of the city in the latter half of the nineteenth century was the expanding population, which nearly tripled in size in less than 70 years. In 1849 there were 7354 inhabitants (3548 of whom were indigenous, 3079 were Swiss from varying cantons, and 727 were foreigners); by 1896 that number soared to 18,339 (breaking down to 7279, 8708 and 2353, respectively). By 1920 there were over 23,000 inhabitants. In his description of the profound social changes of the period, Charly Guyot distinguished between the native view of the continual growth of foreigners as a veritable 'invasion'[7] and the more enlightened view that saw this development as 'an invigorating and reviving force for the electoral body'.[8] The remarkably modern legislation of 1849 granted a voice to all 'residents, regardless of their nationality, in matters pertaining to the levying of taxes'. This right, which was defined in 1850 and attacked in 1861, was strongly defended by the State Council and definitively written into law in 1874; since this time 'Swiss foreigners' at the age of 20 'who have been born in the canton or have lived there for more than five years and for one year in the Municipality, have the right to attend and to vote at the general assembly' of the Municipality.[9] What more tangible sign could there be of the openness that characterized the political institutions in Neuchâtel from the very early years of the republican regime?

The construction industry soared in measure with this vast influx of residents seeking housing. Until 1848 the city boundaries lay at the borders of the old city, but the arrival of the railway in 1859 extended those limits (Neuchâtel was connected to Yverdon and Bienne); the first rails were laid (1860) in the directions of La Chaux-de-Fonds and Le Locle and of Travers and Pontarlier. On 2 July 1901 the 'direct train' to Berne was inaugurated. In 1883 an impressive new train station built of greenish limestone, in contrast to the golden hue of the surrounding chalk buildings, stood out as a thoroughly novel socio-economic monument that drew the expansion of the city first towards itself and then beyond in the direction of the neighbouring mountain of Chaumont. At the same time, new residential quarters were defined: The older bourgeois families stayed in their beautiful urban or country homes, while the new ruling class built residences overlooking the city on the hilly ground of Evole and Port-Roulant, Château or Saint-Nicolas, or in the neighbourhoods of Trois-Portes and the Poudrières, where the Piaget family lived as of 1899. They also settled above the railway and to the east of the Rue de la Côte and its neighbouring streets. The level of the lake shore had sunk by 2.7 metres as a result of the construction work between 1873 and 1879 which redressed the banks and redirected the flow of the water from Lake Neuchâtel towards Lake Bienne and the River Aar. The construction of the train station created vast new building sites. The diversion of the water left 200,000 cubic metres of building lots to be developed according to builders' finances and tastes, while the outlying areas became residential neighbourhoods: Ecluse, Maladière, Parcs, Fahys, etc. A few workers' houses were built by cooperatives, particularly to the northwest of the city. The number of building permits issued during this period reflected this growth. In 1891 the number of permits totalled 19; it had increased to 48 in 1894, and to 50 by 1896.

When Jean Piaget was still a child, the city of Neuchâtel was well endowed with an extensive public transport system. Electric tramways led to the industrial quarter of Serrières and to the neighbouring villages of Saint-Blaise and Valangin; a local railway (electrified in 1902) that ran along the lakeside via Colombier, Auvernier, and Serrières bore passengers from Cortaillod and Boudry to the capital city. In 1890, a hydraulic funicular provided transport from the city down to Ecluse and up to Crêt-du-Plan. By 1910 an electric funicular was ferrying city dwellers to the sunny promontory paths in Chaumont, helping them to escape the fog that would settle on the city from November to March. Enjoyment of Neuchâtel's lakeside setting has been a long-standing tradition among its residents.

The educational system

Ever since the Protestant Reform, schooling had become a public socio-cultural task. According to the best authorities on the matter, the instruction taught in the principality during the eighteenth century was among the finest in all of Europe.[10] One would think that the arrival of democracy in 1848 would have furthered this literacy policy. Primary and secondary education was maintained, but, strangely, the famous Academy of Neuchâtel was closed. This institution, which was hardly ten years old, had the misfortune of being founded with royal subsidies, which in the eyes of the democracy meant it was a hotbed of conservatism, in spite of having progressive science teachers such as Louis Agassiz and Arnold Guyot on the staff. Finally, in 1866, a more confident government authorized the opening of the second Academy of Neuchâtel, where 30 years later, in 1895, Arthur Piaget held the chair of French language and literature in the Faculty of Arts. Although the

Republic opened a 'cantonal grammar school' in 1873, its principal interest lay with primary education. Although they were held on a tight lead by 'pedagogical congresses' (annual two- to three-day meetings that established the 'general conditions of primary education in Neuchâtel'), school teachers actually had a significant role to play in determining educational matters. Many of them were in politics, mainly in the Radical Party (for example, Numa Droz, member of the Neuchâtel government for 27 years, deputy to the federal government at the age of 28, member of the cabinet at 31 years of age,[11] and President of Switzerland at 37, etc.). Among the precursors of the Socialist Party was Daniel Liniger (who was in class with Jean Piaget when he sat for his final exams in the fourth form), the father of one of the future presidents of the City of Neuchâtel, the historian Jean Liniger.[12]

Education establishments and other cultural institutions

Building new schools had to keep step with this institutional development. A burst in such building marked the second half of the nineteenth and the first half of the twentieth century in Neuchâtel. Besides the already sumptuous Latin Grammar School dating from 1835, the girls' primary school from 1854, and the annex on Terreaux in 1893, the city added six new large primary schools and a building for the Academy (1886), which also housed the cantonal grammar school and the commercial college (1900). The new town councillors, taking their example from the beautiful buildings of the *Ancien Régime*, built a palace for the fine arts that was utterly splendid for its time and that, with a slight extension added in 1950, has housed since then the complete municipal collections in what is known today as the Art and History Museum. The beautiful science school, which had been founded and supported by the Coulon family, father and son, as well as some of the most brilliant teachers of the Academy, among whose pioneers was Louis Agassiz, was soon to become a notable natural history museum. At the end of the nineteenth century, thanks to a vast network of Neuchâtel relations spread around the world for commercial or missionary interests, this museum possessed the richest bird collection in Switzerland. Paul Godet (1836–1911), sometime director of the museum, played an influential role in Jean Piaget's youthful scientific vocation. After the First World War, major botanical and geological holdings were transferred to the university institutes, where these subjects were being taught. But then owing to the demands for enlarging local schools, the museum itself fell into neglect for nearly half a century.

The city's library, beside the Art and History Museum, was housed under the roof of the Latin Grammar School, and it offered for the curiosity of its readers a vast collection of scientific works, particularly those by the great scholars of the first Academy. Curiously, access to the reading rooms seems not to have been democratic, for in 1877, at the initiative of the Christian Union of young people, a 'reading room for workers' was created. The initiative was highly successful, and the new reading room had a catalogue of 400 readers per season at the beginning of the next century. This obvious success shows the level of interest in instruction among the working class, whether they were the initiators or the benefactors.

The 'Concert' hall, built in 1769, staged then as now (while waiting for the promised replacement) musical and dramatic productions. The hall was the scene for many an unbridled evening's entertainment, when student societies, which were then greatly in fashion (Belles-Lettres, of which the Piagets, father and son, were made honorary members;[13] Zofingue; the Club of the Friends of Nature, in which Jean Piaget was very active;[14] Etude; Néocomia, etc.), performed some famous 'dress rehearsals'. A 'conference centre', dating from 1884, completed the cultural edifices of Neuchâtel.

On the spiritual plane, Neuchâtel was still in the throes of the disunity into which it had been plunged in 1873 by the grave crisis stirred up by the promulgation of a new ecclesiastical law, the work of Numa Droz. Some Protestants refused to obey the new law, and as a result the Canton split into two Protestant communities, along with several less important religious groups. The National Church of the Canton of Neuchâtel had the majority of the population, which had accepted the law uniting church and state, whereas the Evangelical Church of Neuchâtel, independent from the state, did not. The faithful of the city were divided into two large 'national' parishes: that of the collegiate church (to which the Piaget family belonged) and that of the Temple du Bas. Members of the 'independent' church, around 1800 people at the beginning of the twentieth century, worshipped at the Cassarde chapel (now called the Ermitage). In 1905 the Church of Our Lady was built (according to the neo-Gothic plans of Guillaume Ritter and in an original technique of painted concrete) and offered their own place of worship to the Roman Catholic community, then 20 per cent of the population.

In La Chaux-de-Fonds, under the influence of Charles L'Eplattenier, director of the advanced course at the School of Art since 1910, a group of young artists burst on the scene, giving Neuchâtel a new spirit of artistic creation: Léon Perrin, Charles Humbert, Georges Dessouslavy, André Evard, the Barraud brothers, and the future Le Corbusier were particularly illustrative of this era. In Neuchâtel, descendants of the great families of artists of the nineteenth century, such as Robert and de Meuron, retained their fame thanks to the post-impressionist paintings of Louis de Meuron and the internationally renowned painter Théophile Robert.

From a purely material point of view, Neuchâtel enjoyed a relatively healthy economic development and a political climate favourably disposed to progress. Electricity became publicly and privately available, and between 1896 and 1920 the number of subscriptions to the municipal network rose from 169 to 9318. The number of street lamps went from 288 to 1210 while that of domestic lamps jumped from 3847 to 70,240. Also in 1920, the gas works sold 1,200,000 cubic metres of city gas, delivered for private or industrial use through 60 kilometres of canalization. At the same time, public hygiene – where much work was needed, especially among the less favoured of the population – developed in leaps and bounds. The number of public toilets, which were kept clean by attentive authorities, quadrupled. Finally, the first 20 years of the twentieth century seems to have had all the qualities today's ecologists dream of: Besides the highly developed and well-frequented public transportation system, in 1920 Neuchâtel had seven luxury vehicles, 140 automobiles, 87 motorcycles, and 1670 bicycles! One could thus imagine that Piaget had a taste for bicycles – though the hilly contours of the city hardly favour this form of transport – but we have no definite proof.

Conclusion

Jean Piaget was born in a naturally peaceful environment that was neverthe-less rocked by contemporary historical events that made the capital of a prin-cipality the capital of a Swiss canton – in spite of the wishes of the established elite. Piaget's native Neuchâtel, a humane city for humanists, harboured the rivalry between an intense past built on tradition and a progressive scientific spirit reaching out to the future. He was the son of a man who knew how to retain his independent spirit – in a world that did not always praise such – and of a woman who, though relatively little is known of her, is likely to have been exceptional in her own right.

On that Sunday of 9 August 1896, the average temperature in Neuchâtel was 15.2 degrees Celsius. The sky was cloudy, the winds variable and of moderate force. The barometric pressure reached 719 millibars, and thunder could be heard in the north of the city.[15]

Notes

1 'New castle, royal estate.'
2 G.-A. Matile, *Monuments de l'histoire de Neuchâtel*, 1848, p. 1137. The original parchment manuscript is housed in the Archives départementales de l'Isère (Departmental archives of Isère), Grenoble, shelf mark 1 G 11.
3 Neuchâtel anthem, lyrics by Henri Warnery (1859–1902), music composed by Charles North (1859–1914), written for the 50th anniversary of the Republic in 1898.
4 J.-M. Barrelet and J. Ramseyer (1990). *La Chaux-de-Fonds ou le défi d'une cité horlogère, 1848–1914*. La Chaux-de-Fonds: Ed. d'En Haut.
5 Decision of 1 December 1860, cf. J. Guinand (1986). La succession, un conflit entre la Bourgeoisie et la Ville de Neuchâtel. In L. E. Roulet (Ed.), *David de Pury, 1709–1786* (pp. 99–112). Hauterive (NE), Switzerland: G. Attinger.
6 See Chapter 3 of this volume.
7 Ch. Guyot (1946). *Neuchâtel, Histoire d'une cité* (p. 267). Neuchâtel: La Neuchâteloise.
8 Ibid., p. 267.
9 Philippe Bois (1973). Le droit de vote des étrangers en matière communale. *Musée neuchâtelois*, no. 1, 22–29.
10 This opinion is primarily defended by Pierre Caspard, director of the Service of the History of Education at the Institut National de Recherche Pédagogique in Paris, in correspondence with the present author; and on which he is currently writing.

11 J.-M. Barrelet (1993). Numa Droz. In U. Altermatt (Ed.), *Conseil fédéral: Diction-naire biographique des cent premiers conseillers fédéraux* (pp. 218–223). Yens, Switzerland: Cabédita.

12 J. Liniger (1980). *En toute subjectivité*. Neuchâtel: Messeiller.

13 B. Wavre (Ed.) (1962). *Livre d'or de Belles-lettres de Neuchâtel, 1832–1960*. Arthur Piaget, H. 48, 19 October 1909/Jean Piaget, H. 57, 18 December 1925. Neuchâtel: Société des anciens belletriens neuchâtelois.

14 Archives of the Society of the Friends of Nature, deposited in the History Department of the Art and History Museum of Neuchâtel.

15 *Feuille d'Avis du Neuchâtel*, 10 August 1896, p. 1.

3 Arthur Piaget (1865–1952)

Background of Jean Piaget's father

Maurice de Tribolet

Arthur Piaget[1] was born on 25 November 1865 in Yverdon (Canton of Vaud). His father, Frédéric (1830–1884), remained affiliated with Neuchâtel's *Ancien Régime* after the royalist counter-revolution of 1856 and, as a result, settled in Yverdon soon after that date. He came from a family from La Côte-aux-Fées who have figured in civic records since the seventeenth century. The family belonged to a lineage already mentioned in the middle of the fourteenth century in the Val-de-Travers. The name Piaget is derived from the French word *péager*, which translates as toll-collector, and it is supposed that the family earned its living that way.

Frédéric operated a watch factory and exported his products as far away as America under the brand name Piaget-Allisson. His wife, whom he married in 1857, was born Marie-Adèle Allisson, and it was she that took over operation of the watch factory following the death of her husband in 1884. The watch-making trade was a lucrative activity, and the Piaget family lived very comfortably, having the means to partake in cultural activities such as music and singing. Arthur, who benefited from a modern and open upbringing, even had the opportunity to attend language courses in Leipzig and in London. He spoke very highly of his parents, who were also greatly appreciated in their community of Yverdon. He and his elder brother, Armand, an art instructor, were the only survivors of a family of five children.

Arthur Piaget did his studies at the Gymnase de la Cité in Lausanne alongside the famous philologist Ernest Muret, among others. He obtained his baccalaureate on 24 October 1884. It was most probably in Lausanne that he befriended the future writer Samuel Cornut, well known in French-Swiss literature for his desire 'to express the religious aspirations of a generation of fervent agnostics committed to social brotherhood'.[2] He was eventually to become Jean Piaget's godfather.

Studies in Paris

From 1885 to 1890, Arthur Piaget lived in Paris and studied in Section Four of the Ecole Pratique des Hautes Etudes (philological and historical sciences). He attended courses in Roman and classical philology, Latin epigraphy, and modern Greek, but none of Ferdinand de Saussure, who taught in that school from 1881 to 1891. Thus, Arthur Piaget manifested his preference for the philology and literature of the Middle Ages, and during the academic year of 1887–1888 he studied under Gaston Paris. As of 1886, he followed Gaston Paris's courses at the Collège de France. In 1871, Paris co-founded the internationally acclaimed philological review *Romania*. Advocating the popularization of the sciences and opposing all forms of romanticism, Paris liked to proclaim that whatever the consequences, the only objective of science was truth. Throughout his long career, Arthur Piaget never ceased to gain inspiration from these principles.

Parallel to this programme, and after sitting various exams and presenting a thesis entitled *Martin Le Franc, prévot de Lausanne, auteur du Champion des dames*, Arthur Piaget obtained a master of arts from the Academy of Neuchâtel on 28 October 1887. During the winter of 1887–1888 he continued working on his master's thesis at the National Library in Paris. Towards the end of 1888, he defended the developed thesis as a doctoral dissertation at the Faculty of Letters of the University of Geneva. In 1890 he was awarded a diploma from the Ecole Pratique des Hautes Etudes in Paris after submitting a research paper on Martin Le Franc that demonstrated the laureate's knowledge of fifteenth-century French poetry and, above all, his ability to edit old texts. In 1912 he was appointed editor of texts at the office of the prestigious Société des anciens textes français. Arthur Piaget remained associated with the Ecole Pratique des Hautes Etudes as he gave courses on fourteenth- and fifteenth-century French literature there from 1891 to 1894 alongside such renowned colleagues as Msgr Louis Duchesne (Christian antiquities), Auguste Bréal (comparative grammar), Louis Havet (Latin philology), Gabriel Monod (history), and Arthur Meillet (comparative grammar). This training in Paris was decisive in Arthur Piaget's scientific career, for he would later comment that it was at the Ecole Pratique des Hautes Etudes that he began to work seriously.

As a result of his studies in Paris, Arthur Piaget became a member of the new elite of historical science and took an active part in the revision of French history. This methodical and critical school, which preferred the written document, was characterized by the eminent position of French Protestants, the most illustrious of whom, Gabriel Monod, founded *La Revue historique* (The Historical Review) in 1876. Those same French Protestants would play an important role in establishing the Third Republic and would also contribute to the creation of a secular and tolerant state based on the principles of 1789. This new French science of history was directed by a religious minority and benefited from close ties that the French Protestant intelligentsia established with the Faculties of Theology in Switzerland and especially with those in Germany, where a critical and positive historiography was being developed.

It certainly appears that there was a particular affinity between the spirit of Protestantism and the 'New History' advocated by Gabriel Monod, who can be considered as the founder of a moral epistemology of history.[3] Without openly advocating this school of thought, Arthur Piaget continually demonstrated throughout his work his determination to go to the sources and to remain faithful to a critical thought process that would never support unverified opinions. Arthur Piaget never hid his admiration for Gaston Paris and his method, but neither did he outwardly adhere to the spirit of Protestantism. His growing interest in the history of the Reform in the regions of Neuchâtel and French-speaking Switzerland, which could be observed from 1909 onwards, seemed to indicate that he was also affiliated with Gabriel Monod's school of thought, whose scientific principles showed no contradictions to those advocated by Gaston Paris. Although he never openly professed the Christian faith, instead demonstrating a penchant for scepticism regarding religion, Arthur Piaget, according to his son,[4] was concerned with the gap that existed between science and faith. Towards the end, he acquired the work of August Sabatier entitled *La philosophie de la religion fondée sur la psychologie et l'histoire* (The Philosophy of Religion Based on Psychology and History).

In 1929, Arthur Piaget showed a marked interest in the Reform by creating a seminar on the history of the Reformation, in close collaboration with the Faculty of Theology. With the scientific support of his former student, Gabrielle Berthoud, Arthur Piaget gave decisive impetus to research into the origins of the Reform in the region of Neuchâtel. In 1930, as a result of their mutual and interdisciplinary collaboration, they wrote and published a critical work on Jean Crespin's *Book of Martyrs*, published in 1564, which gave an account of Protestants who had undergone martyrdom for their faith. It is worth noting that the Faculty of Theology acquired this work for its collection. Gabrielle Berthoud became known as a specialist on the origins of the Reform in French-speaking Switzerland and then as a respected scholar of Protestant religious propaganda. There is no doubt that Arthur Piaget, former student of Gaston Paris, was attracted by the Reform's liberating effect, which corresponded well with his independent and critical spirit, typically characteristic of students educated at the Ecole Pratique des Hautes Etudes.

Other aspects of his life in Paris

Arthur Piaget said that what he knew of Paris was only his room at the Sorbonne and the library. During his stay there he worked hard and deliberately avoided the cafés in order to devote himself to his studies. However, if we can believe Jean Rychner,[5] Arthur Piaget had occasion to meet Verlaine, who, as the story goes, borrowed money from him.

It appears that it was also in Paris that, through the intervention of his landlady, Mlle Tabarié, he met his future wife, Rebecca Jackson. This highly intelligent and imaginative woman, who was a pious Protestant, chose to do her studies in primary school education. The Jackson family lived in a mansion in Paris on the Chaussée-d'Antin. Furthermore, one of her sisters married Adolphe Lods, theologian and Hebrew scholar, who was a member of the Académie des inscriptions et belles-lettres (Academy of Historical Records and Literature). Another sister, Madeleine Jackson, married Léon Japy, direct descendant of Fréderic Japy, founder of an industrial dynasty in the region of Montbéliard. It ought to be noted that Rebecca Jackson's godmother was born a Peugeot, which connected the Jacksons with French bourgeois Protestant families closely tied to commercial, industrial, and intellectual interests.

One of Rebecca Jackson's ancestors of English descent settled in France towards the end of the eighteenth or the beginning of the nineteenth century. Armed with the secret of English steelmaking techniques, which were among the best at the time, he established a family business. The Jacksons were also founders of the first steel mills in St-Etienne. With his marriage to Rebecca Jackson, Arthur had the opportunity to climb the social ladder by being introduced into the French upper-class and bourgeois Protestant circles. These ties would last for a long time, and we know that Jean Piaget would later hold these solid connections to his maternal French family close to his heart.

The call to Neuchâtel

During the academic year of 1890–1891 Arthur Piaget set to work on the analysis of Provençal texts at the Academy of Neuchâtel, and in 1894–1895 he gave a course on the Middle Ages. As of 1895, he was given a lectureship for a four-hour weekly course in Romance language and literature, a post that became a chair for French language and literature of the Middle Ages. On 25 October 1895, the young professor devoted his first lecture to the authenticity of the *Chronique des chanoines* (Chronicle of the Canons), a document that had been used by the historians in Neuchâtel since the end of the eighteenth century to prove the age-old ties between the Principality and the Swiss Confederation. This chronicle narrates the high accomplishments of the Neuchâtelois alongside the Swiss from the end of the Middle Ages, and it attributes a noble role to supposed distant ancestors of local patricians. Though barely accessible, this document has a mythical value, for it bears witness to the Swiss patriotism of the Neuchâtel elite during the *Ancien Régime* and thus adds historical depth to the sentiments aroused by the Revolution of 1848. Republicans and old Royalists could identify with this chronicle, which testified to their common love for their Swiss homeland.

In truth, this work, as Arthur Piaget brilliantly proved, was falsely invented in 1765 by the clever Colonel Abram Pury. In effect, relying uniquely on authentic documents, the former student of Gaston Paris succeeded in revealing the mistaken facts and anachronisms of ideas and language contained in this venerable text. Analyzing especially the vocabulary and style of this pseudo-medieval author, Arthur Piaget brilliantly demonstrated that it 'was not the writing style of authors of the Middle Ages'. We should not be surprised that Arthur Piaget's critical analysis was perceived as committing an offence against a certain Neuchâtel historical identity. In Neuchâtel, the Revolution of 1848 and the Royalist counter-revolution of 1856 imposed, as of 1864, a neutral historiography intended to reunite all the opposing political factions. The unusual steps taken by Arthur Piaget were prejudicial to this consensus and risked reviving a historical controversy, which could be perceived as politically destabilizing and as calling into question the new Swiss patrimony that was being promulgated with the establishment of the Republic.[6]

Furthermore, Arthur Piaget was so affected by the polemic his criticism of the *Chronique* had triggered, and which set him on a collision course with local intellectual conformists, that he seriously considered leaving Neuchâtel for places more welcoming and conducive to his independent spirit. This can be seen in a letter addressed to him on 27 September 1902 by Pierre de Meuron, an influential conservative Neuchâtel aristocrat with an extensive cultural and scientific background. He assured Arthur Piaget of his support and his satisfaction to see that:

> thanks to you and your friends, a scientific approach towards history was beginning to make its presence felt. Your free, conscientious approach, which is respectful of facts of our past, is a breath of fresh air; as secular thinkers we are able to foresee a school of history in Neuchâtel free of all the prejudices that weigh on all aspects of public life.

De Meuron was worried to see the historian 'giving up in sheer despair and fleeing to join circles where his work would receive a more intelligent welcome'. He continued:

> you will then feel even better knowing that our country is more in need now than ever of truly independent spirits, and that in spite of the hoards of mediocrity invading us, there is still space for an independent critic free of prejudice.[7]

That a renowned person paid such homage to a debunker of historical myths must have been a balm to the heart of the young historian, who would doubtless have also appreciated de Meuron's remarks on self-righteous milieux.

In the face of this outcry, Arthur Piaget remained resolutely devoted to scientific rigour and spoke out on the need to be straightforward. Several years later, during the winter of 1906, still pursuing the same path, he took on another taboo subject in Neuchâtel history, namely the Revolution of 1848. The public lectures that he gave on the subject were innovative and capable of arousing controversy. Remember that in 1898 the 50th anniversary of the Republic was marked by unanimous festivities that had been designed to eliminate old political rancour. On 5 December 1899, minutes of a meeting of the board of the historical review *Musée neuchâtelois* (Neuchâtel Museum) stated that 'some members of the committee had reservations about looking into the facts of 1848.'

Devoting himself to the study of the most recent history, Arthur Piaget once again demonstrated his intellectual audacity. He realistically judged Prussian politics regarding the principality, without going as far as criticizing the republican historians. This approach was not to the everyone's liking, and some accused the lecturer of prejudice concerning the *Ancien Régime*, as can be observed by the long controversy he carried on with the Neuchâtel patrician Samuel de Chambrier on various aspects of Neuchâtel history. Arthur Piaget thus broke with the political consensus and patriotic approach that had predominated until then, and he showed his public that Neuchâtel, nearly 60 years after the revolution, was politically mature enough to look in the mirror of its most recent history. These quarrels, however, hardly engaged the public, and the debate remained at a high level and involved local personalities of all persuasions and opinions, such as the professor of law Fritz-Henri Mentha, who in 1918 took a stand for the authenticity of the *Chronique des chanoines* in the Radical journal *Le National*.

The reorganization of the State Archives

In line with his primary vocation as a verifier of the authenticity of Neuchâtel history by consulting primary sources, Arthur Piaget became a member of the commission that, on 20 October 1897, presented a report 'on the method to follow in order to complete the classification of State Archive documents'. The government examined this report and, on 19 November 1897, established an archives office with five or six civil servants. Arthur Piaget's candidature was examined, and he was named State Archivist on 20 May 1898. Thus, under the direction of one highly qualified archivist, the service was reorganized to facilitate the centralization of all the documents belonging to the state in the castle of Neuchâtel.

The work of restructuring and classifying was accompanied by the publication of newly disclosed documents. In 1904, Arthur Piaget launched the 'Inventory and Documents' collection, including an edition of the minutes of the General Audiences meeting, the first parliament of Neuchâtel created in 1814. Other volumes followed at regular intervals, leading the new archivist to examine archives abroad to complete the documentation conserved at the State Archives; especially those pertaining to the period 1814 to 1848. Having an interest in the most recent history of his country, Arthur Piaget travelled to Berlin on at least five occasions between the years 1907 and 1913 in order to find documents relative to the Revolution of 1848 in Neuchâtel. Once again, the brilliant student of Gaston Paris demonstrated that it was impossible to revise the historiography of Neuchâtel without examining documents conserved in Neuchâtel as well as in Berlin.

The restructuring of the review *Musée neuchâtelois*

Having been selected as a member of the editorial staff of the cantonal historical review, the *Musée neuchâtelois*, Arthur Piaget made every effort to give a more critical and scientific style to this review, which had been founded in 1864 and was designed to promote an appreciation of history among the citizens of Neuchâtel.

On 13 March 1906, Arthur Piaget was named editor, a privileged position that allowed him control over all the articles appearing in the publication. During his mandate, he seriously committed himself to maintaining a balance between genuine scholarly rigour and the need for a sound popularization that would make the review accessible to amateur historians. Consequently, he made sure that the review's staff kept a self-critical and open mind, yet maintained with vigilance a high standard for articles submitted. It was not long, therefore, before he became the object of a certain animosity among the proponents of 'the futurist school', comprising a 'clan of young people' who had decided to work outside the defined limits of the Historical Society and the *Musée neuchâtelois* by discounting the scientific approach that Arthur Piaget held to so strongly and was unwilling to discard. This skirmish proved that a healthy critical method was not valued by everyone, and again Arthur Piaget had to speak the truth even at the cost of being opposed by a public avid for engaging stories.[8]

An admired master open to youth

Despite his non-negotiable inflexibility on scientific principles, Arthur Piaget did not show a lack of interest in his readers who solicited him or the students who worked under his direction. Numerous letters from students attest to their admiration for a master who was respected for his science and who was always accessible and concerned enough to offer a warm and friendly welcome to the new generation.

For instance, on 9 December 1923 a former student wrote that she had suffered in Switzerland, but that she had also 'had the chance to have met kind-hearted, generous, and open-minded intellects'. In August and December 1924, the future specialist on the history of the Reform, Henri Meylan, who was still at the Ecole des chartes in Paris, thanked him 'for his charming welcome to Neuchâtel', and on 28 December of that same year, Meylan told him of 'the memories of the warm and encouraging welcome he received when just a beginner'.

Another sign of admiration came from a former student from La Chaux-de-Fonds named Madeleine Wasserfallen. On an unmentioned date she wrote the following to her former professor: 'I don't know how to express my recognition for all that you represented to me during my course of study, particularly during my last semester ... I am unable to express how much of an oasis your field was amidst the university desert.' She also recalled his palaeography courses, where he demonstrated his talent as a 'critical jester'.

The same friendly relationship existed between Arthur Piaget and his former student, the scholarly editor Eugénie Droz, who had settled in Paris and wrote to Arthur Piaget addressing him as 'Dear Master', or even 'My Master'. She expressed her dismay at not having had news from him and reproached him for not having wanted to spend several days visiting Paris. It is known that Eugénie Droz was one of Arthur Piaget's most brilliant students and that she loved to claim her membership in the same spiritual family as him. Droz had been welcomed regularly into Arthur Piaget's circle at his home in the company of Gabrielle Berthoud.

No trace of pride or self-satisfaction could be detected in this master of philology, even in the face of an abundance of flattering comments on his work which flowed forth from his peers and could have easily gone to his head. Thus on 25 February 1923, Lucien Havet, director of studies at the Ecole Pratique des Hautes Etudes, asked his colleague to give lectures on romance philology, 'remembering the excellent talks you gave at the school at the request of Gaston Paris in 1891, 1892, and 1893'. In addition, on 30 January 1923, Ernest Hoepfner of Strasbourg recognized his competence in the domain of fifteenth-century language. Also in 1923, the famous Parisian editor and fifteenth-century specialist Pierre Champion inscribed a book to Arthur Piaget, saying: 'he owed him everything'; the book was entitled *L'Histoire poétique du XVe siècle* (The Poetic History of the Fifteenth Century). On that occasion he hailed him 'as an initiator, as a master', while at the same time expressing their spiritual affinity. On 20 December 1925, the same Pierre Champion wrote to him that 'men like you are too rare'.

On 15 March 1924, Charles-Frédéric Ward of Iowa State University informed Piaget that 'he would be happy to have intellectual contact' with him, and an American philologist from Princeton declared that he knew his extraordinary work well and that he was closely following him in 'a sort of intellectual friendship' from which he expected aid and counsel.

With Arthur Piaget, we are dealing not only with an internationally acclaimed scholar but also with an endearing personality who valued close personal relationships. It does not appear that the scholar's mischievous and jesting spirit ever stifled his inner gift of kindness and openness to others. While independent and exacting, taken up mostly with science and impartiality, Arthur Piaget never failed to remain available to his students and to a larger public interested in the history of Neuchâtel.

Arthur Piaget and his son

According to comments we have been able to collect, it is certain that father and son were very close and held great affection for one another. In the words of one observer, Arthur Piaget was a marvellous father, opened-minded and full of understanding for his son's vocation.

Arthur Piaget did, however, exert a great influence on his son, Jean, which the latter recalled fondly in his autobiography of 1976: 'Among many other things, he taught me the value of working systematically down to the last detail.' Jean Piaget mentions as well that his father 'was a man of scrupulous and critical spirit who disliked careless generalizations, and had no fear of prompting controversy when historical fact was altered only for the purpose of respecting tradition'. In its conciseness, his son's judgement is highly relevant and does not contradict comments of others that we have cited.

Jean-Jacques Ducret[9] wrote that one must not 'forget the major role Arthur Piaget played in fostering his son's demanding ideal for truth', while Fernando Vidal insisted in turn on the non-conformist and critical spirit of Arthur Piaget.[10]

The Piaget family and the Protestant tradition

One could hardly deny that Arthur Piaget's liking for turbulent and controversial periods in history stemmed from a rather provocative character. However, it most certainly came as well from the rigorous education he received in Paris, which taught him 'never to accept the arguments of authority and tradition, and to hold true only to that which is based on thoroughly examined proof. This was also the creed of many scientists of the period, from Claude Bernard to Gabriel Monod.'[11]

In this perspective, the emblematic figure of the Protestant Arthur Giry, professor at the Ecole Pratique des Hautes Etudes since 1874 and at the Ecole des chartes in 1885, would resemble Arthur Piaget in that Giry was a Republican free-thinker, although he did not involve himself in politics. He hardly concealed his liberal opinions and showed himself to be sensitive to injustice and persecution. This explains why he committed himself entirely to the Dreyfus cause, applying to 'the affair' what he preached to his students, i.e., 'the acquisition of critical reflexes in the face of any statement'.[12] Note that Arthur Piaget's scientific approach showed a similar attitude: the destruction of the *Chronique des chanoines* took place in 1895 while preparations for the 50th-anniversary celebrations of the Republic were in progress, thus blurring the memory of the royalist and anti-Republican uprising of 1856.

This Protestant tradition manifests itself in a larger sense in Rebecca Jackson, Arthur Piaget's wife, who, as Fernando Vidal remarked, had no fear of expressing her political and religious opinions. During the First World War, she did not conceal her sympathy for the Allied cause. Being the first woman to be elected to the school commission of Neuchâtel in 1912 by the Socialist Party, she put into practice her socio-political convictions by taking a stand for the pacifist theologian Jules Humbert-Droz, who had been imprisoned for being a conscientious objector.[13]

It should also be noted here that Arthur and Rebecca Piaget sided with the pastor Wilfred Monod, partisan (from the end of the nineteenth century) of a faith based on a Christian's personal relationship with the crucified Lord and apostle and which advocated a Social Christianity that most probably influenced Rebecca and her son, Jean. Like Fernando Vidal, we feel it important to point out that Jean Piaget submitted his manuscript of *La mission de l'idée* to Wilfred Monod, who gave him his criticism as well as declaring that Jean was the worthy son of his parents, who were old friends of his.[14]

Thus, as of 1915, Jean Piaget could be said to have been between the centre and the left of Social Christianity.[15] He would not renounce his initial convictions, as can be observed by his defence in March–April 1928 of the French pacifist Pioche, who gave a talk in Neuchâtel. This engagement in favour of the lecturer caused him to be the victim of vehement attacks by the right-wing press.[16] One year later, in 1929, Jean Piaget and his father signed a petition in favour of a woman's right to vote. Jean Piaget therefore remained faithful to the opinions he expressed in *La mission de l'idée* in 1915, where universal suffrage for women was presented as a decisive step towards the restoration of social equality.[17]

According to Jean Liniger,[18] Rebecca Piaget did not hesitate to make her religious feelings known. The quest for scientific truth combined with personal ideals was one of the striking traits of Jean Piaget's family, who held to a moral, intellectual, and social tradition proper to a certain French Protestant ethic at the end of the nineteenth century.

Notes

1 We owe the information on the life of Arthur Piaget to the kindness of Laurent Piaget, who accorded us an interview on 1 June 1994, for which we warmly thank him. Madame Henriette Piaget also gave us precious information in an interview on 16 January 1995. We would like to convey to her our deep recognition. Thanks to the competence of our colleague, Pierre-Yves Favez of the Canton of Vaud Communal Archives, we have been able to obtain numerous details on Arthur Piaget's childhood, for which we express our gratitude.

2 A. Berchtold (1963). *La Suisse romande au cap du XVe siècle Portrait littéraire et moral* (p. 432). Lausanne: Payot.

3 Ch.-O. Carbonell (1979). Les historiens protestants dans le renouveau de l'historiographie française. *Actes du colloque Les Protestants dans les débats de la troisième République (1871–1885)* (pp. 59–67). Paris: Ed. de la S.H.P.F.

4 J. Piaget (1976). Autobiographie. *Cahiers Vilfredo Pareto – Revue européenne des sciences sociales*, Geneva, *XIV*, 1–43.

5 J. Rychner (1952). Arthur Piaget, historien de la littérature française du Moyen Age. In E. Bauer, L. Thévenaz, & J. Rychner, *Arthur Piaget, professeur, archiviste, historien* (p. 32). Neuchâtel: Impr. Centrale.

6 P.-Y. Châtelain (1994). Les manuels d'histoire suisse dans l'école primaire neuchâteloise (1850–1900). *Musée neuchâtelois*, no. 3, 133–144.

7 State Archives, Neuchâtel, Arthur Piaget Collection. Letters cited later in the chapter are from the same collection.

8 State Archives, Neuchâtel, minutes of the review *Musée neuchâtelois*. The polemic began in the spring of 1918 following an unpleasant report by Arthur Piaget on *L'Histoire de la pendulerie neuchâteloise* of Alfred Chapuis, which appeared in 1917.

9 J.-J. Ducret (1984). *Jean Piaget, savant et philosophe. Les années de formation, 1907–1924. Etude sur la formation des connaissances et du sujet de la connaissance* (2 vols; Vol. 1, p. 74). Geneva: Droz.

10 F. Vidal (1994). *Piaget before Piaget* (p. 14). Cambridge, MA: Harvard University Press.

11 B. Joly (1989). L'Ecole des chartes et l'affaire Dreyfus. *Bibliothèque de l'Ecole des chartes, 147*, 626.

12 Ibid., pp. 618–619.

13 Vidal, op. cit., pp. 15–16.

14 Ibid., pp. 98–100, 155–157.

15 Ibid., p. 176.

16 C. Hublard (1987). *La ligue de la paix et de la liberté et l'Association pour la Société des Nations à Neuchâtel: une vision du monde, 1889–1947.* Master's dissertation, Institut d'histoire, Neuchâtel, pp. 54–59.

17 Vidal, op. cit., p. 149; and State Archives, Neuchâtel, Archives of the Swiss Association for Women's Suffrage, Neuchâtel section, dossier 22.

18 J. Liniger (1980). *En toute subjectivité. Cent ans de conquêtes démocratiques et régionales* (pp. 50, 60–61, 74). Neuchâtel: Messeiller.

4   Early schooling

Anne-Françoise Schaller-Jeanneret

This chapter is about Jean Piaget's early schooling in Neuchâtel, from primary through high school.[1] While the general school curriculum may be relatively familiar, the manner in which the course of study was carried out remains vague, as does the quality of the teachers. However, there were a few whose reputations are still remembered and whom Piaget himself credited with having influenced him.

The Neuchâtel school system at the beginning of the twentieth century

The Constitution of the Republic and Canton of Neuchâtel, adopted by the Constitutional Assembly on 25 April 1848, made primary education compulsory and placed it under the auspices of the state. Subsequent laws added to the development of the school system: In 1850, boys and girls between the ages of 7 and 16 were obligated to attend school. Free education was guaranteed by the law of 11 June 1861. In 1872, further legislation introduced lay staff, and state control increased.[2] The law pertaining to primary school of 27 April 1889 extended the period of schooling by adding a year of kindergarten, fixed the number of pupils at a maximum of 50 per class, instituted diplomas to encourage school attendance, and improved the training of teachers. A law proclaimed the following year finally assured the free supply of school materials.

The establishment of secondary schools started in 1853 with the organization of so-called vocational schools that complemented primary education with professionally oriented training for apprenticeships. In 1872, the state set a curriculum of two to three years for this training (practical, technical, industrial, commercial, artistic, pedagogical, agricultural), according to local requirements. The following year saw the introduction of a law providing for classical subjects, such as Latin and Greek, to be taught at the preparatory school level in view of literary studies in high schools.

The status of the grammar school was difficult to determine because it was hard to distinguish it clearly from the Academy, out of which it developed. It was only in 1896 that the baccalaureate was federally accredited, and the law of 26 July 1910, which created the University of Neuchâtel, also clearly relegated the grammar school to the secondary level of education.

Jean Piaget, thus, followed an educational system that had been established in the second half of the nineteenth century.

Jean Piaget's schooling

Primary school

The first traces of Jean Piaget's schooling date from April 1904, when, at the age of eight, he was enrolled for private lessons given by Miss Cécile Berthoud, on Faubourg de l'Hôpital.[3]

There is no evidence regarding Piaget's attendance at kindergarten, for even though it was obligatory, exceptions were made if the child was judged capable of going directly into primary school. Whatever the case, kindergarten was the place to learn the basics of reading, writing, and arithmetic. Founded on the principles of Frédéric Froebel[4] and on educational games, the kindergarten programme offered young children the opportunity to learn manual dexterity and handicraft skills, such as working with paper and clay, drawing, needlework, and singing.

It is not clear why Piaget had been enrolled in a private school since his father was on the school commission and even on the school committee in the neighbourhood of Vauseyon.[5] He did not begin attending public school until 1906, when he was in an all-male class with Jean Beauverd as master. Among his 44 classmates was his future childhood friend, Gustave Juvet.[6]

Jean Piaget was an outstanding pupil, particularly gifted in intellectual work. According to the law of 1889, he studied French, writing, arithmetic, geography, Swiss history, civics, singing, drawing, and gymnastics. His marks for the public school annual examinations that he took even while attending private school are available. In March 1905, at the end of the year with Miss Berthoud, he received full marks, i.e., six out of six in all subjects (dictation, composition, measuring and accounting, and mental arithmetic).

In March 1907, with his teacher Jean Beauverd, Piaget continued to earn exceptionally good marks, getting an average of 5.4 while the class average was 4.26.[7]

A look at the curriculum shows that a pupil who had four years of primary schooling, excluding kindergarten, such as Piaget, spent most of the time learning French (reading and reciting, vocabulary, grammar, and spelling). Many hours were also spent on arithmetic: The pupil, who in the first year learnt to do the four basic operations with the help of an abacus, should by the fourth year have been able to work with decimals and the metric system (not including cubic measures). He would also have been introduced to calculating with fractions. Furthermore, he would have had a basic understanding of local and national geography, and also of Europe and other continents. History would have been restricted to national events covering a vast period, from prehistoric lake dwellings discovered in the area to 1870.[8]

In the fourth year, children studied in greater depth historical events between the fifteenth and twentieth centuries. It is interesting to note that as early as the third year pupils were given some civic education; in the fourth year they would learn about the state government, its election system, and how the state and the towns worked. Such a programme of studies was consistent with the role assigned to public education in a republic where the task was to form its citizens.

Secondary school

Jean Piaget began at the Latin school in 1907, at the age of 11. This was a local secondary school for boys that lasted five years and served as a preparatory school for the cantonal grammar school that delivered the diploma necessary to enter university. In Piaget's time, the secondary school was still under legislation that dated from 1872 and 1873. The curriculum for the secondary level was not reorganized until 1919.

However, the Latin school that Piaget attended was already in the throes of change under the direction of James Paris, who was greatly concerned with the development of children's personalities. Among the many changes introduced was the study of languages: Classical languages were put off for later study in favour of an earlier start in German, and the teaching of French was improved. Natural history, formerly somewhat neglected, came into its own. Paris, convinced of the value of promoting a broad literary education making the students discover France, and of the importance of a familiarity with classical culture, was equally keen on the study of nature, because more than other subjects it gave students an opportunity to be active.

> Would it not be more interesting for young pupils to hear about flowers, animals, physical and meteorological phenomena already by the ages of 11 and 13, on the condition that they are essentially given a practical exposure? We are sure that making a herbarium will enthuse pupils in the fourth or fifth year more than semi-deponent verbs.[9]

The areas of the life sciences studied in each academic year are listed in Table 4.1.

According to the curriculum,[10] the mother language had the highest number of lessons (grammar, spelling, vocabulary, reading, reciting, essay and verse writing, history of the language, written and oral reports, and in the last year 'elements of literature' – extracts of classic and modern texts). In order of importance, Latin was next. The method for teaching the classical language was rapid: Having acquired the basics in the third year, two years later the pupils were already reading extracts from Julius Caesar's *De Bello Gallico*

Table 4.1 Latin school curriculum, 1907–1912

Academic year	Areas studied in life sciences
1907–1908	*Summer:* Introduction to the most important regional plants. Brief description of the parts of the plants. Making herbariums. Outings. *Winter:* Introduction to some types of vertebrates, mammals, and birds.
1908–1909	*Summer:* Introduction to elementary biology (continuation). Introduction to cryptograms. Making herbariums. Outings. *Winter:* Introduction to zoology: reptiles, batrachians, fish, insects, molluscs, worms.
1909–1910	*Summer:* General botany. Classification. *Winter:* Elementary zoology. Classification: invertebrates.
1910–1911	Elements of physics (bodily, acoustical, optical, electrical properties).
1911–1912	Elements of physics (bodily, acoustical, optical, electrical properties).

and Ovid's *Metamorphoses*. By the last year, they were translating passages by Sallust and Virgil, and Cicero's speeches.

The programme for mathematics was spread over the entire secondary schooling, with at least four or five weekly lessons (arithmetic, geometry, accounting, and equations of the first degree with one or several unknowns). In total, the number of lessons in mathematics was identical to that allowed for Latin.

German was not neglected: Lessons were more literary than practical, with the translation of classical authors and the reading of modern ones, although exposure to the literature was limited to conversational practice on literary subjects.

Students studied Greek for two years, reading selected passages of Xenophon's *Anabase* and Homer's *Odyssey*.

The content of the history lessons seems quite ambitious, ranging from antiquity to the twentieth century, including Swiss history since the Reformation. Civic history was not left out: Students studied the federal and cantonal institutions. Also in the curriculum were geography (Switzerland and the five continents, transportation means, introduction to 'geographical economy'), drawing, singing, penmanship, and gymnastics.

In short, the Latin school provided a solid classical education, from which Piaget profited. The five years of the lower secondary school concentrated on classical languages and literary subjects rather than on sciences. Among others, students were expected to know some of the works of Corneille, Racine, Molière, La Fontaine, Bossuet, and La Bruyère. In Latin, Titus Livy replaced Ovid.

Legally, the number of pupils per class at the Latin school was limited to 35 (the total number of pupils at that time ranged between 116 and 130 boys). The number of pupils tended to drop during the course of study, so that in 1911–1912 there were only 16 in class with Piaget. Rolin Wavre[11] was Piaget's schoolmate in the fifth year, as was Maurice Zundel, a companion throughout secondary school.[12]

Others who would go on to grammar school with Piaget were the philologist André Bürger, who married Piaget's younger sister Marthe; the pastor Robert Cand; Georges de Dardel, future manager of La Compagnie Suisse de réassurances (a Swiss insurance company); and Marcel Romy.[13]

Information about Piaget's years at the Latin school is scarce, although school report cards were issued four or even six times a year, and he would have passed comprehensive examinations at the end of his schooling there in order to attend the grammar school.

There is, however, testimony to the fact that in 1907–1908, members of Piaget's class were botanical and zoological enthusiasts, 'some of whom stood out by their zeal and application'.[14] It would probably not be misleading to count Piaget among that number. The report points out that in the following year, 'The class was the best in the school in mathematics and natural history.'[15]

On 9 June 1910, Piaget joined the Club of the Friends of Nature,[16] where he met teachers from the grammar school as well as from the university. Among the Neuchâtel naturalists at that time, little distinction was drawn between amateur and professional. Such extracurricular contact certainly enriched Piaget's scientific development. Pierre Bovet[17] and Eugène Legrandroy[18] attended his trial lecture ('A Special Mollusc in Our Lake'); Théodore Delachaux[19] and Otto Fuhrmann, who later supervised Piaget's doctoral thesis and, owing to his specialization in comparative anatomy, hydrobiology, and helminthology, contributed to the development of the Zoology Institute, were honorary members of the Friends.[20] The sometime Latin school teacher and future grammar school teacher Paul Godet (1836–1911), director of the Natural History Museum, and former high school teacher, was a specialist in malacological taxonomy and a pedagogical force within the Club. It was Godet who reviewed the candidate's trial lecture to the Club. According to Piaget, this was the man who had strongly influenced him years before. Godet, who was himself an expert on Swiss conchological fauna, had been instructing Piaget since 1907 in his methods of describing, classifying, and cataloguing at the Natural History Museum.

To a large extent it was outside school that Piaget cultivated his scientific interests between 1907 and 1912, particularly within the Club of the Friends of Nature, where he read several papers, and by working with Godet. A significant difference between his school work and scientific activities emerged at this time: While the school programme between 1907 and 1910 concentrated on birds, molluscs, and classifying invertebrates, young Piaget, according to Fernando Vidal,[21] was by then a quasi-professional in the classification of molluscs. Piaget's scientific maturity was precocious, even if his activity as a naturalist concentrated only on observation. According to Jean-Jacques Ducret,[22] Piaget's first real article on zoology dates from 1911 and is entitled 'Les limnées des lacs de Neuchâtel, Bienne, Morat et des environs' (The Limnaea of the Lakes of Neuchâtel, Bienne, Morat and the Environs); in 1912, he turned down the post of assistant at the Natural History Museum of Geneva. He was by then a recognized specialist in conchology, capable of striking out on his own.

From that perspective, one wonders how pertinent official schooling was for Piaget, given how much he attained outside the traditional educational system. Nevertheless, it seems worthwhile to look at the masters who marked his youth along the way. They were Henri Borle (French, history, geography), Jules Morgenthaler (also French, history, geography), Marc Nicolet (arithmetic and mathematics, life sciences), Walther Racine (drawing), Samuel Waldvogel (German language), and Charles Zumbach (French, Latin, Greek, history).[23]

The cantonal grammar school

The institution

On 16 September 1912 Jean Piaget began his baccalaureate[24] studies at the Gymnase littéraire (grammar school), from which he graduated on 13 July 1915. This institution had been separated from the Academy of Neuchâtel and was accredited by a nineteenth-century law[25] to confer the federal baccalaureate.[26] With the founding of the Ecole Normale (school of education for primary school teachers)[27] in 1904,[28] the Gymnase was divided into three sections of three years: scientific, literary, and pedagogical. The literary section led to a broader choice of subsequent studies, while the scientific stream limited students to the science faculty at the university, the Federal Polytechnic, or specialized colleges. School attendance was mandatory, and the parents received report cards three times a year. Promotion to the next level depended on marks and teachers' recommendations. The grammar school trained students for academic or technical studies. The student body numbered 100 enrolled students as well as auditors. Although it was a 'co-ed' school, there were in effect very few girls: The first female student enrolled in science in 1908 and the second in literature in 1911. The staff, which was exclusively male at the time, was headed by Ernest DuBois. As of 1912, the headmaster, appointed by the State Council, worked with a school board of seven members on which sat representatives of the four university faculties. Arthur Piaget, Jean's father, became president of the Council in 1919.

The curricula

The weekly course of study at the Gymnase kept students fully occupied.[29] Piaget and his fellow students[30] would also have been expected to do several hours of homework.

Classical languages were in the forefront, followed by French and mathematics. German language, history, chemistry, and physics came next in importance. Life sciences and philosophy had only a limited place in the curriculum. According to the syllabus, Piaget studied Titus Livy, Virgil, Sallust, Circero's speeches, Horace's *Satires* and *Odes*, *Annales* by Tacitus, and select extracts from Plaute, Terence, and Pliny in Latin; in Greek, Homer's *Iliad* and *Odyssey*, Herodotos, Lysias, Xenophon, Plato (*Phaedo*), Euripides (*Iphigenia in Tauris*), Sophocles (*Oedipus at Colonus*), Demosthenes (*On the Crown*), and Thucydides; in French, writing and history of literature from the Middle Ages to the nineteenth century, taking in Corneille (*Le Cid, Cinna*), La Fontaine, Molière (*Le Misanthrophe, L'Avare, Le Malade imaginaire*), Racine (*Britannicus, Phèdre*), and selected passages of Pascal, Boileau, Bossuet, la Bruyère, Saint-Simon, Montesquieu, and Victor Hugo. The German-language syllabus included readings from Goethe (*Faust*) and C.-F. Meyer (*Der Schuss von der Kanzel*).

The history syllabus started with the barbaric invasions and continued up to the nineteenth century, with emphasis on the French Revolution and Swiss political institutions (federal, cantonal, and communal).

Mathematical studies covered algebra, trigonometry, and plane, special, and analytical geometry; in physics the students studied mechanics, acoustics, magnetism, electronics, geometrical optics, and physical optics.

A couple of hours each week were given to organic and inorganic chemistry. But by the third year, geography, which had concentrated on the study of the five continents, was no longer part of the curriculum.

Two subjects that particularly influenced Piaget were natural history, in which he already excelled, and philosophy. The natural history syllabus is outlined in Table 4.2.

This curriculum fit the rules for the baccalaureate examinations for candidates for medical studies of 6 July 1906. At that time, future medical students followed the literary section of study, and all the students benefited from this curriculum. The introduction of geology was due to this law.

The areas covered in philosophy are outlined in Table 4.3.

Table 4.2 Natural history syllabus, 1912–1915

Academic year	Material studied
1912–1913	Winter: invertebrates. Summer: general botany.
1913–1914	Winter: vertebrates. Summer: special botany.
1914–1915	Winter: human anatomy. Summer: geology.

Table 4.3 Philosophy syllabus, 1913–1915

Academic year	Material studied
1913–1914	Psychology, facts of consciousness. Psychological analysis of judgement. The emotions. The will. Reflections.
1914–1915	Descartes: *Discourse on Method*. Aristotle's logic (terms, propositions, syllogisms); elements of modern logic; principles and methods of science.

The examinations

At the end of grammar school, literary studies students sat for examinations in order to obtain the baccalaureate degree. The written examinations were an essay in French, translations from Latin and Greek, an essay in German, and mathematical exercises. These were the major subjects and counted twice in the calculation of the average mark. At the oral examinations, the candidate was questioned on French literature, Latin, Greek, German, philosophy (including psychology and logic), history, geography, mathematics, physics, chemistry, and life sciences.[31] Students also had to earn a mark in drawing. Annual marks counted for one-third of the final grade. The final examination mark awarded could be 'sufficient', 'satisfactory', or 'outstanding'.

The examination papers have been saved only since 1917 so we do not know Piaget's marks for the baccalaureate in 1915. Owing to the Great War, 1914–1915 was an exceptional year because many students were doing military service, and the authorities had to organize a special examination session in September. Ten baccalaureates were awarded in total: five with 'sufficient', four with 'satisfactory', and one with 'outstanding'. It is quite likely that this last was awarded to Jean Piaget, given his yearly marks which were well beyond the average. The report of the Board of Education drew attention 'to the exceptional performance of a few pupils in the first two very small classes which significantly raised the average at the examinations'.[32]

The archival records for the Gymnase show the semester marks awarded to Jean Piaget, as given in Table 4.4.[33] Based on this report of his marks, Piaget was a brilliant student, at the top of his class throughout his grammar school years. Of particular interest are the consistent full marks in philosophy.

In 1912 Piaget belonged to the Neuchâtel Society of Life Sciences; in 1913 he joined the Swiss Zoological Society and in 1914 the Swiss Society of Life Sciences; he continued to work steadfastly for the Friends of Nature, where he took part in high-level debates against his fellow members (Marcel Romy and Gustave Juvet[34]). He cultivated relationships with scientific figures in malacology, such as Emile Yung, professor at Geneva, who entrusted him

Table 4.4 Jean Piaget's semester marks at the grammar school

Subject	1912–1913	1913–1914	1914–1915
Conduct	6 / 6 / 5.5	5.5 / 6 / 6	6 / 6 / 6
French Composition	5.5 / 5.5 / 5.5	5 / 5.5 / 5.5	5.5 / 5.5 / 5.5
Latin	5 / 5.5 / 5.5	5 / 5 / 5	4.5 / 5 / 5
Greek	5 / 5 / 5	4.5 / 5 / 5	5 / 4.5 / 4.5
German	5 / 5 / 4.5	4.5 / 4 / 5	4 / 4 / 4.5
Mathematics	5 / 5 / 5	4.5 / 5 / 5.5	5 / 5 / 5
French Literature	6 / 6 / 6	6 / 5.5 / 6	6 / 5.5
General History	6 / 6 / 6	6 / 6 / 6	6 / 6 / 6
National History	5.5 / 6 / 6	6 / 6 / 6	6 / 6 / 6
Geography	6 / 6 / 6	6 / 6 / 6	–
Physics	5.5 / 6 / 5	5 / 5.5 / 6	5 / 5.5 / 5
Chemistry	6 / 6 / 6	5.5 / 5.5 / 5.5	5 / 5.5 / 5.5
Natural History	6 / 6 / 5.5	6 / 6 / 6	5.5 / 6
Drawing	5 / 5 / 5.5	5 / 5.5 / 5.5	5.5 / 5.5
Philosophy	–	6 / 6 / 6	6 / 6 / 6

with identifying the molluscs collected from his dredging of Lake Geneva, and Maurice Bedot, director of the Natural History Museum of Geneva and founder of the journal *La Revue Suisse de Zoologie* (Swiss Journal of Zoology). He contributed to various European journals and as of 1912 became involved in the controversy about the origins and classification of abyssal limnaea in a published exchange with a doctoral student at the University of Lausanne, Waclaw Roszkwoski, with whom he kept up a private correspondence.[35] This debate between a grammar schoolboy and an advanced postgraduate student proves that Piaget's knowledge far exceeded that taught in the third year of the literary stream of his school; furthermore, this 'school debate' had a formative effect on the young man, who, while still greatly influenced by Paul Godet, realized that he was not sufficiently aware of contemporary theories in zoology.

This was also the time when Piaget developed an interest in moral questions and philosophical issues. From this point, grammar school was perhaps more relevant for him, allowing him access to formidable teachers such as Arnold Reymond, whose strong personalities left lasting impressions.

Jean Piaget's grammar school teachers

Piaget's teachers (see Table 4.5) are of particular interest. According to the law, grammar school teachers were supposed to be university graduates with appropriate teaching qualifications,[36] yet most of the teachers of the day held doctoral degrees. Those of Piaget's teachers who held such a title were Gustave Attinger, William Domeier, Ernest DuBois, Maurice Jaquet, Jules LeCoultre, Alfred Lombard, Arnold Reymond, Henri Rivier, and Fritz

Table 4.5 Jean Piaget's grammar school teachers

Subject	1912–1913	1913–1914	1914–1915
Latin	Gustave Attinger	Fritz Robert	Jules LeCoultre
Greek	Gustave Attinger	Gustave Attinger	William Domeier
French Language	Ernest DuBois	Ernest DuBois	Ernest DuBois
French Literature	Alfred Lombard	Alfred Lombard	Philippe Godet
German Language	Fritz Robert	Fritz Robert	William Domeier
Geography	Charles Knapp	Charles Knapp	Charles Knapp
General History	Alfred Lombard	Alfred Lombard	Alfred Lombard
Swiss History	Adolphe Blanc		
Mathematics	Fritz Rufener	Fritz Rufener	Fritz Rufener
Physics	Fritz Rufener	Fritz Rufener	Fritz Rufener
Chemistry and Mineralogy	Henri Rivier	Henri Rivier	Henri Rivier
Natural History	Maurice Jaquet	Maurice Jaquet	Maurice Jaquet
Artistic Drawing	Théodore Delachaux	Théodore Delachaux	Théodore Delachaux
Philosophy	–	Arnold Reymond	Arnold Reymond

Robert. Closely associated with the Academy and then the university, the grammar school, which was housed in the same building, employed nearly the same staff. Jules LeCoultre, former rector of the Academy, was full professor on the Faculty of Letters, as were William Domeier, Charles Knapp, Philippe Godet, and Arnold Reymond. Later, others were promoted to this level (Alfred Lombard, Henri Rivier, Théodore Delachaux). Piaget himself realized the advantage this held: 'The school programme of my native city was such that professors appointed to the University Faculty also taught at the grammar school, doubtless a heavy duty for them, but an inestimable privilege for the school boys that we were.'[37]

It is impossible to judge the quality of their teaching or of their pedagogical ability, and Piaget claimed, perhaps slyly, that he had been bored at school: 'Thus I have begun to write up my system (one wonders wherever I got the time to do so, but I grab every chance I can, especially during boring lessons).'[38]

However, many of those teachers were anything but banal; in fact they were rather significant scholarly personalities of their day. Ernest DuBois, director of the grammar school and also a French teacher, taught phonetics in the department of modern French at the university. Alfred Lombard, another teacher, earned a doctorate from the Sorbonne in 1913 and was later rector of the university and founding member of the Institut Neuchâtelois.[39] His father-in-law, Philippe Godet, poet, literary critic, essayist, journalist, doctor *honoris causa* at the Universities of Geneva and Lausanne, author of *Histoire littéraire de la Suisse française* (Literary history of French-speaking Switzerland), professor of French literature, and then rector, had a moral authority that made him a leading personality in literary life in Neuchâtel at the time. Charles Knapp, who taught geography at the grammar school and at the Academy, had been curator of the Ethnographic Museum of the city since 1903. In 1915 he held the chair at the university for ethnography and the history of civilizations. Knapp founded the Neuchâtel Society for Geography, of which he became the archivist-librarian and editor of its bulletin, and published the *Dictionnaire géographique de la Suisse* (Geographical Diction-ary of Switzerland), a collective work. Knapp was subsequently awarded a doctorate *honoris causa* by the University of Lausanne. Henri Rivier, profes-sor of chemistry at the Academy and then at the university, an active member of the Neuchâtel Society of Life Sciences, held the post of rector at the university between 1927 and 1929.

The stages of Maurice Jaquet's career are also worth taking a look at. As Carl Vogt's[40] assistant in Geneva he taught anatomy and comparative embry-ology. He then became an assistant at the Anatomy Institute at the University of Bucharest, where he collected molluscs that Paul Godet identified. After serving as curator of the Oceanographic Museum of Monaco, he settled definitively in Neuchâtel. He took part in the life of the Friends of Nature and in his will he provided rooms in his home in Serrières to the Friends so they could hold their meetings.

Paul Godet's nephew, Théodore Delachaux, who taught drawing at the grammar school, was not only a painter and the general secretary of the Swiss Society of Painters, Sculptors, and Architects, but also a naturalist. He became Fuhrmann's assistant at the university's zoological laboratories in 1919. Delachaux published several articles on zoological subjects and in particular on freshwater entomostracan crustaceans. He studied the tiny organisms of underground waters, especially those in the caverns of the nearby Areuse Gorge. He discovered two organisms in the dead expanse of water of the Ver grotto. He was an honorary member of the Club of the Friends of Nature and future president of the Neuchâtel Society of Life Sciences, and of the Neuchâtel Society of Geography. He became curator of the Ethnographic Museum in 1921 and assistant at the Natural History Museum in 1936, curator of the archaeology and prehistorical collections at the History Museum of the city, doctor of science *honoris causa*, and professor of prehistoric archaeology at the university in 1940.

Piaget's godfather, Samuel Cornut, introduced him to philosophy with the teachings of Bergson. However, Arnold Reymond seems to have been the personality to have mostly keenly impressed him in this field, at least accord-ing to his autobiography. Having been his student in philosophy at gram-mar school between 1913 and 1915, Piaget regarded him as someone who could arouse consciousness in a variety of vocations. Reymond for his part had begun his career by studying for a doctorate in theology (*Essai sur le subjectivisme et le problème de la connaissance religieuse* [Essay on Subjectiv-ism and the Problem of Religious Knowledge], 1900), then studied math-ematics, physics, and philosophy before writing a second thesis, this time in philosophy (*Logique et mathématiques. Essai historique et critique sur le nombre infini* [Logic and Mathematics. Historical Essay and Criticism on the Infinite Number], 1908) at the University of Geneva. He was first a privat-docent at the Faculty of Science of the University of Lausanne (history and philosophy of science) and then appointed professor of philosophy and of the history of philosophy at the University and grammar school of Neuchâtel in 1912. He stayed there until 1925, during which time he published his *Histoire des sciences exactes et naturelles dans l'Antiquité gréco-romaine* (History of Exact and Natural Sciences in Greco-Roman Antiquity). Piaget was his successor. Drawn to the idea of a theory of knowledge, Reymond touched upon theology, philosophy, exact and life sciences, pedagogy, and civic life: The quest for truth, reason, and judgement made up the core of his preoccupations. He was interested in the psychology of sciences as well as the relationship between science and faith, between scientific and religious knowledge. According to Piaget, Reymond's critical-historical method exercised a large influence on his students. Taking his student beyond the simple opposition between the vital and the mathematical, Reymond let him perceive the problems of logic. Piaget claimed to have been struck by one of Reymond's lessons on universals and emphasized: 'It was perhaps the first time that I understood, thanks to him, the fundamental union of biology and logic.'[41]

Furthermore, Piaget praised the quality of the personal contact Reymond fostered with his students, inviting them home and reading and commenting on their individual work. Given the small number of students in Piaget's class, Reymond's lessons were 'an unforgettable experience in the initiation to philosophy in small groups, with everything that entails, like spontaneous questions and discussion, besides the regular lectures'.

According to Piaget, Reymond:

> gave especially a commentary on *Discourse on Method*[42] and an initiation into the problems of knowledge. This was where he excelled and managed to impart to us questions arising from the existence of logic and mathematics in a most engaging manner. . . .
>
> In a word, Arnold Reymond was a great master: great by his innate honesty and his profound humanity, and great by the strong and constant effort he puts into fully grasping the scientific origins of philosophical thought. He was anything but just a philosopher of science and one should duly emphasize . . . the metaphysical and religious aspects of his thinking.[43]

As a student at the university, Piaget maintained contact with his grammar school teacher, and many years later, at the installation of the bust of Reymond at the University of Lausanne, Piaget spoke about the major influence of Reymond on his work: 'My own research on the genesis of logic in the child has been inspired to a large extent by his teaching, the genetic study prolonging the historical study itself.'[44]

Reymond seemed to have enjoyed his students, as can be seen in his reply to Piaget's compliments:

> You came into my life at the same time as Rolin Wavre and Gustave Juvet, just as I was starting out teaching at the grammar school and University of Neuchâtel. I could not have asked for better working companions in those beginning stages.[45]

Conclusion

In dealing with a person as talented as Jean Piaget, it would be presumptuous to try to determine just how much was acquired through schooling. Encouraged by a stimulating family environment, Piaget showed early in life a remarkable open-mindedness and a lively intellectual curiosity. But to what extent was the school able to meet the needs of such a child, and then of the adolescent? By the time he started the Latin school his knowledge in life sciences already went beyond that of the average pupil's, and at the grammar school he seemed to have been more influenced by the quality of some teachers than by the actual curriculum. Perhaps one ought to settle for saying that the Neuchâtel school system certainly provided Piaget with solid bases on which he achieved excellent results.

Notes

1 A *gymnase* is the higher secondary school that prepares students for university and the Federal Polytechnic School.
2 In federalist Switzerland, the cantons govern the school system with the exception of certain national degrees (federal baccalaureate, federal medical qualifications, etc.).
3 Archives of the primary school, city of Neuchâtel, Collège de la Promenade, designated status of Neuchâtel classes. Cécile Marie Berthoud (1848–1931) was the sister of the state counsellor and then national counsellor Jean Edouard Berthoud (1846–1916).
4 Frédéric Froebel (1782–1852) was a pedagogue who developed a teaching method for young children.
5 The northwest area of Neuchâtel.
6 Future successor of Eugène Legrandroy, professor of astronomy at the University of Neuchâtel.
7 Archives of the primary schools of the city of Neuchâtel, table of school examinations, 1904–1905 and 1906–1907. The marks in 1907 were for elocution and composition, spelling, reading, grammar and diagramming, memory exercises, vocabulary, practical and mental arithmetic, writing, drawing, geography, history, singing, and gymnastics.
8 Primary school curricula for the school years 1904–1905 and 1905–1906.
9 Report of the organization of the Neuchâtel Latin School, Neuchâtel, 1907, p. 49.
10 Ibid.
11 Mathematics professor at the University of Geneva from 1924 to 1949.
12 Born in Neuchâtel in 1897, died in Lausanne in 1975, Maurice Zundel was also a member of the Friends of Nature as of 1911. Zundel, a Catholic living among

Protestants, left Neuchâtel at the age of 15 in order to study theology at Fribourg and Einsiedeln. He became one of the most important Catholic theologians of the twentieth century.

13 A future lawyer in Lugano and in Basle, Romy published with Piaget, in 1912, *Les mollusques du Lac de Saint-Blaise.*

14 Neuchâtel schools. Report for the school year 1907–1908, p. 53.

15 Ibid., school year 1908–1909.

16 Cf. Fernando Vidal, below.

17 While professor of philosophy at the University of Neuchâtel, Bovet was appointed director of the School for the Science of Education (Rousseau Institute) in Geneva from 1912 to 1944.

18 Astronomy professor at the University of Neuchâtel.

19 Delachaux's career is described later in this chapter.

20 One became an honorary member when one was no longer active yet still paid dues (in principle after graduating from grammar school).

21 F. Vidal (1988). *Piaget adolescent, 1907–1915* (p. 172). Doctoral thesis, University of Geneva.

22 J.-J. Ducret (1984). *Jean Piaget, savant et philosophe. Les années de formation, 1907–1924. Etude sur la formation des connaissances et du sujet de la connaissance.* Geneva: Droz.

23 Classical grammar school curriculum, academic years 1907–1912.

24 Diploma awarded by the state at the end of secondary schooling and allowing bearers entry to university.

25 Law on higher education (Academy and grammar school) of 18 May 1896.

26 A diploma that is like the cantonal baccalaureate but is recognized on the federal level and is required for studying medicine.

27 School for training primary school teachers.

28 Law establishing the cantonal normal school of 21 November 1904. Teacher training had formerly been attached to the Neuchâtel cantonal grammar school.

29 Curricula of the cantonal grammar school of Neuchâtel from 1912 to 1915.

30 They were René Banderet, Edouard Béguelin, Maurice Béguin, Max Berthoud (member of the Friends of Nature), Emile Boller, Gérald Bonhôte, Théodore Borel, André Bürger (id.), Robert Cand (id.), Georges de Dardel, Jean DuBois, René Dubied, Gilbert DuPasquier, Robert Ecklin, Etienne Kruger, Walter Mengel, Bernard Menzel, Jean-Louis Nagel, Willy Oelschläger, Alain de Reynier, and Marcel Romy (id.). Cf. cantonal grammar school of Neuchâtel, students' marks, September 1906–July 1918.

31 General law of 26 September 1905 for Cantonal Grammar School.

32 Report of the Cantonal Board of Education for 1914–1915, Cantonal Grammar School, p. 64.

33 Archives of the Cantonal Grammar School of Neuchâtel. Students' marks, September 1906 to July 1918.

34 See note 6 above.

35 See Ducret, op. cit., pp. 127–138.

36 Law for higher education (Academy and grammar school) of 18 May 1896, art. 14.

37 Letter to Arnold Reymond, *Revue de théologie et de philosophie 9 (1959), Hommage à Arnold Reymond*, p. 44.

38 J. Piaget (1976). Autobiographie (pp. 38–39). *Cahiers Vilfredo Pareto – Revue européenne des sciences sociales*, Geneva, *XIV*, 1–43.

39 A learned society.

40 German naturalist (1817–1895), defended transformism.

41 Letter to Arnold Reymond, op. cit., p. 45.

42 R. Descartes (1637). *Discourse on the method of rightly conducting one's reason and of seeking truth in the sciences.* Cambridge: Cambridge University Press.

43 Letter to Arnold Reymond, op. cit., pp. 44, 46–47.

44 J. Piaget (1945). *Inauguration du buste de M. Arnold Reymond, oeuvre de François L. Simecek, à l'aula de Université de Lausanne le 16 décembre 1944* (p. 20). Lausanne: Rouge.

45 Reply of Arnold Reymond to Jean Piaget, ibid., p. 25.

5 Studies at the University of Neuchâtel

Jean-Paul Schaer

Before entering the university in 1915, Jean Piaget certainly had a good idea of the kind of personalities he would meet there. His father, Arthur Piaget, who had been the first rector, was particularly well placed to judge the advantages and disadvantages a student would have in studying life sciences at a modest institution. Lacking documents that record the reasons for this choice, one must make assumptions on the matter. The war raging in neighbouring countries did not encourage the undertaking of studies outside Switzerland; furthermore, local accommodation would have been easily arranged by his father. Such were the factors that must have contributed to the decision. However, it deprived the young man of a scientific setting better adapted to the discipline in which he had already distinguished himself.

In 1915 Jean Piaget, having received his baccalaureate in humanities at the beginning of the summer, should have begun his studies at the start of the autumn semester. In fact, in order to recover his health, which had been badly affected by bouts of illness and strenuous intellectual work, Piaget was sent off to the mountains for an extended convalescence.

These special circumstances account for the relatively light course load of only 7 hours per week during the winter semesters 1915–1916 and 1916–1917. First-year students normally carried as many as 20 to 30 hours a week.[1] Piaget was not even enrolled as a student for the summer semester of 1916. It was only as of the summer semester of 1917 that he became more or less an ordinary student with a weekly timetable of 18 hours of courses.

Piaget sat, without delay, for the first series of examinations for his degree in life sciences, which included oral and written tests on matter covered in courses that he certainly had not attended; however, he earned full marks in nearly all the subjects, as Table 5.1. shows (scale of 1 to 6, 6 being the maximum).[2]

During the winter semester 1917–1918 and the summer semester 1918, Piaget enrolled respectively for 29 and 24 hours of weekly courses.[3] His accelerated course of scientific studies reflected his determination to satisfy the lecture and laboratory requirements necessary to sit the next series of examinations. As a result, there was almost a total lack of training in chemistry apart from 3 weekly hours of physical chemistry that he followed for one year.

Table 5.1 Piaget's 1917 examination results

Oral examinations	Geology	6
	Palaeontology	6
	Comparative anatomy	6
	Human anatomy and physiology	5
Written examinations	Palaeontology	6
	Botany	6
	Zoology	6

Having regained his health, he broadened his intellectual horizons by attending courses in subjects he felt would be useful for his development (mathematics and philosophy). At the examinations in summer 1918 he was awarded the following marks: 6 in zoology, 5 in botany, and 6 in geology.[4]

In this way, Piaget finished his degree in life sciences with a general average of 5.85 and high honours. The following February, when he was no longer enrolled at the university (once again an exceptional circumstance!), the Faculty had to examine three submitted theses that had been submitted.[5] Professor Otto Fuhrmann, who wrote the report on the two concerning biology (that of Jean Piaget and that of Albert Monard[6]), praised them as outstanding works and gave them the highest mark, i.e., 6. Thus, after little more than five semesters at the Faculty of Sciences, and more than a year spent convalescing at a mountain resort, Piaget finished his university studies with the degree of Doctor of Science.

Nowadays such rapidity would be unheard of, and at the time it was fairly rare, yet at the University of Neuchâtel other students in sciences were also able to defend their theses during the fourth year of their studies. Albert Monard was a similar case and had even earned full marks in all his examinations. However, Piaget's rapidity is more astonishing for two reasons: the lengthy early absence from the university and his participation in two competitions for which he had to submit extra research papers.

It must be noted that Piaget was already a recognized and much appreciated author in malacology when he matriculated at the university. He had published more than 400 pages in scientific journals, some of which had an international circulation. By the time he entered university his thesis was well under way, lacking only specific regional studies and a particular statistical approach. But what kind of training did he receive at this university?

A short history of the University of Neuchâtel

In the Swiss Confederation, each of the 23 cantons is responsible for education from primary school through university. The Confederation coordinates the systems and oversees the training of engineers at the federal polytechnics, the only national schools in the country.

Universities such as those of Basle, Berne, Geneva, and Zurich are long established and benefited from the growth of those cities in the course of their histories. Others, such as Fribourg and Neuchâtel, are much newer institutions. They reflect the cultural and religious regionalism of the country and the determination of the local elite, who, in the nineteenth century, recognized the advantages the small cantons could gain from providing higher education for the managerial needs of their economies.

The University of Neuchâtel was founded only in 1909; it is the heir of two modest academies, the first of which (1838–1848)[7] was remarkable due to the incomparable influence of Louis Agassiz, who transformed the little city where he lived for a while into a scientific centre renowned throughout Europe in its day. Although it had been closed down during the Republican Revolution of 1848, the institution left such a glorious image that it was possible to rekindle the flame without much delay.

The second academy (1866–1909)[8] was a very modest yet hybrid establishment that provided grammar school as well as a basic university education. It fulfilled various functions: As an institution of secondary education, it played a major role in the training of teaching staff for the secondary level, and it also educated local students who intended to go on to university for medical study or for pharmacology or to the polytechnic in Zurich. For many years, the federal government put pressure on the Neuchâtel authorities to ensure that the academy provided adequate training for its students.

The canton's precarious financial circumstances, the irregular number of students, and especially the small number of degrees awarded yearly by the various faculties did not help to strengthen the institution. Yet the number of students continued to grow, from 61 in 1895 to 126 ten years later.

In 1909 the State of Neuchâtel managed to transform the academy into a university, with the hope of improving its influence. This political step was largely due to the State Minister of Education, Edouard Quartier-La-Tente, a former theology professor at the Academy. The new name, however, did not bring with it the changes that had been hoped for: The budget stagnated; no new lecture halls or laboratories were built or even planned, in spite of the chronic lack of space of which everyone complained, especially in the sciences. The change of name did lead, however, to a cleaner administrative separation of the grammar school and the university, even though many professors continued teaching in both institutions and they were still under the same roof.[9]

At the time of its founding, the university had 35 full professors, with widely varying timetables, responsible for its various chairs, 11 lecturers, and 11 privat-docents.[10] There were 169 students and 156 auditors, who were mostly in the Faculty of Arts. While the number of teachers remained nearly constant, the student body increased by 30 per cent over the next ten years, in spite of the drop in foreign students owing to the war of 1914–1918.

In the preceding years, foreign students were an important constituent of the university. They came mostly from Eastern Europe (Bulgaria, Poland,

Romania, and Russia) as well as from Germany and the Scandinavian countries.

Before the war, female students represented nearly 30 per cent of the university community. The majority were in the Faculty of Arts, with an important and large contingent from abroad. There were not many female students in the sciences (22 per cent in 1913, 13 per cent in 1917); a good number of them seemed destined for medical studies and thus stayed for only a year at Neuchâtel. It was not until 1919–1920 that the Faculty of Science awarded its first degree to a Swiss female student, Mercédès Droz (Zahn).[11] However, already as early as the autumn semester 1910–1911, a Swedish female student, Naïma Sahlbom, who had done the first part of her studies at Basle, received the second doctorate of science that the university conferred.[12]

The Faculty of Sciences

In autumn 1915, when Jean Piaget enrolled in the Faculty of Sciences, there were 10 full professors, 3 lecturers, 3 privat-docents, 51 students, and 5 auditors.[13] Even for its time, the Sciences Faculty was a very small establishment. In reply to the critics who accused it of being a luxury from which only an already privileged minority profited, the faculty had set as its primary priority the task of training secondary-school teachers. For this purpose, it established four types of degree: mathematics; physics and chemistry; life sciences (with zoology, botany, and geology); and teaching. The first three degrees required three years of study,[14] while the teaching qualification took only two years.

For each principal subject (mathematics, physics, chemistry, botany, and geology–palaeontology), a single professor taught the basic subjects as well as the specialized courses. In a few rare cases, such as chemistry, the professor would collaborate with a lecturer or a privat-docent. There were three professors on the staff for the zoology department, but this abundance is deceptive because only one of them, Otto Fuhrmann, professor of zoology and comparative anatomy, gave all his time and energy to teaching and administrative duties. Professor Edmond Béraneck, who was absorbed in medical research, taught only two hours a week (general biology and embryology). Professor Auguste Châtelain, who taught a weekly three-hour course in human anatomy, was primarily a practising medical doctor for whom teaching was an ancillary activity. In mathematics, the professor was assisted for two hours weekly by a lecturer. For physics, botany, and the combined subjects of geology–palaeontology, a single professor assumed the duties. For more minor subjects the faculty offered courses in mineralogy, astronomy, and geodesy. The last two subjects were related to the cantonal observatory, which dated from the time of the first academy, and were directly connected to the local watchmaking industry.

The general courses for the first year in chemistry, physics, botany, and zoology were taken by those preparing for the basic degree as well as those going on to study medicine. For many years the latter group made up more than half of the enrolment of new students in the Faculty of Sciences. After successfully accomplishing their first year of studies, students went on to other universities to finish their medical training.

The teaching staff

From the beginning of its existence, the Faculty of Sciences of the new university could depend on a particularly dynamic group of professors for the basic subjects.[15] In general they had been trained at other Swiss universities; many had done internships at institutions of higher education abroad. In 1915, the professors of life sciences who taught the courses that Piaget enrolled in had all been appointed while still young: Otto Fuhrmann (zoology), 22 years old; Henri Spinner (botany), 32; and Emile Argand (geology and palaeontology), 32. The same was the case for the professors of exact sciences. In spite of this context and the rapid development of the sciences, at that time all these professors were able to maintain exemplary research work up to their retirement, which often came after 45 years of teaching and research. The scientific choices made by these devoted men, who had to work under difficult conditions and with mediocre equipment, created the basis for future development in research at the University of Neuchâtel. One wonders if these early appointments did not increase their abilities, which, not being exceptional at the start, went on to become remarkable because they had the drive to achieve influence locally and often outside the country.

Already during the time of the academy, the renowned teaching of the professor of chemistry, Otto Billeter,[16] the oldest member of the Faculty, attracted young students eager to do doctorates that they had to then submit to other universities. Having only the status of an academy, Neuchâtel was not accredited to award such degrees.

From the time of the founding of the university, research was maintained and even strengthened, and a good number of the doctorates awarded by the Faculty of Sciences were for work in chemistry, which is certainly a sign of the dynamism of this laboratory under an ageing, yet active, head. Nevertheless, in 1899 Billeter had expressed reservations, owing to a lack of means, regarding transforming the academy into a university.[17] The attraction of chemistry was certainly due to the presence of Billeter but also to that of two collaborators who achieved renown for their scientific work, particularly Alfred Berthoud,[18] whose reputation in the area of physical chemistry, as well as in thermodynamics, atomic chemistry, and photochemistry, went way beyond the Swiss borders.

The teaching of biology

During the short life of the first Academy of Neuchâtel, Agassiz, by his teaching and especially by his scientific work, made the biological sciences particularly attractive.[19] As of 1881, Edmond Béraneck,[20] who had been specifically trained in animal biology, was appointed to teach zoology. His first works are essentially oriented towards embryology. Afterwards, this remarkable scientist, who had many interests, became passionately engrossed in research on the treatment of tuberculosis. Owing to the intensity of his work and to his weak health, he called upon Otto Fuhrmann[21] in 1897 to temporarily replace him. Fuhrmann then became a special assistant, in 1902 a substitute professor, and finally full professor in 1910.

From the beginning of the century, Fuhrmann took over most of the teaching and the responsibilities of the zoology group. Béraneck taught two hours per week: one in embryology and the other in general zoology. In the latter subject he treated mainly problems of evolution, which attracted students with various views. Fuhrmann and his students' work quickly gave the laboratory an international reputation, particularly in the area of parasitology. As a devoted teacher, he knew how to reach out to the students: 'It is in the laboratory that he gives the best of himself and his advice was that of a master's as well as of a friend's.'[22]

The laboratory work was not exclusively centred on parasitology, because the director always maintained his interest in research in comparative anatomy and hydrobiology, particularly related to Lake Neuchâtel and the alpine lakes in general. Because of his work as professor and in particular his role as curator of the Museum of Natural History of Neuchâtel (a position he took in 1910), as well as his modesty, his commitment, and his counsel, Fuhrmann kept and built up contacts between different naturalists, teachers, and amateurs working in the canton.

Botany came in a poor second in the Faculty of Sciences during the period of the academy and the early decades of the university. Henri Spinner,[23] appointed in 1907, held only a part-time post that he complemented with a teaching job in mathematics at the secondary level. Despite these constraints, Spinner's vitality and idealistic commitment propelled him to continue his own research, and his efforts were rewarded by works of quality furnished by young students seeking to write doctorates. These were works in palynology and plant association studies. The latter became one of the central areas of research in biology at the University of Neuchâtel.

In 1911, Hans Schardt, who had taught geology, was offered a post at the Polytechnic in Zurich. This flattering appointment reflects the high quality of research and teaching that was practised in Neuchâtel.

Emile Argand[24] of Geneva was named successor to Schardt in Neuchâtel. He was in an enviable position through his work in cartography and structural analysis conducted in the Penninic Alps; he appeared to be the rising star in Swiss geology. The vast accomplishments of that ambitious young professor, who in spite of having left school at age 12 had gone on to distinguish himself by his field research, his care in graphical representation, the quality of his writing, and his capability at fund-raising, became the driving force of the small Faculty of Sciences. His awareness of his local and international reputation kept him apart from others, but he was more effective in getting the rooms necessary for teaching and research. On two occasions while Piaget was at the University of Neuchâtel it looked as if Argand would be appointed first in Lausanne and later in Geneva. His rigorous requirements, accompanied by a disdainful air for students, and even for some of his colleagues who did not come up to his exceptional level, compounded an isolation that was already marked by his off-campus office.

Adrien Jaquerod[25] was appointed in 1905 to the Academy of Neuchâtel at the age of only 28 to teach physics. This young researcher had studied in Geneva, where he obtained a doctorate in physical chemistry. He then did an internship in the laboratories of Sir William Ramsay at University College London. Returning to Switzerland, he continued his research on the physics of gas and liquids, first in Geneva and then in Neuchâtel. He was an outstanding experimenter who, undaunted by the lack of financial resources, turned his skill to projects requiring little in the way of infrastructure and a lot of ingenuity and rigour. Although he was the only professor of physics in Neuchâtel, he did not lose track of what was happening in the explosive world of physics at the time. Very early he showed an interest in applied research. In 1919, in his inaugural address[26] as rector of the university, he emphasized the importance of research for the local watchmaking industry in order for it to survive:

> Why not create advanced-level instruction, theoretical as much as practical, for students that would lead to qualifications in clock-making engineering? . . . It will be at a considerable cost. . . . The community will profit from it; the community, that is the State, must do its part, and do it well. The industries will be the first to profit, directly or indirectly . . . thus it is only fair that the industries make large contributions.

It was an ardent plea that formed the basic idea of what would become the Laboratoire Suisse des Recherches Horlogères (Swiss Laboratory of Watchmaking Research) with Adrien Jaquerod as its first director.

With respect to fundamental scientific subjects, the first decades of the new university were not favourable to the development of mathematics. Professor Louis-Gustave DuPasquier, who taught this subject, had studied at the polytechnic in Zurich and then at the University of Zurich, where Albert Einstein and Michel Plancherel were fellow students. Before his appointment in Neuchâtel, DuPasquier had been a lecturer at the polytechnic and a substitute professor at the university. The minutes of meetings held by the Council of the Faculty of Science show that he was an isolated man, and that his initiatives were rarely accepted by his colleagues.

Three lecturers taught ancillary or specialized courses in astronomy, mathematics, botany, and toxicology.

Piaget at the Faculty of Sciences

In his autobiography, Piaget wrote a mere three lines on his student days at the University of Neuchâtel,[27] which indicates how little it mattered in his training. However, it is necessary to mention that he had studied there for only three semesters, and that he was already quite involved in interests other than biology. He indicates that his interest in life sciences remained and that it combined well with his interest in group theory in mathematics, which concerned 'the problem of the totality and its parts'.[28] Perhaps as a way of acknowledging the various subjects he studied, he mentions the professors of zoology, geology, and physical chemistry, but ignores those of botany and mathematics.

In the research in malacology for his doctoral thesis, Piaget visited the sites that figured centrally in the audacious theories that Argand pursued in his lectures. In 1917 Piaget attended those lectures without, it seems, being particularly affected, even though Argand's message was the greatest innovation at that time in Neuchâtel's Sciences Faculty. Although a student at the university, Piaget seems to have pursued a self-teaching course of study that would undoubtedly have isolated him from fellow students. At the secondary level he certainly had taken part in group projects with classmates, but his mastery of subjects set him apart. At the beginning of his specialization in malacology, which occurred well before his university studies, he had received invaluable help from Paul Godet,[29] whose death in 1911 deprived Piaget of genuine support. Thus, Piaget had to conduct his own research, and because of that he quickly made a name for himself as an author in the domain. At the university the professors of biology had at most only a general knowledge of this specialized area, which paled into insignificance when compared with that of the young researcher who had already worked in the field and who had established contacts in Switzerland and abroad.

There is reason to believe that Piaget was not well received in Fuhrmann's famous and welcoming laboratory. His published thesis[30] makes no mention of any ties with the zoology laboratory at Neuchâtel, nor does it acknowledge either the institution or Fuhrmann, its director. This exceptional situation seems to show that relations between the student and the professor who was supposed to direct his research were not the best. The works of Piaget in the holdings of the library of the zoological institution[31] are basically the papers he published while still an undergraduate. These papers came from Fuhrmann's personal collection, and two of them, published in 1913, bear dedications from the author. On the other hand, the works of Piaget dating from his university period are missing or come mostly from external donations.

During the academic year 1917–1918, Jean Piaget won the Léon-DuPasquier Prize, the highest distinction awarded by the university, for a work that begins with the warning that 'It is not such a small field that there is nothing to be gleaned from it' and bears the title *Miscellaneous Swiss Malacology*.[32] Fuhrmann penned the jury's praise, and the paper was awarded the top prize of 500 Swiss francs.[33] This was a sizeable sum for its day, being 100 francs more than state scholarships to needy students or 100 francs less than the annual salary paid to the chemistry laboratory technician. The reporter noted that the award-winning work – which is now unfortunately lost – was a 679-page manuscript in handwriting not always easy to decipher. According to the analysis of the work, it contained a large part of what would become Piaget's doctoral thesis, as well as studies carried out in the Canton of Vaud and in the Neuchâtel Jura, which apparently have not been published since. An important chapter of 84 pages deals with the application of statistics to the malacological zoogeography of the Canton of Valais. It is quite likely that this approach had been influenced by the close contact Piaget maintained with his long-time friend Gustave Juvet, who was working on a thesis in mathematics. This young researcher, full of promise with his openness to modern methods in physics and mathematics, died prematurely of a heart attack.

Piaget's fellow students

Ten students enrolled at the Faculty of Sciences in 1915. Three of them intended to study life sciences, Gustave Juvet came to do mathematics, and the rest had chosen physics with chemistry as their minor. In life sciences, Piaget's fellow naturalists were Albert Morand, a 30-year-old primary school teacher, and Eugène Wegmann[34] from Schaffhouse, who planned to study geology. Both naturalists later had exemplary scientific careers: Morand went on expeditions to Africa and then became an outstanding teacher at the secondary school in La Chaux-de-Fonds. Wegmann, after doing research in Scandinavia and Greenland, returned as a professor to Neuchâtel.

Théodore Delachaux had already matriculated at the Faculty of Sciences in 1914, only to disappear from the register after the summer of 1916 and reappear for the autumn semester of 1918. The young man then committed himself definitively to life sciences. A gifted painter with a sense of humour, Delachaux played an important role in the development of the zoology laboratory, where he served as an assistant beginning in 1919.

Bernard Reichel, another naturalist of international renown and who became professor of palaeontology at the University of Basle, completed the circle of naturalists who trained at this small university that, at the time, lacked funding.

The successful careers of these naturalists who attended the Faculty of Sciences at the same time as Piaget would lead one to believe that the training they received here was at least satisfactory. The influence of the primary and secondary schools, that of their families, and the personal qualities of these young people were also perhaps determining factors in their scientific achievements.

Conclusion

This analysis of Piaget's years at the Faculty of Sciences at Neuchâtel during the Great War shows the dynamism of this institution despite its being understaffed and under-equipped. Improvements that help fill in the most conspicuous gaps were often due to the largess of local patronage.

In recruiting staff, the Faculty of Sciences seemed to be quite open to the outside world. In spite of the low salaries it paid, the faculty found young Swiss scientists of value who were willing to promote research that was in accordance with the international science of the day.

Even though it was principally concerned with training secondary teachers, the Faculty of Sciences did not neglect the importance of its degrees – particularly those in chemistry – and busied itself with integrating its graduates into the economic sector. When a self-taught researcher as accomplished as Piaget applied for admission, the university knew enough to relax its requirements accordingly (perhaps with the intercession of his father) and without raising too much dust. In such a case, the student–teacher relations were likewise adapted to allow the exceptionally gifted student to make what he wanted of what was offered in order to get through as quickly as possible. Piaget attended lectures and laboratory courses for only three semesters, yet managed to earn masters and doctoral degrees. Emile Argand's remark to a friend gives reason to wonder: 'The students are wasting a great deal of our time for nothing: when they are clever, they are ungrateful; when they are grateful, they are nearly always dull.'[35]

Notes

1 Enrolment records.
2 Report of the examining board of the Faculty of Sciences, 13 July 1917.
3 Enrolment records.
4 Report of the examining board of the Faculty of Sciences, 12 July 1918.
5 Ibid., 7 February 1919.
6 Albert Monard (1886–1952), zoologist. He worked as the Conservator of the Musée d'Histoire Naturelle (Museum of Natural History) of La Chaux-de-Fonds between 1920 and 1952. He went on many research expeditions in Africa.
7 *Histoire de l'Université de Neuchâtel*, Vol. 1: *La première Académie, 1838–1848*. (1988). Hauterive, Switzerland: G. Attinger; Neuchâtel; Université de Neuchâtel.
8 Ibid., Vol. 2: *La seconde Académie, 1866–1909*. (1994). Hauterive, Neuchâtel.
9 A.-F. Jeanneret (1994). De l'Académie à l'Université. In *Histoire de l'Université de Neuchâtel*, Vol. 2, op. cit., pp. 225–256.
10 The data on the university in the course of its first decade have been taken from *Autorités, Professeurs, Etudiants, Université de Neuchâtel*, Neuchâtel, 1909–1919. The editing for this chapter is based largely an information communicated by Marie-Jeanne Liengme Bessire.
11 Records of the Council of the Faculty of Science, 28 May 1920.
12 Meeting of the Council of the Faculty of Science, 25 October 1910.
13 *Autorités, Professeurs, Etudiants, Semestre d'hiver 1915–1916. Université de Neuchâtel*, Neuchâtel, 1916.
14 Cf. Chapter 6, this volume.

15 For materials relating to the research and the life of naturalists of the university, it is worthwhile to check G. Dubois (1976). *Naturalistes neuchâtelois du XXe siècle.* Neuchâtel: Ed. de la Baconnière, Cahiers de l'Institut neuchâtelois.

16 H. Rivier (1928). Notice sur la vie et les travaux d'Otto Billeter (1861–1927). *Helvetica Chimica Acta, XI*, 700–710.

17 Jeanneret, op. cit., p. 231. R. Scheurer, 'La Faculté de sciences', ibid., p. 374.

18 M. de Montmollin (1939). Alfred Berthoud, 1874–1939. *Bulletin de la Société neuchâteloise des sciences naturelles, 64*, 63–76.

19 J.-P. Schaer (1988). Louis Agassiz, 1807–1873. In *Histoire de l'Université de Neuchâtel*, Vol. 1, op. cit., pp. 169–188.

20 M. Bedot (1919–1920). Edmond Béraneck, 1859–1920. *Bulletin de la Société neuchâteloise des sciences naturelles, 45*, 125–130.

21 Th. Delachaux and J. G. Baer (1944). Otto Fuhrmann, 1871–1945. *Bulletin de la Société neuchâteloise des sciences naturelles, 69*, 147–167.

22 Ibid, p. 149.

23 A. Ischer (1926). Hommage à M. H. Spinner. *Bulletin de la Société neuchâteloise de géographie, 51*, fasc. 5, 119–126. C. Favarger (1963). Henri Spinner (1875–1962). *Bulletin de la Société neuchâteloise des sciences naturelles, 86*, 155–158.

24 M. Lugeon (1940). Emile Argand. *Bulletin de la société neuchâteloise des sciences naturelles, 65*, 24–53. J.-P. Schaer (1991). Emile Argand 1879–1940. Life and portrait of an inspired geologist. *Eclogae geologicae Helvetiae, 84*, no. 3, 511–534.

25 S. Gagnebin and C. Attinger (1958). Adrien Jaquerod, physicien 1877–1957. *Bulletin de la Société neuchâteloise des sciences naturelles, 81*, pp. 123–140.

26 Ibid., p. 131.

27 J. Piaget (1976). Autobiographie. *Cahiers Vilfredo Pareto – Revue européenne des sciences sociales, XIV*, 1–43.

28 Ibid., p. 35.

29 See Chapter 7, this volume.

30 J. Piaget (1921). *Introduction à la malacologie valaisanne. Thèse présentée à la Faculté des Sciences de l'Université de Neuchâtel.* PhD thesis.

31 Collection of offprints of the Bibliothèque de l'Institut de zoologie de l'Université de Neuchâtel, H910, H912–917, H919–922, H924–926, V1253 and V2618.

32 The work had been submitted during the preceding academic year and then withdrawn because it was in competition with a thesis in physics: *Recherche sur la radioactivité des sources du canton de Neuchâtel.* Report of the Council of the Faculty of Science, 29 January 1917.

33 State Commission for higher education 1917–1918, *Rapport du jury sur un travail de concours pour le prix Léon-DuPasquier*, p. 46.

34 J.-P. Schaer (1995). C.E. Wegmann (1896–1982), Vie et œuvre. *Mémoires de la société géologique de France, 168*, 13–23.

35 Schaer, Emile Argand 1879–1940, op. cit., p. 529.

6 Did Jean Piaget's 'conversion' from malacology to psychology happen in the Faculty of Arts?[1]

Marie-Jeanne Liengme Bessire and
Sylvie Béguelin

The preceding chapters, in describing Jean Piaget's school and university studies, give us a good sense of the official intellectual structures and the general context in which Piaget grew up. There remain, however, a few grey areas related to the genesis and subsequent growth of Piaget's interest in psychology. One might wonder, for instance, whether certain outside influences induced Piaget to turn from malacology to the study of human cognitive processes – without necessarily rejecting the idea that Piaget also went through a personal moral crisis.[2] Such questions tempt one to take a closer look at the relations Piaget had with the Faculty of Arts, the only place in Neuchâtel that gave regular upper-level courses in psychology at this time. Understanding the relations between Piaget and the university, however, presupposes knowing something about that newly created institution. For this reason we begin with a brief history of the Arts Faculty during its youth and then move on to an analysis of the precise role the Arts Faculty played in Jean Piaget's intellectual development.

The Faculty of Letters from 1909 to 1920: Stability or modernity?

The new general charter of the University of Neuchâtel was ratified by the State Council on 19 May 1911. Its rules concerning exams, dated 6 June 1911, set out specific objectives for each faculty within its respective field. The rules were similar to those in effect at other Swiss universities, with the exception of one major innovation, consisting of the possibility of getting a doctoral degree after six semesters of regular study. Four semesters remained necessary for a bachelor's degree.[3]

The Arts Faculty's curriculum was composed of 16 core subjects, as well as other courses given more or less temporarily by associate professors or privat-docents.[4] Compared to the previous Charter,[5] which excluded them, the new Charter officially made psychology and pedagogy part of the faculty's curriculum, but neither discipline had its own professorship independent of philosophy. As of 1914, the Faculty Council actively expressed a desire for the creation of a chair,[6] but its wish was fulfilled only with the nomination of Anne-Nelly Perret-Clermont, in 1979!

The modernity of the Neuchâtel Arts Faculty's approach was manifest: Diverse course offerings emphasized in-depth knowledge in topical, original fields of study. Four types of BA were available, in the following fields: a BA in Classical Letters, which comprised French, Latin Language and Literature, and Greek Language and Literature; a BA in Modern Letters, composed of French Language and Literature as well as two modern languages chosen by the student; a BA in History and Geography; and finally, a BA in the Teaching of Literature, which covered all of the literary disciplines, also included core courses in psychology and pedagogy, and allowed the student to teach in the secondary schools. The first three options included a Latin exam, and all required Latin and philosophy.

At the 20 March 1918 meeting of the Faculty Council, some faculty expressed worries concerning the workload entailed by the programme: The BA in Classical Letters at Neuchâtel was known to be difficult, especially because of the high level at which Old French was taught. It was suggested that such high standards, which students explicitly complained about, might very well incite some prospective students to choose another place of study. Alfred Lombard, Visiting Professor of French Language and Literature, suggested reducing the programme of the BA exam, taking the University of Lausanne's programme as an example. Lausanne's programme, according to Lombard, more closely corresponded to the learning abilities of the students. Jules Jeanjaquet,[7] professor of Medieval Language and Literature, expressed his surprise at all the fuss and replied that the two universities' programmes were too different to be compared.[8] This remark shows the 'federalist' nature of Swiss university education, which tended to vary from one canton to another. For example, at the end of 1918 France had expressed a desire to recognize the universities of French-speaking Switzerland through a series of bilateral agreements, but the Swiss universities themselves could not even reach agreements concerning mutual recognition of their own diplomas, and the French proposal fell through.[9]

In June 1919 the Faculty Council had long debates on a proposed revision of the faculty rules. Among the topics were a possible increase in the number of subjects taught for a BA and the creation of certificates in other areas of study. Among the suggestions was the creation of a BA in philosophy, with psychology, philosophy, and logic as core subjects. Another suggestion was a certificate in practical pedagogy, which would be obligatory for those who wished to teach on the secondary level.[10] Finally, though, only one change was adopted: The extremely difficult written exam on the history of French grammar was dropped from the BA in Classical Letters.[11]

The price of growth

The Faculty of Arts dominated the university as a whole by virtue of its relatively large number of professorial posts. In 1911 there were already 25 professorships. The First World War subsequently slowed down the Faculty's growth,[12] since it forced the canton to reduce spending. For example, Neuchâtel asked professors if they would temporarily give up attending exams for extra money,[13] and Saturday morning classes were cancelled to save on heating.[14] The general mobilization caused by the war disrupted student life and the university's curriculum, since some teaching had to be abandoned and exam sessions had to be moved to accommodate those who left school for the army.

Although the war exacerbated the university's financial problems, it certainly did not cause them: The university had always suffered financially because it was so small. Professorial salaries, for example, had always been low, to the point that it was hard to fill vacant chairs. Thus there were practical limits on the Arts Faculty's dreams of expansion.

One remedy for the lack of government funding was private sponsorship, such as that regularly provided by the Société Académique[15] for lectures. The society, founded on 15 October 1889, was technically independent of the university but included numerous alumni and professors. Many of the former had become important members of the community: lawyers, pastors, doctors, or captains of industry. Their goal was to 'allow this young university to maintain its status relative to its Swiss and foreign rivals, and to help it attract a large student body.'[16] The society organized an annual contest that awarded prizes for the best student work, but this did not raise much interest and in 1915 society president Armand Dupasquier[17] wondered in the yearly report whether the war was also having a negative influence on the intellectual activity of the student body.[18] Finally, in 1917, a student deemed to be particularly brilliant won the prize. The president's reaction was as follows:

> For the last several years no student work had been presented for the contest, so we were pleasantly surprised to receive such a strong paper, entitled *Realism and Nominalism as Seen through the Life Sciences*. This paper, the work of a gifted writer called Jean Piaget, a student at the University, was judged favourably by the contest jury. We have therefore decided to award the maximum possible prize, 100 Frs.[19]

The jury's report,[20] written by Arnold Reymond, Alfred Lombard, and Edmond Béraneck, summarized the essential points of this long paper (320 pages) and emphasized its topical nature: 'In addition, it is directly inspired by the present situation. . . . The war . . . once again, and very acutely, poses the old problem of the relations individuals have to the social organism they belong to.'[21]

The report also noted some methodological problems in Piaget's paper:

For example, 'The author could have provided a list of the works he consulted.'[22] In the report, Arnold Reymond extensively discusses the various theses Piaget defends and the examples he uses in his arguments,[23] and he concludes by regretting Piaget's equivocal definition of God: at times 'a simple ideal', God is in other places presented as 'a reality which would subsist independently of our judgments'. Reymond states that 'the author constantly shifts between these two essential definitions, and this indecision appears to be a consequence of a failure to distinguish the domains of metaphysics and psychology sufficiently.'[24] In Piaget's gradual movement towards psychology, winning this prize for work that was at once malacological, psychological, and philosophical may be seen as an important early step.

Psychology in Neuchâtel between 1909 and 1920: The growth of a discipline

Among the various disciplines within the faculty, French,[25] geography, political economy and philosophy increased their teaching hours between 1909 and 1920, while history and the classical languages made no gains. Certain disciplines were in fashion, such as ethnography, which had only recently appeared as a scientific discipline and no doubt benefited from contemporary colonialism. Psychology, which was developing its fundamental theories, was also in fashion.

Ever since the last decade of the previous century, the Chair of Philosophy[26] had devoted much time to the teaching of psychology. As of the summer of 1901, Professor Ernest Murisier[27] added 'a seventh hour to his [philosophy] teaching, under the title of general pedagogy, but principally devoted to child psychology.'[28]

After Murisier died in 1904 his research was taken up by one of his successors, Pierre Bovet.[29] In 1910 Bovet organized a series of pedagogical lectures on secondary education with the help of several visiting professors. The lectures were a great success. They were published in 1911, under the direction of Bovet himself, in *Actualités pédagogiques*.[30] Bovet organized a similar series in the following semester, for which he requested help from the Neuchâtel Department of Public Instruction. Within his weekly one-hour course on pedagogy, Bovet did not hesitate to include psychological subjects such as mental development (winter 1909–10) and teaching morals and building character at school (winter 1910–11). In the summer of 1910 and the winter of 1910–11 he added two hours devoted explicitly to psychology. Here Bovet took up moral sentiments as well as affective and logical reasoning.

When Bovet resigned in 1912 in order to run the Rousseau Institute in Geneva, Arnold Reymond replaced him[31] under the newly created title of Professor of Philosophy and Pedagogy. Emile Lombard was named privat-docent and taught a course in psychology and religion.[32] Reymond was greatly admired by his colleges 'both as a professor and as a mind', and his teaching skills, which he had amply demonstrated during his career at the

Gymnase (Grammar School) de Neuchâtel, were generally recognized as exceptional.[33] While at the Grammar School Reymond had taught Jean Piaget, and they had kept in touch ever since. Reymond's teaching load was composed of three hours on the history of philosophy, one hour of pedagogy, one hour of psychology, one hour on the philosophy of science, and a one-hour lecture in philosophy each week. Some of the subjects Reymond addressed in these courses were as follows: measuring psychological phenomena and the legitimacy of these measurements (summer 1915); memory (summer 1916); the unconscious (summer 1917); school and children (summer 1917); and a seminar on Edouard Claparède's book *Psychologie de l'enfant* (Child Psychology, published 1911) during 1917 and 1918.[34] The first thesis directed by Reymond was defended on 22 April 1914 by Marguerite Evard, who had written on adolescence. She obtained her doctorate in letters. Reymond's courses and lectures attracted many listeners; indeed, they were among the most heavily attended in the Letters Faculty. Reymond's teaching essentially targeted students who had matriculated in the Letters Faculty and were fol-lowing a traditional course programme,[35] but a look at the sign-up sheets shows that quite a few of the attendees actually came from other faculties, especially the Science Faculty.[36]

From molluscs to children: Did the Faculty of Arts play a role in Piaget's move?

Jean Piaget matriculated in the Faculty of Sciences, and he completed his first semester in that faculty in the winter of 1915–16. His last was the summer semester, 1918. Officially,[37] Piaget studied five semesters, with a break during the summer semester of 1916. For the first two semesters he took only science courses, but starting with the summer semester of 1917 his interests started to vary: He took a sociology course with Professor André de Máday[38] as well as a course in the philosophy of the sciences[39] with Arnold Reymond in the Letters Faculty. In addition, he attended Reymond's lectures on Schopenhauer.[40] The following semester saw Piaget once again signed up for one of Reymond's courses, this time for a three-hour weekly philosophy course.[41] He also took a course on Indian studies taught by Godefroy de Blonay. During his last semester Piaget again signed up for Reymond's philosophy course, for three hours each week,[42] and also took a one-hour class each week on the philosophy of science.[43] In addition, he again took Godefroy de Blonay's class, and a course in Swiss-German literature taught by William Domeier. It is fair to say, then, that throughout his studies Piaget frequented the Letters Faculty. It is nonetheless surprising that on 29 November 1918 he sent a letter to the Arts Faculty Council asking them to recognize his Sciences Degree, in order that he might begin doctoral work in philosophy in the Arts Faculty.[44] A year later, having obtained recognition of his degree, Piaget sent on a thesis project outline under the title *An Essay on Value Judgements and Biological Method in the Sciences of the Mind*.[45] The Arts Faculty accepted the proposal as 'new and interesting' and invited biology professor Edmond Béraneck (of Neuchâtel) to sit on the jury. Piaget never made it to the end of this thesis, however, and we do not know exactly what stopped him. During the same period, however, he did get a Doctorate in Science with a thesis on molluscs.[46] This episode seems to be a critical one in Piaget's development, which of course makes the sketchiness of our knowledge about it all the more frustrating.

A new direction

One way of adding to our understanding of the new direction Piaget's thought seemed to begin to take in 1917–18 was to comb the lending records of the Neuchâtel Library for the period and see what he was reading in addition to the required texts.[47] We noted what Piaget himself borrowed as well as borrowings by his father, Arthur Piaget, when we suspected that they might have been for his son. Piaget borrowed books on 74 occasions between 1908 and 1920 (some books were borrowed more than once), and his father took out books 22 times. The records show that Piaget borrowed irregularly, with spurts of interest in specific subjects. For instance, there was a 'biological phase' in 1913, as well as two 'philosophical phases' in 1914 and 1917. A closer look at the philosophical texts Piaget read in 1914[48] reveals that his curiosity was more precisely centred on moral and metaphysical questions. Among others, Piaget read works by Charles Renouvier,[49] Immanuel Kant,[50] Charles Secrétan,[51] Jean-Marie Guyau,[52] Herbert Spencer,[53] Alfred Fouillée,[54] Henri Bergson,[55] and Armond Sabatier.[56] The last two writers on this list became the topic of the first 'non-biological' article Piaget published, which came out in 1914 in the *Revue chrétienne* and was entitled 'Bergson and Sabatier'.[57]

The second spurt of readings in philosophy centred more specifically on the philosophy of science.[58] Some of the authors whose books Piaget borrowed in 1917 were the French biologist and philosopher Félix Le Dantec,[59] the German philosopher Gottfried Leibniz,[60] and Arnold Reymond.[61]

These readings did not lead directly into any publications for Piaget, but they are nonetheless significant. For one thing, these are the books Piaget was presumably reading as he prepared his prize-winning paper for the Société Académique. In addition, it was roughly one year later that Piaget asked for recognition of his Sciences BA from the Arts Faculty in order to start a PhD in philosophy. There is no mention of Jean Piaget between 4 December 1919, the date on which he submitted his thesis outline, and 19 March 1925, the day he was named Professor of Philosophy, in the records of the Faculty of Arts.[62] The Letters Faculty had lost Arnold Reymond to the University of Lausanne, where he was to take up the Chair in Philosophy. Upon Reymond's resignation eight candidates for the Neuchâtel professorship had been chosen for a shortlist. They were Jean Piaget, Jean de La Harpe, Pierre Bise, Jean Walzburger, Robert Bouvier, Pierre Godet, Antoine Sottile, and Michel

Grodensky. Four of the eight were from Neuchâtel, and the others were from elsewhere in Switzerland. Jean Piaget, the son of the brilliant local professor Arthur, immediately became the favourite for the post. His 'brilliance, impressive publications list, and his youth'[63] stood out. Pierre Godet, who was also the son of a noted local professor, was also among the favourites. Finally the faculty hit upon a compromise, whose goal was obviously to avoid offending either of the two eminent local families: The chair was to be split in half. One half was devoted to teaching the history of philosophy and was given to Godet as of the winter semester of 1925–26. Piaget's half of the professorship comprised pedagogy and psychology. His courses attracted a large number of students,[64] and indeed Piaget managed to keep the wide audience Reymond had drawn to the subjects of psychology and pedagogy. In fact, student numbers for Piaget's classes increased through the years, as sign-up records for his last two semesters at the university indicate.[65]

In addition to his half-post in the Letters Faculty, Piaget had a professorship in sociology in the Faculty of Law and Economics. His nomination was made official by the Neuchâtel State Council on 27 March 1925.[66] The chair had been vacant twice during the period immediately preceding Piaget's appointment, a situation that perfectly illustrates the difficulty the university had in keeping its faculty. Neuchâtel faculty salaries simply were not as attractive as those offered by equivalent institutions in other parts of Switzerland. The first of these vacancies arose when André de Máday, who had been Visiting Professor since 1911, and then Full Professor in the Economy Section of the Law Faculty as of 1917,[67] resigned. Máday had accepted a job as librarian for the International Labour Organization in Geneva, and he gave notice in the middle of 1924. News of Máday's departure upset his peers for several reasons. First, he was a highly valued, dynamic, and loyal co-worker. In addition, Máday had played an active role within a tense political and educative context: In 1924, the Department of Public Instruction had made it known that the BA programme in social, political, and administrative Sciences was to be dropped. The Law Faculty staff, as well as that of the Economics Section, were quick to reject the idea as absurd, but André de Máday stood out among his peers in his firm opposition to a project he termed 'ill-conceived'.[68] His colleagues thought of Máday as an ardent defender of their faculty's interests, and his resignation was considered a great loss. In the beginning of the 1924–25 winter semester, Máday let the others know that his work in Geneva was going to prevent him from teaching in Neuchâtel as of the summer semester. At this point the Neuchâtel State Council decided not to replace him and simply to stop offering those courses. Needless to say, the faculty reacted very negatively, and a compromise was sought by all involved. The solution agreed upon was to break the post into two halves: One would involve social legislation, and the other sociology. The two posts were offered to Tell Perrin[69] and Arnold Reymond, who accepted under a few conditions in January 1925.[70] Reymond, however, would resign in March of the same year, when he was appointed in Lausanne. Faced with the same problem only three months after having 'solved' it, certain members of the faculty appeared to be almost at wits' end, as excerpts from the minutes illustrate: 'The issue is the Chair in Sociology, which Arnold Reymond's departure has once again reduced to vacuity. Oh fickle lovers! Newlyweds separated before their time! Let us console the widow, exempt her from the ten months' mourning period . . .'[71] Jean Piaget and five other candidates[72] made offers for the post. Professors Reymond and Emmanuel Junod[73] backed Piaget, who was deemed to be 'by far, the most qualified candidate', and he got the professorship. Once ensconced[74] Piaget immediately sought to modify the post's teaching profile, reducing hours in sociology in favour of more psychology. The two faculties involved were unenthusiastic about the proposed changes, and the rector was asked to recommend a 'no' to the Department of Public Instruction. Arnold Reymond wrote to Piaget, informing him of the various 'arguments made for keeping all three hours of sociology'.[75]

Piaget taught for eight semesters at the University of Neuchâtel, but he always kept in touch with Professor Pierre Bovet and the Rousseau Institute in Geneva, which he visited every two weeks.[76] Right from the start Piaget proved to have a dynamic, resolutely scientific approach to his teaching, and he quickly introduced two hours of *Travaux Pratiques* (laboratory work) in psychology. Both the topics he taught[77] and the works he took up in colloquia[78] attest to Piaget's interest in contemporary innovations. His own previous publications, as well as the ongoing research projects that he conducted contemporaneously at the Rousseau Institute, were the source of much of his teaching material, especially for the courses in pedagogy.[79]

Piaget was named Visiting Professor of the History of Scientific Thought at the Sciences Faculty of the University of Geneva, and promoted to the post of Director of the Rousseau Institute,[80] in the winter of 1929–30. Jean de La Harpe replaced him in Neuchâtel.

The above overview shows the intellectual vitality of the world in which Jean Piaget undertook his university studies and started off on his academic career. Such a lively intellectual context is perhaps surprising, given the First World War, and it is perhaps necessary to temper the enthusiastic image of a young and dynamic university with the observation that for the first ten years of its existence, the Arts Faculty was more or less cut off from the rest of world, if by that term we understand everything beyond the frontiers of Neuchâtel Canton. One possible explanation for the University of Neuchâtel's isolation is to be found in its very limited resources, which often forced the university to settle for less than it might have wanted. The First World War only reinforced this tendency. That said, it was not just for financial reasons that the University of Neuchâtel tended not to go outside the canton when it recruited new professors: Plain small-mindedness also appears to have played a role, as the minutes of several faculty meetings attest. Professorships were frequently filled as a function of local 'dynasties', from father to son or within the same family, and a traditional, almost familial conception of the university appears to have predominated. This seems to have played a role in the establishment of a teaching programme that was certainly demanding and innovative, but it had the additional purpose of providing local intellectuals with the wherewithal necessary for their development. The faculty members could then in turn become a source of recognition and respect for their employer, the university. Such a way of operating inevitably entailed the disadvantages that come with provincialism, but it also made for an intimate campus atmosphere with a personal touch and finally proved to be an intellectually fertile strategy as well: The generation of researchers that emerged from this milieu included many who attained national and even international renown.

Jean Piaget's own story was somewhat academically unconventional, since he was something of an autodidact, but both his father and his circle of friends also helped him along. Piaget's early academic career now looks like something from another era, one in which academic success was possible while one was still young, and in which an academic career did not yet mean homing in on one highly specialized subdiscipline and publishing, or perishing, within its strict limits.

Notes

1 This chapter was translated by David Jemielitly, with minor revisions by Anne-Nelly Perret-Clermont.
2 Jean-Jacques Ducret (1990) makes the hypothesis of a personal crisis in *J. Piaget, Biographie et parcours intellectuel*. Neuchâtel and Paris: Delachaux et Niestlé.
3 The first doctoral degree was given to Lydie Morel for a thesis on Jean Ogier de Gombauld, on 3 November 1910.
4 See Articles 9 and 12 of the Charter, 19 May 1911.
5 Law on Superior Education of 18 May and 24 July 1896.
6 Minutes of the meetings of the Letters Faculty Council for 18 June 1914, and 16 November 1916.
7 For more details on the life of this lively professor, see E. Bauer (1947) Jules Jeanjaquet, philologue et historien Neuchâtelois. *Musée neuchâtelois*, (unnumbered), 5–11.
8 Minutes of the 20 March 1918 meeting of the Letters Faculty Council.
9 Ibid., 4 November 1918.
10 Ibid., 5 June 1919.
11 Ibid., 10 November 1919.
12 'Many of the students from the belligerent powers had to leave the classroom when their countries called them. And once the war ended many of the young people could not return to the university because their countries' currencies had lost too much value.' A. Dupasquier (1933) *L'Université de Neuchâtel* (pp. 12–13). Neuchâtel. Jean Piaget was not indifferent to the war, as two of his publications show: (1915) *La mission de l'idée*. Lausanne: Ed. la Concorde; (1918) La biologie et la guerre. *Feuille centrale de la société suisse de Zofingue, 58*, 374–380.
13 Minutes of the Letters Faculty Meeting, 13 January 1915.
14 Ibid., 31 October 1917.
15 For the history and the goals of this group see Dupasquier, op. cit., pp. 14–18.
16 Yearly Report of the Societé Académique, 1910, p. 3.

17 Doctor in Law (Leipzig, 1895) and lawyer (1897), Dupasquier worked for a great number of Neuchâtel organizations and institutions. He presided over the Société Académique from 1908 to 1930. Cf. L. Thévenaz (1947) Armand Dupasquier (1869–1946). *Musée neuchâtelois* (unnumbered), 111–112.

18 Yearly Report of the Société Académique, 1915, p. 4.

19 Ibid., 1917, p. 5.

20 A. Reymond (1917) Rapport du jury sur le prix de la société académique. *Département de l'Instruction publique, Première partie: Enseignement supérieur*, pp. 53–63.

21 Ibid., p. 53.

22 Ibid., p. 57.

23 Here there is an abundance of examples, and our author conjures up an entire world of molluscs with weird names and appears to know them all. Ibid., p. 59.

24 Reymond, op. cit., pp. 62–63.

25 The French Department was reorganized in 1911 and obtained two new professorial posts in literature.

26 This chair was created with the founding of the first academy, in 1848, and was occupied by Alphonse Guillebert, Ferdinand Buisson, Adrien Naville, and Ernest Murisier.

27 Murisier wrote *Maine de Biran: esquisse d'une psychologie religieuse*. Paris: H. Jouve, 1892; and *Les maladies du sentiment religieux*. Paris: F. Alcan, 1901.

28 R. Scheurer (1994) La Faculté des Lettres. In *Histoire de l'Université de Neuchâtel: la seconde Académie (1866–1909)* (p. 339). Neuchâtel: Université de Neuchâtel; Hauterive: Ed. G. Attinger.

29 Murisier was replaced by Georges Godet (1845–1907) and Pierre Bovet, who admitted that he 'was appointed at 25 years of age, less for my merits than for the confidence and the gratitude that the memory of my father inspired'. P. Bovet (1932) *Vingt ans de vie. L'Institut Jean-Jacques Rousseau de 1912 à 1932* (p. 15). Neuchâtel and Paris: Delachaux & Niestlé. The teaching hour devoted to pedagogy was at times given to someone else, such as in the summer of 1904 with Auguste Hillebrand, and in the summer of 1905 with P. Dumont. See R. Scheurer, La Faculté des Lettres, op. cit., p. 340. As of 1907, Pierre Bovet occupied the Chair of Philosophy alone, and he maintained Murisier's curriculum without making any large changes.

30 This collection was first edited at St.-Blaise by the Foyer Solidariste and printed by Delachaux & Niestlé in Neuchâtel, who took over the editing as well in 1912 when the Foyer Solidariste disappeared. In the same year the J.-J. Rousseau Foundation, which was officially created in Geneva on 14 February 1912, took over the *Actualités pédagogiques*. The Rousseau Foundation was the result of initiatives taken by a group composed of Edmond Bossier, Bernard Bouvier, Edouard Claparède, Adrien Naville, and Cornille Vidart. They hoped to promote research in education. The Institute opened in autumn of the same year, under the direction of Bovet, whom Claparède had convinced to leave his post at the University of Neuchâtel. Bovet brought with him the collection *Actualités pédagogiques*, which was henceforth published by the Institute. The loss hastened the demise of the Foyer Solidariste, which had been founded on 1 December 1906 in St.-Blaise by James Meuron, the theologian René Guisan, the mathematician and philosopher Samuel Gagnebin, and Pierre Bovet. The Foyer had been conceived as a bookselling and editing centre. See M. Schlup, 'Les Editions Delachaux et Niestlé' and S. Roller, 'Pédagogie et pschologie', *Editeurs neuchâtelois du XXème siècle*, Neuchâtel, 1987, pp. 47–58 and 93–103; as well as P. Bovet (1932) *Vingt ans de vie*. Neuchâtel and Paris: Delachaux & Niestlé.

31 There was a brief period during the summer semester in 1912 during which the chair was vacant.

32 Lombard stopped teaching this course after the summer semester of 1917 when he

was named Extraordinary Professor in the Theology Faculty of the University of Lausanne.

33 Minutes of the Letters Faculty Meeting, 28 February 1912.

34 A search of the Neuchâtel Library's records reveals that Jean Piaget borrowed this book on 2 February 1920. (The Professor of French Literature, Philippe Godet, had donated it to the library in 1913.) Of course, Piaget may well have been familiar with the book before he borrowed it.

35 The history of philosophy course was part of the required programme in all four types of BA offered by the Letters Faculty.

36 Most of these students took the courses in the philosophy of science. The numbers are as follows: one in summer 1913; three in winter 1913–14; four in summer 1914; one in winter 1914–15; three in summer 1915; four, including Piaget's friend Gustave Juvet, in winter 1915–16; six, including Juvet and three other students who followed science courses with Piaget, in winter 1916–17; five, including Juvet and Piaget, in summer 1917; four, all of whom followed courses with Piaget, in winter 1917–18; six, including Juvet and Piaget, in summer 1918; seven in winter 1918–19; one in summer 1919; nine in winter 1919–20; four in summer 1920.

37 Cf. the hypotheses of Jean-Paul Schaer, Chapter 5 of this volume, on the possibility that what Piaget was officially signed up for might not correspond to what he actually attended.

38 The title of this course is not mentioned in the course schedule

39 The title of this course is not mentioned in the course schedule.

40 The lectures dealt with free will. Note that Piaget won his Société Académique prize for the essay on realism and nominalism just after attending these lectures.

41 The course title is not mentioned in the course schedule.

42 The course title is not mentioned in the course schedule.

43 The course was called 'History and the Philosophy of Science in Greece and Rome'.

44 It is of course tempting to see a link between the coursework Piaget did with Reymond during the preceding semester and this request, but this cannot be sufficiently substantiated for lack of primary-source evidence.

45 Minutes of the Letters Faculty Meeting, 4 December 1919.

46 See Chapter 5 of this volume.

47 This source of information must naturally be used cautiously, and we certainly would not claim that it provides a complete list of Piaget's reading during the period. However, the library records can help fill in some gaps, adding to the research done by Jean-Jacques Ducret, who examined what Piaget himself had to say about writers and works who influenced him. See J.-J. Ducret (1984) *Jean Piaget, savant et philosophe. Les années de formation 1907–1924. Etude sur la formation des connaissances et du sujet de la connaissance.* Geneva: Droz; and J.-J. Ducret (1990) *Jean Piaget. Biographie et parcours intellectuel.* Neuchâtel. Paris: Delachaux & Niestlé. His research leads Ducret to conclude that 'when Piaget decided in 1918 to get trained as a scientific psychologist . . . his goal was to verify the hypotheses in the *Recherche*. In a word, he wished to find scientific explanations for biological structures in the most general sense of the term, a sense which includes the structures of thought.' J.-J. Ducret, *Jean Piaget. Biographie*, op cit., p. 75.

48 A total of 19 books borrowed.

49 *Histoire et solution des problèmes métaphysiques.* Paris: F. Alcan, 1901.

50 *The Critique of Practical Reason.* London: Longmans, Green & Co., 1909.

51 *Recherche de la méthode.* Neuchâtel: C. Leidecker; Paris, Geneva: J. Cherbuliez, 1857.

52 *Essai d'une Morale sociale* and *Morale sociale.*

53 *The Data of Ethics.* London and Edinburgh: Williams and Norgate, 1881.

54 *La Morale, l'Art et la Religion.* Paris: F. Alcan, 1892; *La Liberté et le déterminisme.* Paris: F. Alcan, 1907 (borrowed by Arthur Piaget).

55 *Matière et mémoire.* Paris: F. Alcan, 1896; *Essai sur les données.* Paris: F. Alcan, 1889 (borrowed by Arthur Piaget).

56 *Philosophie de l'effort.* Paris: F. Alcan, 1903 (borrowed by Arthur Piaget).

57 This was followed by another publication of the same sort, in 1915 (*La mission de l'idée*, Lausanne: Ed. La Concorde, 1915). There was then a three-year gap before the next such publication, *Recherche* (Lausanne: Ed. La Concorde, 1918). The first essentially psychological publication appeared in 1920 (La psychanalyse dans ses rapports avec la psychologie de l'enfant/Psychoanalysis and child psychology. *Psychologie de l'enfant et pédagogie expérimentale.* 1920, *20*, 18–34, 41–58.)

58 Piaget borrowed 17 books during this period.

59 *Evolution individuelle et hérédité.* Paris: F. Alcan, 1913; *L'Unité de l'être vivant.* Paris: F. Alcan, 1902; *Les Limites du connaissable.* Paris: F. Alcan, 1903; *Stabilité dans la vie.* Paris: F. Alcan, 1910; *L'Athéisme.* Paris: E. Flammarion, 1916.

60 *Monadologie.* Paris: E. Belin, 1886.

61 *Logique et mathématique.* Saint-Blaise: Foyer Solidariste, 1908.

62 During this time Piaget had been away from Neuchâtel, first in Zurich, where he studied psychology (winter 1918–19) and took courses from G. Lipps and A. Wreschner as well as courses in psychiatry and lectures by E. Bleuler and C. Jung. In the summer of 1919 Piaget hiked the trails of the Valais region and devoted himself to malacology. In autumn 1919 he went to Paris and did coursework in the philosophy of logic and psychology. He also did lab work with Binet and participated in the psychiatrist G. Dumas's labs. In the summer semester of 1921 Piaget accepted a post as senior lecturer in the Rousseau Institute. The job had been offered to him by Edouard Claparède.

63 Minutes of the Letters Faculty Meeting, 19 March 1925.

64 The University of Neuchâtel redistributed sign-up fees to its teachers as a function of how many students attended class, so we can draw conclusions as to the size of Piaget's groups from the records of these redistributions. In 1909 a course-hour cost 3 Fr. for students and 5 Fr. for auditors, and as of 1911 the fee was raised to 5 Fr. for everyone, with a 50 per cent reduction for teachers with a Swiss degree. Optional course fees went directly to the professors who taught the courses, while required course fees were split evenly between the teacher and the university.

65 Winter 1927–28, 75 sign-ups; winter 1928–29, 97 sign-ups; summer 1929, 101 sign-ups.

66 Minutes of the Law Faculty Meeting, 27 June 1925.

67 Section created in 1910.

68 Minutes of the Law Faculty Meeting, 26 April 1924.

69 Professor of Swiss Public Law and Federal Administrative Law in the Law Faculty.

70 Minutes of the Law Faculty, 4 January 1925.

71 Ibid., 20 March 1925.

72 The six of them made offers for all of the posts held by Reymond and were among the eight listed above. Only Jean de La Harpe and Pierre Godet did not apply for the post in sociology.

73 Professor of Political Economy and Statistics in the Letters Faculty.

74 Decree of 27 March 1925.

75 Minutes of the Law Faculty Meeting, 2 April 1925.

76 Bovet, op cit., p. 78.

77 The topics of the courses taught in psychology were as follows: intelligence (winter 1925–26 and 1928–29); judgement and reasoning (summer of 1926 and 1929); autism and symbolic thought (winter 1926–27); autism and affectivity (summer

1927); the development of thought and genetic logic (winter 1927–28 and summer 1928).

78 Piaget discussed Lucien Lévy-Bruhl's *L'âme primitive*, which came out in 1927, in the winter semester of 1928. Jean Lagneau's *Les leçons sur l'existence de Dieu*, which had been published in 1925, was the topic of a lecture in the summer of 1928.

79 The course topics show this pretty clearly: the stages of knowledge (winter 1926–27 and winter 1928–29); children's explanations (summer 1927, summer 1929); intelligence and social life in children (winter 1927–28); the logic of the child (summer 1928).

80 The Rousseau Institute was established, largely thanks to Edouard Claparède, in Geneva in 1912. Claparède, Professor and Director of the Laboratory of Psychology in the University of Geneva's Science Faculty, felt that the Institute could address two major problem areas in education: first, teachers were thought to have an insufficient background in psychology, and second, not enough progress was being made in the science of education. Named 'Institut J.-J. Rousseau', it was considered to be an institute of 'Hautes Etudes pédagogiques' (Advanced Studies in Pedagogy) and was conceived of as at once a school, a research centre, and a source of information and of propaganda. Legally, the Rousseau Institute was a corporation with a start-up capital of 67,500 Fr. after the sale of stocks at 500 Fr. each. It quickly ran into cash problems, which the war exacerbated. In 1919 the Director, Pierre Bovet, accepted the post of Director of the Neuchâtel Secondary Schools in order to lighten the burden his salary represented for the Rousseau Institute. In 1920 Bovet was named to the Chair of Philosophy and Pedagogy at the University of Basle. Knowing that to accept this post would mean the end of the Rousseau Institute, Bovet turned it down. Basle's interest in him rekindled that of Geneva, however, and on the advice of an *ad hoc* commission of the Letters Faculty the State Council of Geneva Canton finally named Bovet Professor of Educational Science and Experimental Pedagogy on 24 February 1920. This saved the Rousseau Institute, which changed its by-laws in 1921 to become an association of collaborating and subscribing members. The association's still shaky finances were notably improved in November 1925 by a 5,000 dollar grant (worth 25,000 Fr. then) from the Rockefeller Foundation, spread over three years. This generous grant was renewed for three more years and even increased to 10,000 dollars over five years in 1930. In 1928 the Department of Public Instruction suggested that the Rousseau Institute be integrated within the Letters Faculty. The institute was officially affiliated with the university in a decree signed on 9 April 1929, but it remained private and was run independently. For more information see Pierre Bovet, *Vingt ans de vie*, op. cit. (especially pp. 126–131 on institute-university relations). See also E. Claparède (1912) Un Institut des sciences de l'éducation et des besoins auxquels il répond, *Archives de psychologie, XII*.

7   Jean Piaget, 'friend of nature'

Fernando Vidal

It is a well-known fact that Jean Piaget was a precocious naturalist. At the age of 15, he was already a recognized expert in the field of mollusc taxonomy and the author of a number of articles in specialized journals. Piaget himself considered his early training an essential aspect of his intellectual biography, and he never forgot the importance of his years working with the malacologist Paul Godet (1836–1911), director of the Natural History Museum in Neuchâtel:

> When I was eleven years old [1907], I had the chance to publish some remarks on an albino sparrow, then to present myself to the director of the zoological museum of my native town to ask permission to work there during my days off from school. . . . He took me for 'famulus', made me stick labels, taught me about collecting and about terrestrial and fresh-water molluscs. . . . These beginnings were important for me. While some may get their school education in mathematics or in Latin, I received hands-on training working on a precise problem, that of the species and their innumerable variations according to their habitat, of the relations between genotypes and phenotypes, with a preference for studying adaptations to altitude . . . fresh-water, etc. In short, ever since this experience I have thought in terms of forms and the evolution of forms.[1]

This passage provides a certain amount of biographical information, but above all it tells us something about the way Piaget viewed his intellectual development and the image that he wished to leave of himself.

On the one hand, Piaget gives continuity to his thinking, so as to account for the 'biological' dimension of his psychological and epistemological work. As has been said, Piaget 'went from the snail's adaptive forms to that of man'.[2] However, although such an image of continuity may fit an auto-biographical account, it does not match a historical rendering of the facts.[3]

On the other hand, Piaget's description of his early scientific years leads us to believe that he was a solitary young scholar. But he was not. From 1910 to 1915, he developed in the midst of a Neuchâtel group of amateur naturalists, the Club of the Friends of Nature, which he failed to mention in his autobiographical writings. A look at this club modifies the image of Piaget as a lonely figure, provides a better understanding of the biographical significance of his early scientific activities, and shows that some oft-repeated ideas are more or less mythical clichés.

The albino sparrow is a good starting point. In his autobiography, Piaget writes: 'Having spotted an albino sparrow in a public park, I submitted a single page article to a journal of natural history in Neuchâtel. The article was published and I was "launched"!'[4] The 'article' in question was no more than a hundred words long and appeared in 1907 in a journal for amateur naturalists.[5] Although Piaget gives no information about the 'journal' in question, he relativizes the event by placing 'launched' in quotation marks. A number of commentators have nevertheless given that short text the rank of a unique event, an expression of early genius and the starting point of Piaget's career.

Throughout the world, there seems to have been a need to compensate for the modesty of such a beginning. Thus it has been written: 'Piaget schrieb bereits mit 11 Jahren einen wissenschaftlichen Artikel über einen Albino-Spatzen'; 'niño prodigio que a los once años publicó un pequeño trabajo de ornitología sobre el gorrión albino'; 'se destacó en el campo de la biología. Contaba apenas diez años cuando publicó un estudio sobre la golondrina albina'; 'à dix ans il publiait son premier article sur les moineaux albinos du parc de Neuchâtel'; 'il fut en effet d'abord un jeune biologiste, qui publia à onze ans un premier travail sur les moineaux albinos'; 'at age ten he wrote and published a monograph on a rare part-albino sparrow'; 'surpreendeu a comunidade científica da sua cidade ao apresentar um trabalho para uma revista sobre um pardal totalmente albino que observara num parque público'; 'inizió presto a interessarsi ai problemi scientifici. Risale a quando aveva solo dieci anni una memoria scientifica nata dalla sua passione di collezionista.' All of this led to a mystification of the event: Piaget is even said to have devoted his first publication to an albino sparrow he saw from his zoology laboratory in Neuchâtel ('consacré sa première publication au moineau albinos qu'il voyait de son laboratoire de zoologie neuchâtelois')![6]

These quotations, with their comical hyperboles and distortions, come from newspapers, but numerous books about Piaget's work provide other examples that are equally enthusiastic in conveying the idea that the origin of his work is marked by the seal of a precocious genius. Yet, spotting an albino sparrow is not what distinguishes Piaget – for other youths published similar observations in the same journal – but rather the fact of becoming a professional naturalist at an early age and then of extrapolating into natural history his first philosophical concerns.[7]

Naturalists and natural history societies

The image of Piaget, Friend of Nature, is naturally linked to that of his first teacher in natural history, Paul Godet. In his autobiography, Piaget writes that he owes Godet 'the privilege of taking up science' early enough to have been saved 'from the demon of philosophy'.[8]

Paul Godet was born in 1836 in Neuchâtel to a bourgeois and royalist family, at a time when Neuchâtel was already a Swiss canton, but still a Prussian principality. His grandfather, born in Berlin, came to Neuchâtel after serving as secretary to the Russian ambassador in Constantinople. His grandmother was governess of the future Prussian king Frederick III. Frédéric Godet, Paul's uncle, was the prince's tutor before going on to become an eminent theologian. Paul's father was Charles-Henri Godet (1797–1879), Frédéric's elder brother. He led an itinerant life, especially as a tutor, before settling in Neuchâtel. He worked for years on *flore du Jura* (flora of the Jura region) and was one of the founders of the Neuchâtel Horticultural Society and Botanical Gardens. He was, above all, his son's first natural history teacher.

The tradition that Charles-Henri Godet taught his son Paul, who in turn taught it to Piaget and the Friends of Nature, was that knowing nature consisted essentially of knowing how to recognize and classify species, and that the means of doing so was to examine immediately observable external characteristics. Paul Godet's work, concerned primarily with the taxonomy of Neuchâtel and Jura molluscs, belonged to this tradition, as did Piaget's youthful studies.

The benefits that Piaget would reap from such early exposure to the natural sciences extended beyond the scientific aspect of the tradition handed down by the Godet family. As a child he found in this 'serious work' and 'non-fictive, personal world' an escape from a difficult family life.[9] Godet enjoyed recounting his father's adventures in Russia, where he had managed to overcome a 'violent homesickness' thanks to an old botany book that encouraged him to collect plants and herbs.[10] Natural history provided him with 'an excellent means of shaking off longing'.[11] Such commentaries are typical of a time and context in which the cognitive value of the natural sciences was being complemented by their psychological and moral functions. In these functions lay the true worth of such groups of amateur naturalists and the reason why they were unconditionally supported by the social structure of science as practised in Neuchâtel at the end of the nineteenth century.

The investiture ceremony in which Jean Piaget became a member of the Friends of Nature in June 1910 provides a perfect illustration of the social and intellectual context to which the club belonged. After the candidate's lecture, in which the influence of Paul Godet's interests and teaching was particularly acknowledged,[12] several honorary members took the podium. Godet, the dean of Neuchâtel naturalists, was the son of an outstanding citizen, nephew of a distinguished theologian, and cousin of Philippe Godet, a writer and politician well known at the time. Another honorary member was Pierre Bovet (1873–1965), psychologist, pedagogue, and philosopher as well as co-founder of the Club of the Friends of Nature. He also came from an eminent Neuchâtel family. In 1910, Bovet was a colleague of Philippe Godet at the University of Neuchâtel, whose rector was Jean's father, Arthur Piaget. Two years later Bovet became director of the Jean-Jacques Rousseau Institute in Geneva, where Piaget himself started his career in 1921. The third honorary member, Eugène Legrandroy, was professor of astronomy at the university. His successor was Gustave Juvet (1896–1936), a member of the Club and one of Piaget's closest friends.

Thus the ceremony of 9 June 1910 reflected the social network of the city, where a limited number of persons of similar standing formed an educated elite. The same individuals crossed paths at the university and in scholarly and amateur societies, creating a scientific atmosphere of freely moving members, ideas, information, and values through the halls of learned institutions, as well as private homes. These institutions formed a hierarchy, the intellectual and social centre of which revolved round scholarly societies. At a young age, Piaget became a member of the Neuchâtel Natural Sciences Society (1912), the Swiss Zoological Society (1913), and the Swiss Natural Sciences Society (1914).

During the restoration ushered in by Napoleon's defeat in 1815, naturalist groups were created throughout Switzerland with the patriotic aim of exploring their country. The Neuchâtel Natural Sciences Society, founded in 1832, was part of that general movement. From then on, in spite of the emigration of Louis Agassiz and others to America after 1848, the society remained the centre for local scientific pursuits. Many of its members also belonged to groups aimed at fostering through natural science the moral and civic education of youth.

The oldest of these groups was the *Club Jurassien* (Jura Club), established in 1865 at the initiative of a medical doctor, Louis Guillaume (1833–1924), who served first as deputy, then as director of the state penitentiary and of the Federal Bureau for Statistics, as well as Professor of Hygiene at the Academy of Neuchâtel. In 1864 Guillaume helped create the History and Archaeology Society and its journal *Musée neuchâtelois*. The Jura Club and the History Society pursued common goals. In fact, the founders of the *Musée* were eager to incite the population to learn about their country's history, considered 'the basis of political life'.[13] For them, participation in political life did not depend on specialized knowledge, but on the capacity to read intelligently the local press, remain attentive to significant matters of ordinary life, and communicate about them.[14] Because the Jura Club was the counterpart of the Historical Society, they had many members in common.

The founders of the Club wanted to occupy young people with 'healthy, elevated matters so necessary during that transition period when dangers often lurk, when after leaving school an adolescent has not yet found his place in society and may be lured by frivolous attractions and material pleasures'[15]. The Jura Club published *Le Rameau de Sapin* (The Fir Branch), a monthly journal printed by a procedure akin to lithography; many local youths, including Piaget, made their scientific and literary beginnings in *Le Rameau de Sapin*.

Through his various activities in education and public health, Guillaume was one of many contemporaries who treated the problem of moral and civic education in a context in which teaching was becoming increasingly secular. Nothing is more indicative of this fact than the praise of the Jura Club that appeared in the famous pedagogical dictionary published by the French educational reformer Ferdinand Buisson (1841–1932).[16]

During his appointment as Professor of Philosophy and Comparative Literature at the Academy of Neuchâtel (1866–1870), Buisson had criticized religious teaching in the primary schools. He returned to France full of admiration for Switzerland's 'authentic democracy', which he claimed to have seen put into practice in education.[17] As head of primary education in France, he drafted the laws for the creation of a new lay and obligatory educational system. From the point of view of French educational reform, Buisson considered the Jura Club a model of an ingenious intellectual and moral pedagogy.

At the end of the nineteenth century, a stroll in nature was no longer a Rousseauian occasion for solitary reverie, but the source of moral and intellectual value for the individual and the group. An example of such ideology can be found in the local bestseller *Robinson de la Tène* (1875), whose author, Louis Favre (1822–1904), filled pages of his novel with lessons on natural history, geography, and prehistoric lacustrian environments. Favre, a prolific historian, naturalist, and novelist, had co-founded and worked assiduously for the *Musée neuchâtelois* and the *Rameau de Sapin*.

The birth of the Friends of Nature

The Club of the Friends of Nature was founded in 1893 by two 15-year-old schoolboys, Pierre Bovet and his friend Carl-Albert Loosli (1877–1959), who went on to become an art critic, biographer of the Swiss artist Ferdinand Hodler, and a political polemicist. According to Bovet, it was Loosli who had the idea of beginning a natural history society for secondary, Latin, or grammar school students aged at least 14.[18] From the beginning, the club set itself apart from the kind of groups inspired by German student societies that had become common in Swiss high schools and universities at the end of the nineteenth century. These student societies required their members to wear uniforms and obey strict rules and regulations; in contrast, the Friends of Nature were interested in science and wanted to work discreetly and without constraints.

From the beginning, the Friends of Nature received the support of established naturalists, whom they thanked by bestowing on them the title of honorary member. Paul Godet was one of the first. He taught the members the importance of a hands-on approach to studying nature through the practices and principles of natural history and classification. He demanded 'not youths who talk, but youths who act'; he warned that 'Anyone who limits himself to a few books about natural history and does not feel the need to have an immediate contact with nature will never be anything else than a failed naturalist.'[19] This conviction became the Friends' intellectual creed.

The club met every fortnight on Thursday afternoons. Botanical, palae-ontological, and zoological excursions were organized regularly. During the meetings, the members listened to reports on observations of animals, plants, or other natural phenomena. More formal lectures or informal chats were also part of the proceedings. The Friends occasionally undertook a common project that would then be published. As one of its former members said, 'The Club was scientific and its goal was to work'; its motto was 'To live happily, let us live in hiding.'[20]

Approved by parents and supported by distinguished men of science who took an interest in the education of youth, the club had an important social-izing role. In 1901, for example, the Friends invited the Minister of State Education to their 150th meeting. Not knowing whether he would be able to attend, the minister nevertheless replied that he would like to: 'It is not neces-sary to tell you', he wrote to the Friends, 'that I am most pleased to know that the young take an interest in nature and that my support will never be failing for a Club such as yours.' He added: 'Nature has such riches to teach us and what one can learn from it is so precious that I congratulate you in your pursuit of this goal.'[21] For those who were involved in educating young people, the Club of the Friends of Nature was a reassuring institution that inspired confidence.

The young Piaget, who was greatly attached to the club and its ideals, was an active member in all its functions and became, as Bovet said, its ornament.[22] In 1912, he successfully proposed a new article to the rules forbidding Friends from belonging to the above-mentioned student societies of Germanic inspir-ation (Minutes, 19 September 1912).[23] Later, during his stay in Neuchâtel from 1925 to 1929, Piaget, along with Juvet, attended club meetings and left 'unforgettable memories' among the members of the day.[24]

Piaget among the Friends of Nature

Piaget was a member of the Club of the Friends of Nature from June 1910 to September 1915, from ages 14 to 19, during his last two years at the Latin high school and throughout his grammar school years.

In February 1910, when Piaget was admitted to the Club as 'guest' or future candidate, the minutes reported that he was already known as 'profes-sor of conchology', as well as author of a 'famous dictionary' and 'of many articles' (Minutes, 10 and 24 February 1910). In fact, Piaget had merely penned a simple malacological note for *Le Rameau de Sapin*. However, his passion for molluscs was well known; at his 'baptism' it was declared that being a 'great collector of shells, snails, etc., he will take the name of the slug' (Minutes, 28 September 1910). At the time, the Friends of Nature were given nicknames taken from the medieval *Roman de Renart*. Piaget's name came from Tardif the slug, and he thus became 'Tardieu'.

The 'official critique' of the work Piaget presented for his candidature stated that he 'showed a group of grammar school students that the research of a second-year Latin school student was worth that of a so-called scientist'.[25] A few months later, the Friends thought that Piaget had surpassed them all in science: 'We have all decided that apart from conchology, an area in which only one of them is greatly gifted, the members are rather mediocre Friends of Nature' (Minutes, 13 July 1911). Compared with others, whose papers were also 'excellent', Piaget was considered 'more scientific, more learned' (Minutes, 27 January 1911). When criticized for using Latin terminology too much, he responded 'that one can only call a shell by its proper name' (Minutes, 13 July 1911). According to tradition, at the first meeting of the year the secretary would deliver a 'philosophical discourse' about his peers; Piaget invariable fared the best: 'good adjunct secretary, perfect toad secretary, admirable conchologist, and one could say much more' (Minutes, 12 January 1911).

The 'toad committee', whose secretary was Piaget, dated from the first years of the club and was revived in 1912 by Juvet. In the following year, he and Piaget published a classification of Neuchâtel batrachians.[26] Belonging to the toad committee was almost a scientific virtue:

> Piaget's work is consistently good and very conscientiously done; nothing astonishing in that, for as I have said, he is on the toad committee. Piaget has given us a complete catalogue of the molluscs of the Val d'Hérens, and to this day it is the only one of its kind. Knowing our crass ignorance, Piaget had the happy and intelligent idea to bring a lovely collection of samples gathered *in situ* to enlighten the poor members who had never had an idea of what the Latin name of a mollusc meant. Piaget is to be warmly and deservedly congratulated.
>
> (Minutes, 27 January 1911)

In every instance, Piaget's work is 'perfect in content, style, and length' (Minutes, 23 February 1911); his minutes are also 'admirably' recorded.

A few years later, at a time when the Friends lamented that they had become somewhat lax about life sciences, Piaget presented one of his research projects, which was about to be published. It caused an enthusiastic reaction: 'His work is obviously excellent! It's by Piaget.' One called it 'impressive', while describing it as 'totally in keeping with the Club's spirit: 1. it is personal; 2. it concerns local fauna; and 3. it is serious' (Minutes, 19 November 1914).

Apart from his active participation at club meetings as president, secretary, recording secretary, or speaker, Piaget played a major role in carrying out two collective projects: the catalogue of batrachians already mentioned and the study of the Loclat (or Lake Saint-Blaise), a small lake near Neuchâtel that had long interested the club. In 1912, Marcel Romy, another Friend of Nature, and Piaget completed a catalogue of the Loclat molluscs, thus continuing what the Club had already published in 1907.[27]

Piaget's contributions to the Friends of Nature reflect the fact that the club was the centre of the social life of an autonomous group of male students between the ages of 14 and 19. The social dimension can be seen in the minutes of meetings, which were organized around the reading of a paper and followed by noisy, yet never malicious or aggressive, discussions. Time was also reserved for administrative business (committees, distribution of work, courses, outings, Christmas celebrations), which included the reading and approval of the minutes and, of course, singing. The minutes were written in a caustic, ironically formal style. Thus, far from being purely scholarly, the meetings provided a convivial occasion in a tone that the members themselves set and maintained.

Piaget seems to have been a central figure in the entertaining atmosphere that occasionally reigned. For example, in a picturesque tale of moving house in December 1912, which took three journeys 'with carts drawn by members, loaded with specimen bottles and stuffed animals, and everybody singing', there is an amusing description of Piaget wearing a necklace made of 'a shell of a respectable size, sea horses, various skeletons and many other things'.[28] Once, after an excursion when he was asked to deliver a 'presidential discourse', Piaget 'started emptying his pockets to make himself comfortable, then started laughing with an uncontrollable and contagious laugh. Finally, he took a seat and mumbled some senseless words.'[29] The minutes that he recorded were without doubt some of the most entertaining, and at the same time his intellectual presence was always greatly appreciated.

From its founding in 1893, the Club of the Friends of Nature gave its members the opportunity to discuss non-scientific subjects. Though the most popular topic was natural history, the members also took an interest in biography, philosophy, and history. Compared with other periods of the club's history, the years 1910 to 1915 were particularly marked by philosophical discussions. At the end of 1912, the club was divided into sections. Piaget belonged (with Romy) to the malacology section and Juvet was in the mathematical–physical–chemical and botanical sections. Together Piaget and Juvet made up the philosophy section. A 'literary section for the study of Nature among writers' was created two weeks later during a turbulent meeting at which Piaget defended the new section against Juvet's adamant refusal (Minutes, 21 November 1912).

In 1915, after listening to two public lectures given by Piaget and Juvet, 'Biology and Philosophy' and 'The Neo-Darwin Tendency in Biology', one of the club's founders protested that their ideal 'had not been to philosophize but to observe' and that the club had not been created 'to do metaphysics' (Minutes, 29 April 1915). The remark was legitimate over and above the lectures in question, for the members of the club were spending a good part of the time discussing biological theories and the philosophy of science.

The Friends of Nature loved philosophizing, in particular about the status of science compared with other forms of knowledge, and involved themselves in the controversy between scientism and pragmatism. At the time, the 'pragmatic' philosophy of Henri Bergson (1859–1941) was inciting lively debate. Opposed to Bergson was an exemplary adept of scientism, the French biologist Félix Le Dantec (1869–1917), militantly Lamarckian, monistic, materialistic, deterministic, and atheistic. Piaget and Juvet, the two most philosophically inclined of the members, used to carry on the Bergson–Le Dantec debate between themselves.

The Bergsonian biology of the young Piaget

Born the same year as Piaget and, like him, from a family of La Côte-au-Fées, Juvet was, like his friend, a student of the philosopher Arnold Reymond at the cantonal grammar school; furthermore, just after the Great War he too went to Paris before returning to Neuchâtel as professor at the university. The friendship between the two men dates from the period that interests us here – 'the happy years', as Piaget called them, 'when we passionately united the cult of life sciences . . . philosophical discussion and friendship'.[30]

Juvet was a member of the Club of the Friends of Nature from 1912 to 1916, where, like Piaget, he was a dynamic force. He was known as a 'hardened mathematician' and a 'materialist philosopher' inspired by Le Dantec. Piaget, on the other hand, had allied himself with Bergson.

In 1911 Piaget read at the club a series of papers on the embryos of molluscs, the relations between molluscs and other animals, and the zoological geography of the octopus. In 1913 he spoke extemporaneously about the molluscs of Lake Annecy. In the meantime, he also started to deal with the evolution of organized creatures and creative evolution.

Piaget's papers reflected the influence of Bergson's ideas on his own development. Most of them were about malacology, but in September 1912 Piaget used Bergsonian philosophy to demonstrate 'the vanity of nomenclature'.[31] In 1913 he developed a critique of what he believed to be the idea of the species 'according to the Mendelian school'.[32] In 1915, he gave the above-mentioned lecture, 'Biology and Philosophy'. The frequency of his papers on malacology diminished as his interest in philosophy increased and as he distanced himself from the natural history Godet had taught him. Nevertheless, as his publications show, Piaget did not completely abandon his scientific interests; his last work on malacological taxonomy was the doctoral thesis he submitted to the University of Neuchâtel in 1918.

Piaget first learned about Bergson's philosophy in the summer of 1912, and by September his paper on 'the vanity of nomenclature' revealed the extent of his assimilation of Bergsonian ideas. But the club as a whole began giving a significant place to philosophy only in 1913, when Juvet became an active member. Juvet's first paper on transformism, read in February 1913, generated great interest.[33] In the discussion, Piaget compared life 'to an arm thrust into a bucket of metal pellets' (Minutes, 13 February 1913). This comparison reproduced a famous image from Bergson's *Creative Evolution*. The philosopher wanted to explain how nature creates structures as complex as an eye by describing for his readers the image of a hand passing through a bucket of iron filings 'that squeeze themselves together and resist'. He went on to explain:

> The relation of sight to its organ is like that of the hand to a mass of iron filings that determines, channels, and limits its movement . . . so that wherever it [the hand] stops, instantly and automatically, the granules take their respective places. So it is for sight and the organ of sight.[34]

The fact that Piaget was able to spontaneously use such an image to challenge Le Dantec shows to what extent he had assimilated Bergson's philosophy. As long as Piaget and Juvet were members of the Friends of Nature, the club's life was largely animated by their debates over the philosophy of the *élan vital* and mechanistic reductionism. This fact nuances Piaget's autobiographical memories.

Reading Bergson, he said, 'was somewhat disappointing. Instead of finding up-to-date scientific ideas . . . I had the impression of an ingenious construction that lacked an experimental basis.'[35] In his autobiography, Piaget claims that his scientific epistemological project dated from an early stage. In fact, by 1913 he was in the grip of Bergsonian ideas. In October of that year, when Piaget read passages from *Creative Evolution* 'against mechanists', Juvet argued:

> This reading is a fine example of finalist style and scholastic wording. Phrases such as the Progress of Sight or the *élan vital* are meaningless . . . Richeux [Juvet] then criticized the finalism of this text, and everything in it that runs against the determinism without which science would not be possible; but the pragmatists, whose French leader is Bergson, with the pretence of thinking science, deny it completely. As Mr Leuba [an honorary member] put it, these are matters of conviction. That does not keep one from drawing up a list of facts that are fatal to Bergson's arguments, and prove that determinism can be applied equally well to vital phenomena and to chemical reactions. He [Juvet] refutes Piaget so well, that Piaget is thoroughly troubled, and Romy pitifully exclaims: 'Ah! But it is . . . it is negation of . . . of . . . how shall I put it? of . . . the soul.' Yet, I must congratulate Piaget for the highly interesting discussion he provoked. Let us hope to have more of the like, for from the clash of ideas surges light.
>
> (Minutes, 9 October 1913, recorded by Juvet)

Once again the debate between the Bergsonian and the determinist seems to have been at the core of the intellectual life of the Friends of Nature.

Philosophical questions stimulated great discussions. In 1913, for example, when Piaget explained 'the idea of the species according to the Mendelian school', he made several conceptual errors that stemmed from his Bergsonian point of view; nevertheless, the paper was considered 'very good' (Minutes, 4 December 1913). That was due to the fact that the Bergsonian ideas remained hidden, while his Lamarckian, anti-Mendelian argument met with general agreement. It was a different matter in October 1914, when Piaget read texts by Alfred Fouillée (1838–1912) on 'the origins of thought from the biological point of view'. The excerpts were listened to 'with religious attention', and the reading 'was enthusiastically applauded' and 'found to be interesting'. The minutes did not give the source of the texts, but these doubtless came from Fouillée's major book, *L'évolutionnisme des idées-force* (1890). Both the notions and the style of this philosophy match the young Piaget's Bergsonian inclination. But Juvet was not in agreement with Fouillée, and 'found furthermore that it was a wordy text delivered in a preachy style' (Minutes, 22 October 1914).

At two public meetings of the Club, Juvet and Piaget both gave lectures. On the first occasion, in 1913, Juvet spoke on transformism, and Piaget on animal life in the depths of oceans and lakes. The second time, for the celebration of the 400th meeting of the club in April 1915, Juvet read 'The Neo-Darwinian Tendency in Biology' and Piaget read 'Biology and Philosophy'. Juvet recorded the minutes of this meeting, which he claimed was 'splendid, magnificent, idyllic, erotic, comical', and described his own work as a 'somewhat pretentious thing'. Under the circumstances, Piaget was also expected to give an appraisal of Juvet's contribution, which he qualified as 'good, scientific, philosophical, etc., etc., but read too fast'.

Piaget then read his paper, which Juvet characterized as a 'good work, scientific, philosophical, etc., etc., but delivered largely with the support of lofty words like determinism, gushing reality, etc., etc.'. When asked what he thought of the lecture, Juvet busied himself with his notes and 'mumbled some polite noises to thank Tardieu for his good speech'. 'What an irony!', he wrote, for he 'was far from agreeing with the lecturer's personal, metaphysical, transcendental conclusions based on Bergson and Piaget, two philosophers who might lead the world for a short while, but will end up either in hell or in the garbage' (Minutes, 29 April 1915).

Tardieu's individuality

Even though the manuscript of 'Biology and Philosophy' has been lost, it was obviously a defence of Bergson's ideas, so much so in fact that the title was taken from the first chapter of Bergson's *Creative Evolution*. Bergson stated that neither mechanism nor finalism is a proper tool for studying life. According to him, both fall into the error of applying too extensively certain scientific concepts to our intelligence; whereas, once we leave the framework where these concepts straitjacket our thoughts, 'Reality appears to us like a spring of ongoing novelties.'[36] Bergson spoke about evolving novelties in 1915, when, it must be remembered, the Great War had already been raging for eight months. In the sheltered enclave of Switzerland, in the meantime, Piaget had joined a movement of young Christians, sympathized with the young socialists, and wanted to put his mix of 'Bergson and Piaget' in the service of a humankind that seemed to be headed for extinction, and which he hoped to recreate on new foundations.[37]

Until then, the Club of the Friends of Nature had been Piaget's intellectual milieu. Drawn to both science and philosophy (seen mainly as a way of 'thinking about science'), the Friends of Nature practised a descriptive science that was quite unlike the philosophies they enjoyed discussing. Their metaphysical disagreements were offset by a fundamental agreement on the cognitive value of science. That is why Piaget's position was so peculiar. Although he did not question the value of science, he adopted a philosophy that someone like Juvet saw as contradicting it. Piaget preferred Bergson to mechanistic and scientistic philosophies. Like the other Friends of Nature, he rejected Darwinism, the theory of mutation, and Mendelism; but he was the only one to defend his scientific opinions by using the philosophy of creative evolution and of the *élan vital*.

Piaget's intellectual development between 1910 and 1915 can be measured by the contrast between the work he presented as candidate to the Club of the Friends of Nature and the last paper he read there. From the detailed description and exhaustive cataloguing of 'A Mollusc Particular to Our Lake', he reached towards the cosmic sources of creative evolution. The path he travelled as a Friend of Nature thus led him to the fields of knowledge that nourished all his later work.

Notes

1 J. Piaget (1959) Les modèles abstraits sont-ils opposés aux interprétations psycho-physiologiques dans l'explication en psychologie? Esquisse d'autobiographie intellectuelle. *Bulletin de psychologie, 13*, 7–13, p. 9.
2 G. Meili-Dworetzki (1978) Piaget im Verhältnis zu seinen Lehrern Pierre Janet und Edouard Claparède. In G. Steiner (Ed.), *Piaget und die Folgen* (p. 508). Zurich: Kindler.
3 See F. Vidal (1994) *Piaget before Piaget*. Cambridge, MA: Harvard University Press (a detailed study of Piaget up to 1918); (1996) *Piaget Neuchâtelois*. Neuchâtel: Bibliothèque publique et universitaire.
4 J. Piaget (1976) Autobiographie. *Cahiers Vilfredo Pareto – Revue européenne des sciences sociales, XIV*, 1–43, p. 2. Appeared originally in English in 1952.
5 J. Piaget (1907) Un moineau albinos. *Le Rameau de Sapin, 41*, 36.
6 Quotations in newspapers from Europe, North America, and South America taken from articles reproduced in *Hommage à Jean Piaget* (University of Geneva, June 1982), pp. 44, 65, 117, 78, 81, 101, 109, 86, 36, respectively.
7 The manuscripts of the young Piaget deposited at the Club of the Friends of Nature are especially revealing on this matter. See F. Vidal (1999) *'La vanité de la nomenclature' et autres écrits de jeunesse de Jean Piaget*, www.piaget.org/piaget (henceforth: *Inédits*).
8 Piaget, Autobiographie, op. cit., p. 3.
9 Ibid., p. 2. On Piaget's mother (who, according to Piaget's autobiography, was the source of family problems), see Vidal, *Piaget before Piaget*, op. cit.

10 P. Godet (1879) Charles-Henri Godet, botaniste neuchâtelois. *Bulletin de la Société des sciences naturelles de Neuchâtel*, *12*, 166–175, pp. 166–167.

11 'What wonderful hours I spent among my dear snails, those calm and patient creatures, that produce a calming effect, so different from that which one experiences under the influence of the feverish, tormented existence, the torrent of which rules our lives. Blessed be those peaceful "hard-shelled creatures"!' P. Godet, letter to the Friends of Nature, 26 October 1894. Collection of the Friends of Nature (City Archives, Musée d'Art et d'Histoire, Neuchâtel), Correspondence. Collection henceforth referred to as F.C.A.N.

12 J. Piaget, Un mollusque spécial à notre lac. Delivered at the Club of the Friends of Nature, 9 June 1919; published in *Inédits*.

13 J. Petitpierre (1935). Une date dans la vie du canton. Soixante-dix ans du Musée neuchâtelois. In *Patrie neuchâteloise, Recueil illustré de chroniques d'histoire régionale* (Vol. 2, p. 82). Neuchâtel.

14 E. Junod (1923). Les étapes de la Société d'histoire. *Nouvelles étrennes neuchâteloises*, p. 15.

15 L. Favre, A. Bachelin, & Dr Guillaume (1874) A nos lecteurs. *Le Rameau de Sapin*, 1874, no. 1, January, 1.

16 F. Buisson (Ed.) (1882) *Dictionnaire de pédagogie et d'instruction primaire* (Part I, Vol. 1). Paris: Hachette.

17 F. Buisson (1916) *Souvenir (1866–1916)* (p. 11). Paris: Fischbacher. Lecture delivered at the University of Neuchâtel, 10 January.

18 P. Bovet (1943) *La fondation et les quatre premières années (1893–1897) des Amis de la Nature*. Lecture delivered at the fiftieth anniversary of the Club of the Friends of Nature, 12 June. Mimeographed text (deposited at the Bibliothèque publique et universitaire, Neuchâtel).

19 P. Godet (1875) Les collections d'histoire naturelle. *Le Rameau de Sapin*, no. 2, 5–6, p. 6.

20 P. Ducommun (1943) *Historique du Club des Amis de la Nature* (p. 24). Lecture delivered at the fiftieth anniversary of the Club, 12 June. Mimeographed text, bound with Bovet, La fondation, op. cit.

21 E. Quartier-la-Tente (1901) Reply to the Friends of Nature, 20 October. CFN, Correspondence.

22 P. Bovet (1932) *Vingt ans de vie. L'Institut J.-J. Rousseau de 1912 à 1932* (p. 74). Neuchâtel/Paris: Delachaux & Niestlé.

23 'Minutes' henceforth refers to the 'Procès-verbaux' (Minutes) of the Club of the Friends of Nature, manuscript copies, CFN.

24 The following are almost complete, Pierre-Ernest Meystre's 'Quelques souvenirs de Jean Piaget' (*Feuille d'Avis du Neuchâtel*, 19 September 1980): 'Jean Piaget, among others, left unforgettable memories at the time when he was professor at Neuchâtel (1925–1929) with the grammar school students who were then members of the Club of the Friends of Nature. . . . Among our honorary members and on more than one occasion, a triumvirate would arrive in a whirlwind, shifting about furniture "procured" at garage-sales, in order to find a place at the old table scarred with cigar and pipe burns or with graffiti chiselled by old and new members. They were Professor Jean Piaget, the mathematics professor Gustave Juvet and the architect Edmond Calame. They would immediately order rounds of the traditional mulled wine. . . . On those occasions, the member designated to report on his work was not much at ease confronted by this triumvirate known for their dialectic skills. However, the traditional, yet nonetheless merited, praise relieved the speaker, giving credit to the good reputation of the club and the grammar school. During the second round of mulled wine, while Piaget puffed on his pipe, Juvet and Calame would lead lofty scholarly discussions on matters of world importance and foreshadowing future developments. We were ecstatic (the word is

not excessive) in the presence of such men learned in all the areas of science in general, and in view of their eloquence on contemporary philosophical issues. The rebuttals were like firework displays, one more convincing than the other, to our great enjoyment as much as to our profit. It was often only after midnight, when the "Chanson de fin de semestre" composed by Philippe Godet had been sung, that we closed down the local pub.'

25　J. Béguin, *Critique officielle du travail de Jean Piaget*, preserved with Piaget's manuscript *Un mollusque spécial*; published in *Inédits*.

26　J. Piaget & G. Juvet (1912–13) Catalogue des batraciens du canton de Neuchâtel. *Bulletin de la Société neuchâteloise des sciences naturelles*, *40*, 172–186.

27　J. Piaget & M. Romy (1914) Notes malacologiques sur le Jura bernois. *Revue suisse de zoologie*, *22*, 365–406.

28　Notebook no. 6, 19 December 1912. This is a manuscript notebook entitled *Procès-verbaux des courses, arbres de Noël, déménagements, conférences, 1912–1916*, CFN.

29　Ibid., 24 March 1913.

30　J. Piaget (1937) La philosophie de Gustave Juvet. In *A la mémoire de Gustave Juvet, 1896–1936* (p. 38). Lausanne: La Concorde.

31　J. Piaget (1912) *La vanité de la nomenclature*, read at the Club of the Friends of Nature, 26 September; published in *Inédits*. See also F. Vidal (1984) *La vanité de la nomenclature*. Un manuscrit inédit de Jean Piaget. *History and philosophy of the life sciences*, *6*, 75–106.

32　J. Piaget (1913) *La notion de l'espèce suivant l'école mendélienne*, read at the Club of the Friends of Nature, 4 December 1913; published in *Inédits*. See also F. Vidal (1992) Jean Piaget's early critique of Mendelism: 'La notion de l'espèce suivant l'école mendélienne' (A 1913 manuscript). *History and philosophy of the life sciences*, *14*, 121–143.

33　G. Juvet, 'Le transformisme', CFN, ms. no. 596.

34　H. Bergson (1963) L'évolution créatrice. In *Oeuvres* (pp. 575–577). Paris: Presses universitaires de France. [English translation: *Creative Evolution*. New York: Henry Holt and Company, 1911.] (Original work published 1907.)

35　Piaget, Autobiographie, op. cit., p. 5.

36　H. Bergson, *L'évolution créatrice*, op. cit., pp. 532–534.

37　See Vidal, *Piaget before Piaget*, op. cit. On Piaget's spiritual and political development and its connections to his scientific and philosophical work, see also F. Vidal (1994) 'Les mystères de la douleur divine'. Une 'prière' du jeune Jean Piaget pour l'année 1916. *Revue de théologie et de philosophie*, *126*, 97–118; (1994) Piaget poète. Avec deux sonnets oubliés de 1918. *Archives de psychologie*, *64*, 3–7; (1996) L'oeuvre de Jean Piaget. Un engagement social et religieux. *Psychoscope*, *17*, no. 6, pp. 12–15; (1997) L'éducation nouvelle et l'esprit de Genève. Une utopie politico-pédagogique des années 1920. *Equinoxe. Revue de sciences humaines*, no. 17, 81–98; (1998) Immanence, affectivité et démocratie dans *Le jugement moral chez l'enfant*. *Bulletin de psychologie*, *51*(5), no. 437, 585–597.

8 Christian and social commitment

Charles Thomann

Piaget the Christian

Jean Piaget was born into a divided family. His father, an agnostic who was a distinguished historian, certainly had a strong influence on his son, exposing him to multiple aspects of culture. By contrast, his mother was an ardent believer. She belonged to an independent church, one of the two factions that came out of the schism that disrupted Neuchâtel Protestantism at the end of the nineteenth century. This church, which was separated from the state, had been founded by men who were stricter and more attached to dogma than the parishioners who remained faithful to the national church.

In 1868 a strong liberal Christian movement had demanded a profound modification of the status of the Neuchâtel reformed church. It favoured a church without ministry, a religion without catechism, a morality without theology. With the support of a number of sympathizers, liberal Christianity took hold in the state church, and liberal pastors were appointed to the parishes. In recommending the suppression of the church budget, it did away with the state religion.

Aware of this evolution and concerned about keeping in close contact with its citizens, the cantonal government gave in to the liberal minority and let them take control of ecclesiastical matters. A law was drawn up that defined what it meant to be a member of the church and a citizen, and it gave the state authority over theological studies, which guaranteed freedom of conscience. The new law tended to confuse the church with civil society by distancing the reformed church from the doctrine of its synod and thus breaking the unity of faith of its ecclesiastics and its faithful. The law, which was promulgated in 1873, had been accepted by a majority of only 16 votes.

A large group of Protestants, convinced that their church could no longer stay faithful to its Master and its mission, founded an evangelical church independent of the state. But the majority of the population remained faithful to the national church.

Jean Piaget had a rigorous Protestant upbringing. He had religious instruction and renewed his baptismal vows on Whit Sunday in 1912. Although he was interested in catechism lessons, his critical spirit often rebelled against the intransigent precepts and the complex problems created by a world preparing for war. Nevertheless, this contact with religion strengthened his faith.

The young man with a passion for life sciences admired nature and joined clubs that fostered his scientific aspirations and his personal tastes. Caught up in religion, he became a member of the Swiss Christian Student Association in 1914. His scientific and philosophical tendencies did not interfere with his Christian commitment. Being a strongly committed Protestant, he boldly proclaimed his convictions. He loudly and publicly stood by his faith in Jesus Christ in two texts that had an important impact: *La mission de l'idée* and *Recherche*.

La mission de l'idée

Jean Piaget was apparently strongly affected by the opening lines of the Gospel of St John. For him, the Word of the gospel became the Idea, the mission of which he laid out in his first work, which appeared in 1915. The young man bore witness by his ardent faith, but he rejected the traditions and dogmas of the church. Only the Gospel could satisfy the human being; only the message of Jesus Christ should be one's guide. He had hardly any interest in the other books of the Bible.

'It is the deepest part of our being from which the Idea emerges, from this fertile and mysterious region which man on his own never reaches. It is this vital source from which emanations well up only under a sublime influence.' 'The Idea is the kernel of life.' 'Jesus is the Idea made flesh.' 'Dogma is a dead Idea.'

Piaget was referring here to the web of lies that surrounded the young, the hypocrisy and egotism of society that smothers the Idea just when it begins to germinate within their hearts. Piaget also disclaimed the need for action. For him it was clear that the Reform had come from the silence of the cloisters and not from councils and clashes, that the revolution came from Rousseau's wanderings and not from meetings and demonstrations.

While the war laid waste to Europe, the Christian youths cursed the leaders, the orthodox, the reactionary, the utilitarian, and the sceptic. The amorphous herd of conservatives who complacently clung to their narrow world and rejected any kind of progress were to blame for the conflict. The pettiness of the traditionalist measured the fatherland by the national army or by personal interests. Detesting all levelling dogmatism that smothered the Idea, the author foresaw an era when social Christianity, founded on the message of Jesus Christ, would reign.

The young author was attacking the unflinching institutions of the churches, the gregariousness of Christians, but not the clergy who were prisoners of the system. The churches were closed off by a stagnant morality and by a static spirit of orthodoxy. They had betrayed Christ. If Christ were to come back, He would be seized with holy indignation:

Cursed are the great of this world for they have fought against me for 20 centuries! Cursed are the conservatives for they have shackled me for 20 centuries! But seven times cursed are you the Christians for you have denied me for 20 centuries! I came to bring the struggle to earth, and you have only thought of yourselves and your own salvation.[1]

The salvation of Christians is a synonym for damnation, for they have thought only of a heavenly kingdom and eternal happiness without looking after the problems here below. The churches have silenced the atheist as guilty; they have denied God forgiveness by making themselves judge; they have smothered themselves in their own moral sanction. The dogma has killed the Christian Idea; 'religion is dead by wanting to stay faithful to itself'.

As a Christian committed to a social vocation, Jean Piaget attacked the church for having reduced its social concerns to the bare minimum in order to give the best of itself to the hereafter. The conservative church had neglected to defend the poor, to deliver men from degradation, to rescue children from oppressive labour, to liberate women. Science in no way goes against God's designs. It should be put to the service of people. Piaget argued that the church had the obligation to promote feminism. He was giving in to a juvenile wish and let himself be taken in by his dreams when he declared: 'From the women's vote will come peace, death to the politics of self-interest, patriotic idealism, humanitarian laws, social regeneration, the rise of the proletariat.'[2]

The mission of the Idea was the rebirth of Christianity.

Recherche

Jean Piaget was barely 20 years old when he published this new essay. The war was raging, and he suffered deeply from it. He confirmed the convictions expressed in his first work, but now the effects of the vast knowledge acquired as he matured deepened his thoughts, which he articulated less spontaneously, less absolutely, but with the same conviction and resolve.

Piaget wrote 210 pages entitled *Recherche* in an attempt to reconcile science and faith and to restore the moral dimension of society; these were, in his eyes, the essential problems of his time, as the debate between faith and philosophy had been in the eighteenth century. Piaget also wanted to deal with the problems of the good and true in the light of Kant, Pascal, and especially Rousseau, and with the questions of Catholicism and Protestantism enlightened by Vinet, Secrétan, Amiel, and Félix Bovet. The author referred to Henri Bergson, Claude Bernard, and Auguste Comte, all great minds who had understood the beauty and humanity of science and who enthusiastically endeavoured to bring about a Platonic conquest of what was true over pretentious scholasticism empty of tolerance and respect. According to the author, literature was also full of examples that treated these ills. Tolstoy, Péguy, Romain Rolland, Claudel, and Gide projected vast sites of ruins lying next to scaffoldings, where a mysterious impulse would draw a new order out of the present chaos.

In 1917, at the heart of the detestable German nationalism and the exasperating French patriotism, hatred became a state virtue and imperialism reigned. Each one wanted to identify his God with the endangered home-lands. Many atheistic groups tried to free people of all belief and put into their proselytizing a religious fervour to seek the truth and the good. A common ideal, the patrimony of the human race, to which many socialists aspired, appeared as a fragile hope. 'Socialism ought to be a science, an art and a moral according to Jaurès' teaching, whose death was a tragedy. Romain Rolland spoke; Jaurès would have acted.'[3]

Atheistic thought, incapable of making sense of life, created a terrible imbalance. Both literature and philosophy were affected, though the latter retained metaphysical beliefs. The mass of believers huddled in the churches, hothouses of stale air where some rare plants grew.

All research is an act of faith, and doubt paralyzes action. There is solidar-ity between science and faith. The first needs value and the second needs truth; each provides the other with what it lacks. Equilibrium alone leads to the concept of truth: biological, aesthetic, moral, and religious truth. Piaget's faith drove him to research. The endless recommencement process of the research is the good desired by God. Faith is enlivened by joy. There had been enough of morose believing, cramped asceticism, fakes who dishonoured faith! Unfortunately, the youth of the day turned towards nationalism in politics, Catholicism in religion, pragmatism in philosophy – towards every-thing that held up the past at the expense of moving towards solutions to problems for the future.

The equilibrium of qualities is the basis of psychology on the individual level and of sociology on the moral level. The social order is disturbed by the imbalance of individuals and of the society itself. The true Christian moral is a condemnation of all egotism, of all pride, and of all passion. Science only confirms these observations.

Piaget, the young Christian, claimed that the socialism of his elders had failed because of dogmatism. He based his hopes on a liberal socialism to forge a new church. The new socialism is without doubt a synonym of social Christianity. It is in no way whatsoever a strict doctrine or a political strategy, but, rather, a search for the truth, respect for the laws of nature, solidarity, and respect and love for the other. Jean Piaget purposely titled his study *Recherche* (Research) because in it he tries to analyse the fabric of society and the function of science, but he refrains from offering hasty answers. He ended the study by foreseeing a general federalist system in order to establish an equilibrium between the diverse political forces, and cooperation to abolish privileges. Cooperation would channel capital to the profit of the collective and not to the state, and it would protect the personality and the autonomy of the individual.

If the revolt of the young man against the established order was still present, his faith no longer seemed unshaken. His attempts – particularly to reconcile religion and science, to found a moral on objectively recognized principles – hardly came to anything, in spite of worthy efforts. Doubt gradually took hold of his spirit.

Social Christianity[4]

This political movement found fertile ground at the beginning of the twentieth century in the populous, industrialized city of La Chaux-de-Fonds, not far from Neuchâtel. Its members did not belong to the Socialist Party like the Christian socialists, but they had adopted a similar path and aimed at raising the living standards of workers. They sought to instruct workers, to let them take responsibilities; they were concerned with the improvement of professional training and tried to get the workers involved in the city's political and cultural life. In this industrial city, the need to improve the lot of workers accounts for the success of this education inspired by the Gospel.

The elderly doctor Pierre Coullery (1819–1903) had charitably treated his patients. He was also concerned about the lot of the disinherited and wanted to help them lead a decent life and to integrate into society. He is considered the founder of the Neuchâtel Socialist Party. A fervent Christian, Coullery had always refused to join a religious community, yet he never stopped proclaiming his faith.

Paul Pettavel (1861–1934), who belonged to the next generation, was an enthusiastic pastor. His personality and ideas attracted a crowd of friends and people from different walks of life. He loudly proclaimed that though he was a liberal, he was voting with the workers. He was forever involved in the lives of the people; he organized demonstrations and spoke out on many occasions. In the *Feuille du Dimanche*, a small weekly journal that he edited alone for 34 years, he advocated an improvement of the workers' social status through a bold political action that nevertheless respected democratic rules.

The socialist leaders Charles Naine and Ernest-Paul Graber had both followed the religious instruction of Paul Pettavel, who had a strong influence on the two catechumens. They had become members of the Young Men's Christian Association, led by the pastor, which was trying to make Protestants aware of the social problems and to get them active in life outside the church, particularly civic and professional life. Later, Naine and Graber distanced themselves from religion and followed the struggle at the heart of the Socialist Party.

Along with Pettavel, the bubbling, eloquent, witty, and joyful Christian, another pastor to leave a profound mark on La Chaux-de-Fonds in the course of his short time there was Jules Humbert-Droz. After his theological studies he was appointed minister, a function he fulfilled with little orthodoxy and much provocation. As a member of the Socialist Party, he wanted to change the society radically, while his older and more level-headed colleague advocated reforms within the established legal channels. Humbert-Droz broke with his friends and turned towards communism.[5]

From the beginning of the century until the rise of fascism, La-Chaux-de-Fonds was shaken by constant political unrest. Workers laboured 10 hours a day in the factories, yet their wages barely provided their families with a living, even if by today's standards the cost of living was low. There was no question of social security insurance or paid holidays. The workers gathered round the dynamic, rallying Socialist Party, which united the majority of voters in 1912. Six years later, the misery of the workers was aggravated by the war, and their political hopes, particularly their wish to install proportional representation, ended in a general strike throughout Switzerland.

The atmosphere was different in Neuchâtel. It was a learning site, an administrative centre, a city dedicated to commerce, with only a few factories. Many families lived in ease, if not actual opulence. Workers hardly dared to meet, and they lacked means of expression. Those who did raise their voices were in general neither the dissatisfied nor the aggressive, but Christians haunted by the idea of social justice. The presence of the church weighed heavily on civil life. In Neuchâtel a large number of citizens, often severe and orthodox, formed an independent parish. Its members came from families of different political stripes and social classes, but the parish identified itself with the Liberal Party. In La Chaux-de-Fonds, many socialists distanced themselves from the state church and turned towards agnosticism.

The burning hearth created by Paul Pettavel aroused the interest of many young Neuchâtelois and profoundly influenced them. Groups were formed, and the city itself was affected by this wave of social renewal that called the status quo into question. Some young Christians proclaimed their faith and took on the task of relieving the material penury of the people: Human relations and the social, economical, and political status of the citizens ought henceforth to be marked by the spirit of the Gospel. Jean Piaget figured among these idealists.

The young friend of Paul Pettavel

Besides *La Feuille du Dimanche*, *L'Essor*,[6] a small Protestant journal published in Geneva but intended for the whole French-speaking Swiss community, dealt with the social problems that it tried to resolve in light of the Gospel, which was Pettavel's preoccupation. One finds essentially in this modest publication claims for fairness in work and housing conditions, reports on relevant achievements, proposals, and wishes. The pastor of La Chaux-de-Fonds was appointed to edit the journal from 1916 to 1918. He insisted on the importance of the Bible and its demands in community life. He also took up the question of conscientious objectors and vigorously defended them. Charles Naine had earlier refused to serve in the army. During the First World War, most of the workers thought that the Swiss Army, with a highly authoritarian commander, was not defending a country so much as an old-fashion regime.

Jean Piaget regularly read *L'Essor*. He agreed with the editor's opinions and the ideas advocated therein. Convinced that he had to make a personal contribution and that he had an obligation to express his faith publicly, he wanted to participate in this movement to create a fairer society.

On 22 December 1915 the young Piaget wrote to Paul Pettavel to ask him to publish in *L'Essor* an article on the Bible and the problem of suffering. The editor gladly accepted this request. He loved ardent youth with vibrant faith and appreciated spontaneous suggestions. Instead of placing the article in the editorial pages of the journal, he created a special section called 'young people's corner' which enabled *L'Essor* to retain its vitality and regenerate itself from outside contributions. This section regularly appeared in the first issue of each month.

Jean Piaget wrote an article that filled up the entire 'young people's corner'. He sent it with a letter thanking the editor for having accepted his request. The text appeared on 5 February 1916 under the title 'Les mystères de la douleur divine' (The mysteries of divine suffering). The author bore witness to his faith without the least philanthropic intention. In fact, he wrote a prayer full of feeling and in a poetical style: 'Un homme, que l'approche de l'année nouvelle mettait dans l'angoisse, était monté dans le temple de Dieu pour gémir et prier au sein de la nature . . .' (A man, who was troubled by the upcoming new year, went up to the temple of the Lord to wail and pray in the bosom of nature . . .).

We do not know of any other contributions from Piaget in subsequent issues of *L'Essor*, but it is possible that he submitted articles that were not signed. In any case, he continued to support the convictions of the journal. On 17 May 1916 he agreed to join the editorial board.

La Feuille du Dimanche and *L'Essor* always proclaimed the Gospel courageously and advocated unceasingly for major reforms to be brought about within the law. The two journals regularly aroused a large response. However, some dynamic and impulsive youths were unsatisfied with the pacifist manner of the journals; they wanted to react more forcefully and more quickly. It seems that Jean Piaget belonged to this enthusiastic and impatient group. With some Christian socialists he decided to launch a new journal, probably less traditional but more incisive. He politely told Paul Pettavel about his decision, because he had always held him in great esteem.[7]

No new journal appeared, and the project undoubtedly stayed at the level of intent. Had the young man been solicited by the editors of the *Voix des Jeunes*? (As of 1914 this had become *Organe de propagande et d'éducation des jeunes socialistes suisses* [Organ of Propaganda and Education for Young Swiss Socialists] and in 1916 it became the *Organe de la Fédération romande de la Jeunesse socialiste* [Organ of the French-Swiss Federation of Socialist Youth].) This journal, published in La Chaux-de-Fonds, and filled with some religiously oriented articles at its inception, never contained anything signed by Piaget.

This small publication indicated the existence in Neuchâtel of a sluggish section of the party that was made up of irregular members and reduced activity. Professor Pierre Reymond would soon reanimate it. Nevertheless, Piaget did not want to walk on the dangerous path some intransigent socialists were following. He kept himself apart from the rousing Jules Humbert-Droz, who, having become president of the central committee and editor of the *Voix des jeunes*, eagerly greeted the Bolshevik Revolution.

The mutual respect between the future intellectual and the pastor Paul Pettavel never changed. Many years later, *La Feuille du Dimanche*[8] announced that 'The University of Neuchâtel has delegated Dr Jean Piaget, son of the eminent cantonal archivist, to La Chaux-de-Fonds . . . He will give in the lecture room a course of six lessons on the subject: Child Psychology.' The journal praised the professor and recommended its readers not to miss the great occasion.

In 1927, when Jean Piaget asked Paul Pettavel to convince his mother to go to a psychiatric hospital, the two men had already chosen different paths. Nevertheless, their friendship and mutual esteem never failed. Jean Piaget had fond memories of his youthful enthusiasms. Social Christian or Christian Socialist, he probably never belonged to a political party, but he was part of the generous and innovative movements that attracted just individuals willing to share their convictions. What they had in common was the ideal to bring about social justice with zeal.

Notes

1 J. Piaget (1915) *La mission de l'idée* (p. 31). Lausanne: La Concorde.
2 Ibid., p. 63.
3 J. Piaget (1918) *Recherche* (p. 82). Lausanne: La Concorde.
4 Ch. Thomann (1988) *Une chronique insolite de la Chaux-de-Fonds* (La-Chaux-de-Fonds: Ed. d'en Haut) deals to a large extent with Social Christianity, particularly Paul Pettavel, *La Feuille du Dimanche*, and the Young Men's Christian Association. Short biographies of Pierre Coullery, Charles Naine, Ernest-Paul Graber, and Jules Humbert-Droz are to be found on pp. 118 to 120.
5 J. Humbert-Droz (1969) *Mémoires. Mon évolution du tolstoïsme au communisme 1891–1921* (pp. 251ff.). Neuchâtel: A La Baconnière.
6 For information about its founding and the first 13 years of its existence, consult A. Schmitt (1980) *L'Essor 1905–1980* (pp. 3–10). La Chaux-de-Fonds: L'Essor.
7 Jean Piaget, letter of 9 January 1917.
8 7 November 1926.

9   Grandchamp and Pierre Bovet

Carlo Robert-Grandpierre

Among all the influences on the young Piaget that contributed to his spiritual, moral, and intellectual development and that he drew on and referred to, one influence is especially important: that of Pierre Bovet. Behind this person lay the entire milieu of Grandchamp and a cluster of people who formed a true network of intellectual dialogue whose echo can be discerned in some revealing texts about Piaget's journey. I would like to evoke this magisterial milieu and try to identify the steps of the student's progressive distancing of himself from it, and, in so doing, to describe a more general problem.

The mentors that Piaget acknowledged in his earlier years (Pierre Bovet, Arnold Reymond, Théodore Flournoy, etc.) all had a religious dimension as well as their scientific interests. Reason and faith, according to the various forms they took, had to be taken into account. This is clear in the young Piaget, but the rationalist demands would get the upper hand over the Christian commitments. One sees the growing influence of an immanentist theology on Piaget's thinking: He tried to integrate it into his scientific thoughts, but towards the end the immanentist theology became a kind of moral guarantee for the scientific programme. One could say that Piaget did on a personal level what Western society has done in the modern era, namely a process of secularization. Piaget's thinking became *secularized*. Neither the how nor the why is particularly pertinent in terms of personal motivation and secrets, but I would like to ask these questions on another level, that of an 'epistemological' nature: Can one understand the inherent logic of this evolution? Is it there from the start? More precisely, after the informative and descriptive part, I wonder how much of Piaget's development is due to Protestantism (which, as has often been remarked, contains a germ of secularism) and especially to the form of Protestantism that was represented at Grandchamp by Pierre Bovet and other influential personalities.

A certain moral climate

At the end of the nineteenth century and the beginning of the twentieth, French-speaking Switzerland was a breeding ground for highly moral intellectuals who were simultaneously open to the world and to universal questions.

They were confined to a country that is so small that whatever was said would become known and have multiple effects. From Alexandre Vinet to the founders of the Rousseau Institute there was a profusion of thinkers, researchers, sometimes prophets even, and reformists – without counting the artists and poets. This is what strikes the reader of Alfred Berchtold's beautiful book.[1] It was anything but a dull and boring land, though it has been accused of being conservative in the extreme. When one sees the intellectual exchanges that took place between Secrétan, Pettavel, Claparède, Bovet, Ferrière, Ceresole, Humbert-Droz, and Flournoy, as well as many renowned foreigners, one might get the impression that the whole world had its eyes on these illustrious predecessors. The second thing that strikes one is the omnipresence of the religious dimension. Whatever the matter was, be it education, medicine, politics, or literature, there was always the concern to respect what was God's. That these great minds came together in this small country and produced such astonishing as well as stimulating things is a surprise for those who had not suspected such wealth.

Moral concern dominated. The Christian message of charity was primary. One did not have to wait for Denis de Rougemont 'to think with one's hands'. Paradoxically the heirs to the Reform, who believed in salvation by faith rather than by 'good works' as the Catholics preached, believed with their hands. Since Vinet, being Christian meant personal commitment as followers of Christ. And if such Christianity is called liberal, it is a form of liberation from the church and its dogma. It is a matter of taking on the task of being human according to the Christian model. Piaget's arrival was predicted by this shift from dogma to practice, from theology to the moral. But let us not jump ahead.

Felix Bovet (1824–1903)

Pierre Bovet's father was a particularly attractive personality: cultivated and refined, curious and scrupulous, tortured to the point of calling himself 'a believing agnostic', a man of prayer, expressed in actions rather than words. A vaguely mystical personal piety had turned him away from orthodox theology (i.e., Protestant orthodoxy), which was too caught up with explanations. He refused to choose between Jesus and Plato, between Athens and Jerusalem. It is thus not surprising that he had a very good relationship with Ferdinand Buisson, the champion of liberal Christianity, who played a major role, along with Jules Ferry, in creating the French state school free of religious affiliation. Buisson later wrote a biography of Sébastien Castellion, a dissident collaborator of Calvin in Geneva. I mention it only because of the great spiritual tie between these two men. Castellion became an impassioned defender of tolerance at the height of the Reform. Castellion and Buisson not only shared a passion for poetry and ancient literature but were also concerned about not raising themselves above the Lord's service. I have no idea whether Bovet knew of this book, or whether he had the opportunity to read

Kierkegaard, who was translated into French only in the twentieth century, but he would have found there a common point of view as well as a kindred soul.

Grandchamp is a beautiful riverside hamlet that lies one kilometre from the mouth of the River Areuse. In the second half of the nineteenth century, the Bovet family estate was turned into a major centre of teaching, a sort of foundling home offering welcome and refuge. Félix Bovet ran the establishment, rearing and providing religious instruction to orphaned boys and girls. The children led regulated, simple lives organized around work, on the model and in the spirit of institutions run by the United Brethren, which Bovet had visited and admired in Herrnhut. He then wrote a biography of Zinzendorf, who had been the principal inspiration of homes such as Grandchamp in the eighteenth century. The story of the Bovets at Grandchamp is a long and beautiful one, a true epic.[2] The image of this home is not unlike that of Stans or Yverdon in the previous century with Pestalozzi.

Besides this establishment, there was a hospital supported by relief funds for those in need and an evangelical school founded and directed by Jules Paroz, who had inherited the property and trained a contingent of teachers before it was moved to Peseux. Its confessional and militant character, in protest against the rise of rationalism that was creeping into Protestant churches, armed young teachers with a form of religious piety attached to a rather conservative theology. Given the orthodox strain of this movement, it is a wonder that Félix Bovet was a part of it. Yet he was not content just to house this institution; he was also active in it. Doubtless he was part of Paroz's project, owing to that man's spiritual commitment and the generosity of his pedagogical views. Paroz, in fact, was not of a sectarian spirit. Educated at the Catholic school in Porrentruy, he became a defender of the Christian cause by engaging himself fully in a variety of activities that ranged from visiting prisoners to writing a book entitled *Histoire universelle de la pédagogie*,[3] which was translated into many languages.

One of Grandchamp[4]

Pierre Bovet, Félix's son who continued his works, played a major role in Jean Piaget's life. Although the younger Bovet exceeded his father on the international level with his public career and his writings on the theory of the New Education, it was to Grandchamp and the spirit of the place that he owed his success. When he was appointed, in 1912, the first director of the Rousseau Institute, the authors of *La Geste des Bovet de Grandchamp* wittily remarked that the famous Geneva institute had some important roots in the hamlet bordering the Areuse. Pierre Bovet studied literature and philosophy and wrote a doctoral thesis on *Le Dieu de Platon d'après la chronologie des dialogues* (1902). He taught philosophy at the college and then at the University of Neuchâtel, where he occupied the chair previously held by Ferdinand Buisson. Bovet did not confine himself to the history of ideas, but was given rather to scientific rigour. The psychology that he taught, along with philosophy, was based more on factual observations and analysis than on speculation. Following Théodore Flournoy, who had founded a laboratory for experimental psychology in Geneva, and as a precursor of Piaget's work, Bovet undertook the search for a real knowledge of children. Not knowledge for its own sake, but knowledge that served pedagogy. Using a metaphor with which we are less comfortable today, he said, using Claparède's words: 'It is as important for the teacher to know the laws that govern the mind as it is for the botanist to know biology of plants, and the doctor to know the physiology of the organs.'[5] In the two principal studies that he published in psychology, he preached about neither the religious sentiment[6] nor the combative instinct;[7] rather, he investigated, observed, hypothesized, and verified.

In Emile's shadow

In Geneva, Claparède wanted to seize the occasion of the 200th anniversary of J. J. Rousseau's birth, in 1912, and found an institute for research and teaching pedagogy. He had just published an important article on Rousseau, seeing him as the 'Copernicus of pedagogy', a precursor of all the modern ideas which he then made his own. He focused in particular on the concept that the child is not a miniature adult and should be at the centre of the educative process: the child as he really is, which meant finding out what he truly *was*, freed of all expectations and projections (I am slightly stressing the scientific rigour in order to show the connection that goes from Rousseau to Piaget and the Geneva school, noting in passing another similarity in expression and spirit between the concern of focusing education on the child and the dictate from Rogerian psychology to be 'centred on the child', which has become the attitude of being 'non-directive' in pedagogy). In any case, one tends to give the child responsibility for his own learning, conquering and constructing what will be his knowledge. Pierre Bovet's 'active school' (New Education) intended nothing other. Thus it is not surprising that Claparède thought of Bovet to direct the institute.

All of this ought to have brought about a change in the status and the function of teaching. The teacher should no longer be expected to be omniscient or a dispenser of knowledge, but should stimulate interest, awaken needs, arouse curiosity more than produce erudition. Bovet even wanted to abolish school textbooks, where knowledge is pre-digested and ready for consumption. In place of that he would make dictionaries, encyclopaedias, and resource materials available for consultation so that the individual pupil could advance along a path that had not been a laid out beforehand, guided of course by the teacher but nevertheless remaining the principal actor in the play. Functional education, active school, non-directive pedagogy – they were all the same struggle! That at least is the impression we get: Seen from a certain distance, all the doctrines seem to say the same thing, from Rabelais to Decroly and from Montaigne to Freinet, passing by Comenius, Pestalozzi, or those at the Rousseau Institute . . . Without doubt it is an optical illusion, the impression of a layman; without doubt the topic merits much more rigour and nuance. Just consider the dizzying effect caused by the history of peda- gogical ideas . . . Has there been any progress in education? What of our current practices, still far from the simple and good things that have been forever recommended? Why so slow, so much inertia? Was Samuel Roller right? At the end of a lecture on the active school delivered in Neuchâtel in 1978 – Pierre Bovet's 100th birthday – Roller named a single fault: taking too little account of social and political inertia. He suspected that behind the conscious and explicit official talk that always wants the child to be expansive and the citizen critical was another discourse, perhaps unconscious but def- initely secret, which is that of denial: 'One does not want man to be free . . . one wants him to conform to norms.'

Educate: The source (or the end) and the means

We have spoken of Bovet's openness to the human sciences. Psychology, however scientific, does not create pedagogy (in this respect the name 'sci- ences de l'éducation' [educational sciences], is ambiguous – unless it means that these sciences are *in the service* of education). The educational project entails aspects other than scientific, and Bovet said as much in his last lesson in July 1944:[8] 'One cannot look after children without being led to believe in something greater than ourselves.' His references and his spiritual horizon were something he shared with his father. As we have seen, the latter had written a book on Zinzendorf, the Moravian reformer of the eighteenth cen- tury, also an educator and founder of educational institutions. The younger Bovet went on to study another Moravian, whose span of influence exceeded Zinzendorf's: Jan Amos Komensky, called Comenius, a genial precursor in pedagogy from the seventeenth century. Comenius was an admirable, cour- ageous person who paid dearly for his commitment to the service of human freedom, of responsible and generous Christianity, and of prophetic ecumen- ism. Moravian piety, a religion of the heart, addresses committed individuals, fervent and active – yet open and tolerant. This was the spirituality fostered at Grandchamp and was the source of inspiration for Pierre Bovet's thinking and vision of humanity.

At Grandchamp, the child was seen as free, unique, and thoroughly res- pected. There were no recipes to educate him, nor tools to mechanize his life. The 'active school' (a name that Bovet coined) indicates more a spirit than a doctrine, more an attitude than a method (which is exactly what Hameline says about 'non-directiveness'). But if scientific data cannot equip and motiv- ate the teacher, the school must still, however free it may be, develop methods in accord with the facts actually seen and treated. According to Bovet, even if pedagogy is more often called an art than a science and even if it relies more on the personal qualities of the teacher than on the methods used, it must be empirically based. Personal freedom does not contradict reason.

What should be the frame of reference for training 'man'? Bovet answered in the words of Vinet: Man himself! Not an ideal, universal model, or pure product of the mind, but a real 'man' that is at the heart of everyone. The criterion for evaluating pedagogy is the interior, intimate accord, felt more than thought, with oneself. Bovet seemed to work in the spirit of personalism and under the influence of a non-intellectualistic philosophy like that of Bergson. And the denial of the doctrine in philosophy, parallel to the distancing from all theology in an effort to theorize about the child and education, suggests the possible influence of Bovet on Piaget.

But which humanism?

Bovet's principle of separating faith and reason remained constant. Logically this means secular schooling (give up wanting to teach 'that which cannot be taught' was already Flournoy's argument) as well as the separation of the church and state (following that of Vinet). Neuchâtel Protestantism had been divided into two churches since 1873: the State Church, which advocated the rationalism of the Enlightenment and as such was open to humanitarian and political ideas, and the Free Church, which was theologically orthodox and denominational. Besides these churches, diverse communities sprung up: The United Brethren (Moravian) had been established at Montmirail for over a century, the Salvationists had just arrived, the Librists were born of an earlier dissension (1840), etc. It is not easy to place the Bovets of Grandchamp in this ecclesiastical landscape. We have seen their debt to Moravian piety, their support of Salvationists unfairly exiled from certain places (and the admiration Bovet had for their founder, William Booth), the openness towards ecumenism (in spite of being Protestant, Bovet had an audacious admiration for the founder of the Jesuit order, Ignatius Loyola), and their sympathy for the Jewish cause. By his openness to modernity, to the sciences, to pacifism (his friendship with Pierre Ceresole), Bovet would without doubt be in good company with the liberal side. But then his personal piety and spiritual avowal would put him with the independent movement. In reality he was . . . from Grandchamp!

Regarding the twin allegiance to humanism and Christianity and the paradox that entails, Bovet had so much confidence in the nature of the child and was so sure of the child's instincts, even in regard to religion, that one could suspect him of Pelagianism. But he preached conversion. Further, he hailed the combative instinct in man, capable of a life susceptible to restraint and sublimation, which could be harnessed for the better: He speaks Esperanto, believes in a 'school for peace', takes up the pilgrim's staff and goes to spread the good news around the world. In the end, one has the impression that for him what was made explicit was that man must (and can) do everything without God; but at the same time, more implicitly, in the words of Bergson, 'everything is grace'. In light of this astonishing presence–absence of God, of the mixture of what is said and what is not, of a fervent belief intimately lived but integrated into a background of all intellectual effort that it fertilized, I would like to shed some light, briefly, on the direction of Jean Piaget's career.

The stages of a deconversion

'The child explains the man as much, and often more, than the man explains the child', our author said.[9] This permits us to explore the sources of Piaget's training, certainly not to 'explain Piaget' but to try to capture a certain postulated logic of his evolution. Educated as a traditional Protestant, he renewed his baptismal vow as an adolescent. Later he enthusiastically discovered Bergson: In a 'sort of euphoria', as he himself described it, he perceived a God at the heart of life whom he identified as an *élan vital*. Studying biology would be a way of 'reading' God, a privileged (perhaps the only?) path to knowledge. He was a member of the Club of the Friends of Nature, an association to which its founder, Pierre Bovet in 1893, continued to pay attention and to visit. It was apparently through this association that the two men met, but it was at the Rousseau Institute, where Piaget, a young professor, and Bovet, the director, worked together. In 1916, when Piaget was 20 years old, he published a remarkable article entitled *La mission de l'idée*, a sort of ideological romantic–Hegelian theological dissertation that sang the praises of the Gospel as an Idea making its way through the history of humankind, triumphing (or called to triumph) over structures and dogmatism (the churches' especially), a bearer of progress and freedom. Though it may be full of inspiration, it leaves the reader who began at the other end of Piaget's career rather nonplussed. The second step that followed the pantheistic biology of adolescence was the immanentist stage.

This evolution was written up in a highly interesting text published in 1928[10] in which the author argues explicitly for an immanentist interpretation of the divine. Based on Bovet's work, he shows how the moral judgement of the child is first of all heteronymous and unilateral (it is based on a feeling of respect that a child has for someone superior, the adult), to become later, by a process of maturing and rationalizing, autonomous and bilateral: a moral of the good and no longer of obligation; mutual and no longer dependent. The superiority of the second over the first is immediately striking. Further, Piaget related these two moral attitudes to two religious attitudes, that of transcendence and that of immanence. The parallel is obvious: The self-respecting adult would not believe in the heavenly Father who is a symbol of the child's mythic imagination. Psychology and sociology undo the illusion of the supernatural. Piaget is on firm ground to declare himself an immanentist. One sees how he chose a metaphysical option over an empirical fact. After the biological fervour of adolescence and the idealism of youth, psychology and science appear with maturity. He was rather bothered by this and addressed the matter before making what to me seems a definite break: 'Without doubt these sciences seem on principle to exclude the idea of transcendence, and thus it is understandable that what is not in the premises will not be found in the conclusions.'[11] We could not say it better! But immanentism does not mean atheism: Piaget rejected the God of classical theology in order to venerate better 'the God of spirit and truth who is postulated by the conscience'. Some years later, in his study on the child's moral judgement,[12] he refers principally to Durkheim and to 'Mr Bovet', to whose views and observations on the origins of the feeling of obligation and of religious conscience Piaget always deferred. Concerning religious psychology, both Bovet and Piaget certainly had in mind the methodological principle advocated by Ribot: 'Religious feeling is a fact that it simply has to analyze and to follow in its transformations, without assuming competence to discuss its value or its legitimacy.'

The victory of science – or of scientism?

While it is doubtless impossible to measure the influence Pierre Bovet and others must have had on Piaget, we can establish several similar points. There is a plethora of common ideas: the intention to read the sign of the divine in the human, thus becoming a possible object of scientific investigation; the rejection of theology as an autonomous discourse (for Piaget it was not theology but philosophy that was rejected as a distinct body of knowledge) and all dogmatism; distrust of the institutional church and rejection of the principle of authority; and finally, the emphasis on human activity, which for Bovet showed interior commitment and belief, and for Piaget indicated growing intelligence and knowledge. For Bovet (and Reymond and Flournoy) methodologically formal autonomy, which is rationally treated, becomes ontologically total autonomy in the pupil. The duality that his teachers had established by separating belief (intimate) and knowledge (rational and communicable) produced a morality (in the most noble sense of the term). Piaget kept only the moral. This 'deconversion' (the term he himself used to describe his progress and ineluctable distancing from philosophy[13]) must have taken place relatively early. But in the small text of 1928 cited above, his immanentism retained a strong religious tenor. God reveals himself to those who humbly and patiently (i.e., scientifically) seek to know the rational norms of thought, with which God concurs, and that is a 'supreme mystical experience'. It was the beginning of a magnificent career: Piaget entered science as others entered religion.

Piaget was heir – and this seems logical – to a certain secularized and secularizing Protestantism. Faith that existed in the early years was lost along the way. What more can be said? There is nothing to add about the ups and downs of Jean Piaget's faith, which now belong to his secret sphere. But a more general question of historical and cultural interest can be asked about this uncertain transmission of values and faith from one generation to another. Berchtold claims a certain theological deficiency in the period he analyses in his book.[14] By failing to link theology with their view of humanity and their scientific endeavours, and by failing to develop a genuine theology that takes faith into account, but that also critically addresses rationalism and science, these Protestant scholars make their concerns irrelevant. Theology should have been rehabilitated, as Berchtold notes.[15] As we know, Karl Barth took on the task: in an irony of history, at the same time as Piaget was vigorously distancing himself from his childhood faith. I do not know whether these two men ever met . . .

Notes

1 A. Berchtold (1963). *La Suisse romande au cap du XXe siècle. Portrait littéraire et moral.* Lausanne: Payot.
2 G. de Rougemont & G. Bovet (1992). *La geste des Bovet de Grandchamp.* Areuse, Boudry, Switzerland: Baillod.
3 J. Paroz (1880). *Histoire universelle de la pédagogie.* Paris: Delagrave.
4 Parody of *Un de Baumugnes*, a novel by Jean Giono (Paris: Gallimard, 1968).
5 Cited by Berchtold, op. cit., p. 173.
6 P. Bovet (1925). *Le sentiment religieux et la psychologie de l'enfant.* Neuchâtel: Delachaux & Niestlé.
7 P. Bovet (1917). *L'instinct combatif, psychologie, éducation.* Neuchâtel: Delachaux & Niestlé.
8 S. Roller (1978). *Pierre Bovet et l'école active* (p. 32). Neuchâtel: Ed. de la Baconnière.
9 J. Piaget & B. Inhelder (1966). *La psychologie de l'enfant.* Paris: Presses Universitaires de France. [English translation: *The Psychology of the Child.* New York: Basic Books, 1969.]
10 J. Piaget (1928). *Deux types d'attitudes religieuses: immanence et transcendance.* Geneva: Ed. de l'Association chrétienne d'étudiants de Suisse romande.
11 Ibid., p. 27.
12 J. Piaget (1932). *Le jugement moral chez l'enfant.* Paris: Delachaux & Niestlé. [English translation: *The Moral Judgement of the Child.* London: Routledge & Kegan Paul, 1956.]
13 J. Piaget (1965). *Sagesse et illusions de la philosophie.* Paris: Gonthier. [English translation: *Insights and Illusions of Philosophy.* New York & Cleveland: The World Publishing Company, 1971.]
14 Berchtold, op. cit., pp. 204–207.
15 Ibid., p. 207.

Part II
A savant of his age

10 The socio-intellectual genealogy of Jean Piaget

Tania Zittoun,[1] *Anne-Nelly Perret-Clermont, and Jean-Marc Barrelet*

Scientific openings and discussions

What was the historical context at the heart of which Jean Piaget's thought emerged? The first part of this work aims at sketching a view of Neuchâtel at the beginning of the twentieth century in order to give an idea of Piaget's family background, his school milieu, and his friends and masters who would become his interlocutors in science well as in philosophy. In the second part, we will address the intellectual context of his century in order to understand how Jean Piaget fits into the extraordinary scientific blossoming that, in the second half of the twentieth century, extended beyond his native city and country to embrace France, Belgium, Germany, Austria, and later, beyond his linguistic range, the whole of Europe and North America. Piaget was able to make extensive contacts throughout the world owing to his university life and his personal travels. Correspondence, congresses, and lecturing opened the path for ideas to circulate which then instigated challenge and debate. Piaget actively participated in such events by adding his observations and analyses and thus contributed to reformulating certain questions and to ignoring others.

We shall accompany Piaget on this intellectual journey in order to outline the history of the human sciences from the beginning of the last century. The 'Piagetian' persona, including its reception and its effect, will thus emerge from the path he made first in Switzerland and then elsewhere. Distance allows us to put some of his choices into perspective and even to probe their sources: Where did his radical distrust of the socio-historic stem from, or his search for the universal and his preoccupation with logic as a precious (quasi-divine) ethical source? How did he relate to authority?

In the present chapter, we shall lay a kind of bridge between the two parts of this work. First, there are the professors who occupied successively the chair of psychology[2] at the University of Neuchâtel; then there are the predominant areas of research in Neuchâtel and other French-speaking parts of Switzerland. This gives us an understanding of where Piaget fits in a particular intellectual genealogy, which, in spite of the rigour in the Piagetian subject, had further ramifications in the field of science. This passage from the specificity of the Neuchâtel influence to the richness of an era will introduce the subject matter of the second part of this work: the diverse aspects of the larger question of the role of Jean Piaget, the learned scholar, in his century.

The following brief intellectual history, which places Piaget among the heirs of his time, is not a defence of socio-cultural determinism. Rather, it is a picture of how intellectuals from Neuchâtel, whether they were partners, collaborators, or successors, were for a while at least taken up with the same questions and how they went on to study domains Piaget would forsake. Areas of common interest reveal three converging points that give an epistemological coherence to this genealogy.

Science, religion, philosophy, and commitment

At the end of the nineteenth century, when Piaget was born, the recently united Swiss Confederation lent a strong coherence to the Canton of Neuchâtel, which eagerly sought out its European neighbours and participated in the economic and cultural boom of the period. These circumstances gave students the opportunity to benefit from a broad freedom of thought, encouraged by the tradition of complementary studies in the great university cities throughout Europe. In effect, it was customary to spend six months or a year studying with a 'mentor': Sigmund Freud, for example, was a pupil of Jean Martin Charcot, and Carl Jung one of Pierre Janet's. Such internships were a part of life for Piaget's contemporaries, a fact which in itself lent coherence to scientific and philosophical work being done by a diverse range of European intellectuals. On a different level, Maurice de Tribolet[3] has already shown how the multifarious activities of Piaget's family, who had been not only intellectual and militant in their scientific commitment but also politically and religiously minded, were representative of this openness.

Such was the context in which Pierre Bovet became professor of psychology, philosophy, and pedagogy at the Academy of Neuchâtel. A leader in local affairs, he founded, while still an adolescent, the Club of the Friends of Nature; some years later he translated the writings of Robert Baden-Powell, founder of the Boy Scouts, and contributed to introducing the Scouts to Switzerland. Bovet was also active in developing the religious centre at Grandchamp, still known today for its work and for its openness to interconfessional dialogue. Bovet wrote a work on the origins of religious feelings in children,[4] which brought together his three areas of interest. Such spiritual, scholarly, and social commitment characterized several generations of the university community in Neuchâtel, which was the first meeting point of intellectual activity in the region. Piaget was too young to be a student of Bovet's, but both the Club of the Friends of Nature[5] (which kept him in touch with Bovet) and his participation in Christian movements provided the starting point for his queries. His activities as a naturalist and his exposure to the philosophy of Henri Bergson in 1912 led to his writing his first texts, which predated *Biologie et connaissance*,[6] and were seen by teachers and peers alike as having a clearly mystical–metaphysical slant.[7]

Arnold Reymond, who had been Jean Piaget's teacher at grammar school, held the chair of philosophy and psychology after Pierre Bovet at the University of Neuchâtel (1912–1925), where his former pupil would become his student. Reymond had acquired a strong scientific training by travelling to Berlin, London, and Paris, where he studied physics and philosophy under the tutelage of Emile Boutroux and Bergson. Later, Reymond played a role in introducing a new approach to logic[8] at the university. Apart from his work as a historian of science, Reymond pursued two important parallel approaches: one religious and the other philosophical.[9] He took part in discussing such French thinkers as Léon Brunschvicg and André Lalande. In this post-Kantian period, Reymond developed a major theory of judgement – a weighty matter in the Kantian structure. The principal idea is that the act of judgement is itself neither true nor false, but is first of all determined by a particular 'view of reality' among other coherent views of reality, and before which the mind adopts a particular position that is part of a rational system of subjective positions. This idea led to the notions of the relativity of judgement and of the diversity of points of view about the world. Such notions were instrumental in breaking through certain dogmatisms and in recognizing the relativity of science. Piaget would take up this idea in psychology. Although Reymond considered him 'one of his illustrious students', Piaget had to overcome his reticence before this rigorous professor – which was hardly compatible with a juvenile fascination for Bergson – before recognizing, in 1942, the major role Reymond had on French-Swiss thinking.[10] Having, on the one hand, 'lived profoundly the different movements of modern thought', Reymond become a 'conciliator', rigorously distinguishing 'values of faith of speculative theology' and subjecting those values to a rational critique. On the other hand, he examined the connections between the exact sciences and reason, mathematics, and logic. Piaget adds that Reymond 'had profoundly influenced us and was thus the vital centre for our society [Société romande de philosophie], whether we were theologians, moralists, logicians, historians or psychologists'. In fact, it was with scientific rigour at the beginning of the last century that Reymond made his way in Neuchâtel, where the logico-psychological connection had a lasting influence on subsequent work.

Beyond the problem of faith and reason, Reymond inspired Piaget's interest in logic and the philosophy of Brunschvicg, whose philosophical ideas, which Piaget had studied for two years in Paris, would later underlie his own system of thought. After studying in Paris and in Zurich, and concomitant with his appointment at the Jean-Jacques Rousseau Institute in Geneva, Piaget succeeded Reymond at the University of Neuchâtel, where he taught psychology, the philosophy of sciences, and soon thereafter sociology[11] (1925–1929).

However, Piaget was not Bovet and Reymond's only student. Jean de La Harpe, who held the chair of philosophy and psychology after Piaget, had also been their student. After rigorous studies with Lalande, Meyerson, and

Brunschvicg, La Harpe worked at the same time as Piaget, sometimes collaborating and sometimes opposing him on such matters as religious sentiment, post-critical philosophy, and the genetic perspective of epistemology. One is thus not surprised to find in their writings implicit or explicit references to the philosophy of Brunschvicg, the anthropology of Lucien Lévy-Bruhl, the sociology of Emile Durkheim, and the psychology of Janet – of the importance of the social milieu in the development of relations between phylogenesis and ontogenesis.

The problem of time

The second point of convergence in the intellectual life around Neuchâtel can be seen in particular in La Harpe's years (after 1930) spent teaching, publishing, and finally producing a thesis on the subject of time. Titled *Genèse et mesure du temps* (1941),[12] this thesis of philosophical interest drew support for its arguments, on the one hand, from Janet's work in psychology and, on the other, from sociology. It added, not without humour, common sense to this temporal problem: A nomadic hunter's relation to time is different from that of an inhabitant of a watchmaking region. This thesis, beyond its critical aspect, well illustrated the confluence of approaches mentioned above. The first half of it, which is from a resolutely genetic perspective, locates the origin of the sensation of time in the child's sensorimotor behaviour. This sensation integrates first the notion of habit and thus memory, then the notion of waiting and thus 'prospective memory', i.e., the future. When the subject adds imagination to that future, a 'mythical' time is created, in the sense described by early oriental civilizations. With language, time becomes the object and the structure of the narrative. Finally, owing to the need for consensus that socialization requires, time is then something to be measured. What had originally been a 'need to agree among priests' became measured time and led to the emergence of metrics. Time passed from an unconscious sense of continuity to a conscious measure. The second part of this thesis deals with the formal articulation of metric time and from that to objectivity in logical language. La Harpe reflected on the connection between time lived, its existential profundity, and formal time.

There are two reasons for presenting this thesis here. On the one hand, this thesis, which appeared after Piaget's early work on the child's conception of the world (1926)[13] but before *The Child's Conception of Time* (1941)[14] – work made possible by the theoretical clarification given by La Harpe? – is an example of the contact between Neuchâtel researchers and interdisciplinary collaboration, as well as of the common ground of theoretical presuppositions of the period. On the other hand, La Harpe's thesis led to other works on the subject of time. In fact, the mathematician and logician Jean-Blaise Grize, who was a student both of La Harpe and of Piaget as well as a brilliant collaborator, wrote a thesis on science, at La Harpe's suggestion, that was also on this subject. Grize's work laid the premises of a vigorous intellectual movement to which we shall return later. The starting point of this thesis, *Essai sur le rôle du temps en analyse mathématique classique*,[15] is the irrepressible appearance of 'common' language in any attempt at mathematical formulation. From there Grize proceeds to examine first the significance of this irruption and then the suppression of notions referring to time in mathematical analysis. One discovers, thereby, that natural, or common, language generally slips temporal images into abstract scientific discourse when a formal framework reaches its limits. This presence of common language proves that formal language fails to describe reality sufficiently, and it makes evident the consequent need for conceptual reformulation. From this a more powerful system emerges, which is to say that science progresses. Scientists then try to eliminate this embarrassing temporal dimension and the natural language that translates it. On the one hand, this thesis demonstrates the significant presence of register in a certain language (here, formal versus informal) for a 'given state of civilization'; on the other hand, it sets the requirement for a non-bivalent logic, which can be expressed in a language explicitly able to find a place for temporal elements, which are present in any reflection.[16]

Introducing socio-cultural time to the theoretical

After this thesis, Jean-Blaise Grize, who contributed for a long time to Piaget's work (particularly to the second edition of *Traité de logique*[17] and to the studies of genetic epistemology), continued his own research, examining areas that Piaget had chosen – from lack of interest? – to lay aside. Grize developed logic and semiological studies, 'in order to found a true science of man in society'.[18] From the beginning his questioning the limits of a form of logic exposed how everyday language was an irreducible part of all formal language. Grize laid out the basis of a 'natural logic' that analysed the logico-discursive acts operating in all language production: not only mathematical, a privileged domain in Piagetian studies, but also in ordinary and non-formal language. Beyond initial observations about 'shared meaning' and awareness of the creative aspect of the subject in articulating and communicating in context – the manner by which one reasons 'daily' – lies the whole problem of the social dimension and its meaning, which became the researchers' concern.

In order to continue his work, Grize, who was later rector of the University of Neuchâtel, founded the Centre for Semiological Research in Neuchâtel in 1969. The founding postulate for the centre was 'One never reasons about things themselves, but about the signs that replace them; and one never communicates without signs.'[19] This well-known theory of semiotics had its place in discussions led by figures such as Umberto Eco and Julia Kristeva, though it clearly distanced itself from their semiological theories. Besides the obvious interest of semiology in studies of speech acts, logic, and psychology, a remark made by a sociologist reveals a further application. In the mid-1960s, when sociology faded with the collapse of social structures, 'natural logic' offered a new basis for the realities of the time and an adaptation to the new social dynamic.[20] The integration of the societal at the level of the theoretical marks the third point where the intellectual activity of the Neuchâtel region merged. A quick look at history shows that the historian Arthur Piaget, Jean's father, had led the way, in spite of resistance, in requiring a historical critique of history (one owns the history that one reads); yet Jean Piaget left out the 'socio-critical' dimension in his own work. It is true that history, or more precisely a temporal course, was not completely forsaken in his work. The historical dimension can be seen in his work on the history of ontogenesis, where Piaget – 'historically critical' in his way – showed that the child always thinks within the limits of his ability to reason governed by the stage of development that he has reached. However, this interpretation owes more to Kant than to a historical perspective, ignoring as it does the impact of the time of social history on the subject. While it is true that as a young man Piaget had been sensitive to the historical events of his time, his socio-political and Christian-associated engagements in the aftermath of the First World War were relegated to the back burner by the time he was launching himself into research on fundamental clinical psychology. From then on, the historical social was supplanted by the goal – as if it were contradictory – to find the universal processes of thought.[21] In spite of this turn, two other researchers who succeeded Piaget explicitly integrated contemporary history into their theoretical reflections.

Philippe Muller, who was appointed to the chair of philosophy and psychology after Jean de La Harpe at the University of Neuchâtel (1954–1973), was trained in both philosophy and psychology. He also reflected on the relation between religion and philosophical thought. Nevertheless, from 1933 to the time before the Second World War, Muller was not concerned enough with the limits of his predecessor's theory to take account of the subject's cognitive operation in making sense of his surroundings. He deplored the hiatus that separated 'man assured by a certain type of knowledge coming from the sciences' (such as Piaget, logicians, and philosophers) from 'universal man who is thrown into disarray by current circumstances'.[22] In effect, the tensions and conflicts that tore apart Europe in the first half of the twentieth century affected students even without the historical and existential dimensions actually being part of scientific research itself. Muller himself could no longer separate science and conscience from those events, and his initial thesis led to the point of view that Max Scheler encapsulated: 'For the first time in history, man no longer knows who he is. And worse, he knows that he does not know it.'[23] Thus, with a rigorous training in Anglo-Saxon experimental psychology on the one hand and in French existential philosophy on the other, Muller's work sought to integrate the contemporary problematic into his theoretical reflections. From the 1940s to the 1970s, apart from his major political and social commitments, Muller wrote a work on industrial psychology, subject matter that treated the situations that were one's daily struggle in the contemporary world, child development, and in particular the psychology of modern man. This psychology needed to address socio-cultural and anthropological factors.[24] His publications, widely translated (even into Japanese), found an international readership. Besides his philosophical and psychological engagements, his research on the psychology of work led to the creation of two university chairs in the subject at the faculty of economics and sociology. These university posts fostered active involvement in contemporary problems, which was faithful to Muller's desire to integrate the existential dimension into theory.

We have tried to set forth here the university's 'fathers of thought' who influenced Piaget and others like him. Against the socio-economic and political background of the era, we have been able to trace ways of thinking that ran parallel to Piaget's, used him as a source, and then often diverged.

Intellectual dynamics and ruptures

The second part of this work starts off with the seething intellectual spirit that characterized Europe at the time. Piaget grew up amid this intellectual European climate, which helps to account for the role his native Neuchâtel played in fostering the development of the lively, curious intelligence that characterized the researcher he became. The historical and social tensions of the period were reflected in theoretical discussions and in social science research. Like the political turbulence of the day, Piaget's own course of development underwent various ruptures, some of which will be examined in the following chapters.

On a local level we can see that the same background, without being deterministic, led to different ideas that may lie outside the Piagetian scope but nevertheless have an importance to this study. We have already seen how the young science of semiology, among others, followed in the wake of Piaget's own work.

But what has been the intellectual reception worldwide? How has the intellectual climate developed since the beginning of the last century? In Chapter 11 John Rijsman presents the *Zeitgeist* of an era filled with hope in the galloping progress of science. Frequent contacts between European intellectuals, from a largely common humanist and scientific background of shared tensions and contradictions, formed a platform for exchange and for extensive dissemination, which led to the re-emergence of philosophical and theological questions. The century, however, was also jolted by the worst wars and by the aftermath of decolonization, a time when strategies of power were transformed and an Iron Curtain raised.

The connections between the young Piaget and Russian psychology are perhaps illustrative, on the intellectual level, of certain tensions of this period. In fact, when Piaget was still young, the nascent discipline of psychology – which some attribute to Wundt in Leipzig, and others to Freud in Vienna, or even to the milieu of pedagogy with Decroly, Montessori, and Claparède – was also enjoying a dynamic debut in Russia. Researchers and students mixed and discussed the same authors. The young Piaget was quickly recognized and published in Russian by his contemporary, Lev Vygotsky. In Chapter 14, René van der Veer retraces the ideological and political circumstances in which Piaget's work was read and criticized in Moscow. The differences with the 'bourgeois' Swiss author that Soviet psychology loudly and frequently espoused badly disguised the Russian readers' infatuation with Piaget's work and its impact on their own research. There was without doubt a polemic, but beyond it there were also fundamental questions about psychology, which remain today. These questions concern the conditions of cultural transmission, the role of the interlocutor in developing thought, and the functions of language and of semiotic tools. Why did Piaget seem to duck this challenge and not reply to the Soviet criticisms that he knew existed? Did these criticisms touch deeply on fundamental points in his own system? Did he fear the censorship of his ideas, which would then be circulated in a distorted form? Or was it, rather, a matter of Piaget taking a political and ideological stance against Communist Russia, refusing to enter into intellectual contact with potential enemies (but are intellectuals such enemies?[25]) of his ethical and democratic positions? In a Piagetian perspective, true science is possible only between people who share intellectual positions that respect the democratic principle of equality and horizontal reciprocity, which a dictatorial regime perverts. This was the beginning of the European divide that the Iron Curtain would exploit . . . It is striking to see today the pertinence of these questions at the heart of the discussions opened by the new configuration of contacts between East and West. The centenary celebrations for both Piaget and Vygotsky in 1996 (in Switzerland and Russia, as well as in Great Britain, in Portugal, at the major meeting of the International Society for the Study of Behavioural Development in Canada, in Paris, and elsewhere) demonstrated this point.

Another interesting breakthrough is that of the relations between human sciences founded on the basis of education. In Chapter 12, Jürgen Oelkers writes of the pedagogical movements that reflected the energetic initiatives and discussions in the field of education. State recognition of the growing importance of education at the turn of the last century is of particular interest. Ideas of humanity, God, and society challenged each other. Durkheim, professor of pedagogy, founded a flourishing school of sociology; paediatrics developed; Freud located the origins of mental problems in childhood education; and the respective roles of nature, the state, the church, and even of faith in children's education were discussed. These movements affected Piaget: he benefited from them in his own education; he found his first employment with Bovet and Claparède at the Jean-Jacques Rousseau Institute in Geneva; and to a certain degree he even became the emblem of these movements. But Piaget always refused to let himself be labelled a pedagogue (even if the *Petit Larousse* identified him for a long time as 'Swiss pedagogue') and showed a certain disdain for educational practices, particularly the activity of school teaching, which was never sufficiently noble in its execution to reach the level of epistemology. We shall see how Piaget distanced himself from some of his own masters' positions in this regard and how he sought to learn about the child outside the pedagogical domains – while nevertheless being known as the first director of the International Bureau of Education.

Piaget seemed to advance imperturbably in the midst of the unrest he stirred up. It is interesting to see the different 'images' of Piaget by Daniel Hameline in Chapter 15. Our hero is a person who did not allow himself to be easily categorized; he even saw to it that such could not be done. From his adolescence, he reflected (meta-reflected on himself!) on the mission he was undertaking, on the meaning of his system, on the importance of his work, all the while contributing to the maintenance of a faithful self-image.

Let these texts contribute not to an abstract image, but to the rediscovery of the richness of a human being with an unmistakable magnetism! The reader will find here not only a challenge to his moral and psychic strengths but also an invitation to take a fresh look at some fundamental questions.

Notes

1 Tania Zittoun is the author of the part of this chapter that deals with the intellectual genealogy of Neuchâtel and Jean Piaget.
2 More precisely, this chair of philosophy was responsible for teaching psychology. The title of the chair had changed and besides philosophy included, on occasion explicitly, logic, the history of sciences and psychology. Psychology chairs, as such, did not appear at the University of Neuchâtel until the 1970s.
3 Chapter 3 of the present volume.
4 P. Bovet (1925). *Le sentiment religieux et la psychologie de l'enfant*. Neuchâtel: Delachaux & Niestlé.
5 See Chapter 7 and the epilogue in the present volume.
6 J. Piaget (1967). *Biologie et connaissance*. Paris: Gallimard. [English translation: *Biology and knowledge: An essay on the relations between organic regulations and cognitive processes*. Chicago: University of Chicago Press, 1971.]
7 See also F. Vidal (1996). *Piaget Neuchâtelois*. Neuchâtel: Bibliothèque publique et universitaire.
8 A. Reymond (1932). *Les principes de la logique et la critique contemporaine*, Paris: Boivin.
9 A. Virieux-Reymond, R. Blanché, G. Widmer, & F. Brunner (1956). *Arnold Reymond*. Torino, Italy: Ed. de Filosofia.
10 J. Piaget (1942). Note complémentaire à 'Questions historiques'. In A. Reymond, *Philosophie spiritualiste*. Lausanne: F. Rouge, and Paris: J. Vrin.
11 See Chapter 6 in the present volume.
12 J. de La Harpe (1941). *Genèse et mesure du temps*. Neuchâtel: Secrétariat de l'Université.
13 J. Piaget (1926). *La représentation du monde chez l'enfant*. Paris: Alcan. [English translation: *The child's conception of the world*. London: Routledge & Kegan Paul, 1929.]
14 J. Piaget (1946). *Le développement de la notion de temps chez l'enfant*. Paris: Presses Universitaires de France. [English translation: *The child's conception of time*. London: Routledge & Kegan Paul, 1969.]
15 J.-B. Grize (1954). *Essai sur le rôle du temps en analyse mathématique classique*. Neuchâtel: Impr. nouvelle L.-A. Monnier.
16 For more information on these lines of thought, see A.N. Perret-Clermont et al.

(Eds.) (2005). *Thinking time: A multidisciplinary perspective on time*. Cambridge, MA: Hogrefe.

17 J. Piaget (1972). *Essai de logique opératoire*. Paris: Dunod (2nd revised and completed edition of *Traité de logique* by Jean Piaget, 1949, arranged by Jean-Blaise Grize).

18 A step that, according to Busino, can be praised as the result of 'probably the most profound, innovative and original work that a French Swiss university has developed owing to the exceptional greatness of Jean Piaget'. G. Busino (1982). Préface. In J.-B. Grize, *De la logique à l'argumentation*. Geneva: Droz.

19 J.-B. Grize (1992), cited in D. Miéville (Ed.) (1993). *Approches sémiologiques dans les sciences humaines*. Lausanne: Payot.

20 Busino, op. cit.

21 This is all the more striking due to the fact that Jean Piaget taught sociology and expressed his opinions on this matter (see also J. Piaget (1965). *Etudes sociologiques*. Geneva and Paris: Droz (3rd ed. 1977)), but he never referred to the two problems!

22 See Philippe Muller's discussion of this matter in *Options philosophiques*. Lausanne: L'Age d'homme, 1976.

23 Ibid.

24 See particularly P. Muller (1974). *La psychologie dans le monde moderne*. Brussels: Ch. Dessart.

25 For a description of the situation of Soviet psychology, see for example D. Joravsky (1987). L.S. Vygotskii: The muffled deity of Soviet psychology. In M. G. Ash & W. R. Woodward (Eds.), *Psychology in twentieth-century thought and society* (pp. 89–211). New York: Cambridge University Press.

11 An intellectual and technological panorama of Piaget's world

John Rijsman

It is no small thing to sketch the scientific *Zeitgeist* of a man whose publications cover almost three quarters of a century, who was himself for several years a professor of the history of science, and who wrote with clear sympathy about his father: 'He did not like hasty judgements and he did not hesitate to defend a polemic when he saw the historical truth deformed.'[1] I will nevertheless take a chance, which of course, in a short chapter like this, cannot be more than a rough sketch. It might resemble the bizarre lines of the constructivist painters Picasso and Braque, who worked largely in the same period as Piaget but who, remarkably enough, were convinced that they represented the true nature of the visible reality better than the realist painters (an intriguing relationship with the genetic constructivism of Jean Piaget, which I will come back to later in this chapter).

I will also speak almost exclusively of the *Zeitgeist* in psychology, which is a significant restriction. In effect, we would need to paint a vast fresco covering science as well as philosophy to evoke a man like Piaget, who started as a biology student; then became a doctor in science; followed by a professor in philosophy, history of science, sociology,[2] and experimental psychology. He also created a centre for genetic epistemology. Nor shall I deal with those who are inclined to see Piaget as a pedagogue or cultural politician who made many contributions to international organizations, such as UNESCO, and who, during the Second World War, aspired to put science aside temporarily to fight against dictatorship.

But it is precisely this characteristic of Piaget as a 'generalist' that inspires the first lines in my constructivist sketch of his worldview. Towards the end of the nineteenth century, psychology as a science emerged out of a strange union between philosophy and the life sciences. This psychology had a different orientation from that of Piaget, which we shall examine in greater detail.

Life sciences and human sciences

By examining the history of science in Europe at the end of the nineteenth century, we shall show how the physiologists made a decisive step in turning towards psychology. On another level, Jean Piaget did the same thing when he moved from biology to genetic epistemology.

Wilhelm Wundt and the first institute of psychology

In 1897 the University of Leipzig constructed a completely new building for Wilhelm Wundt's work in experimental psychology. Shortly after his appointment in Leipzig in 1875 as a professor in philosophy, Wundt paid for a small workshop that he rather pompously called the 'Psychologisches Institut'. The university did not recognize his 'Institut' officially until 1885. Twelve years later, when students from all over the world were coming to Wundt, the university made up for its original reservations and offered Wundt a grand new institute, the first of its kind in Europe.

These facts have nothing to do with the birth of Piaget in 1896, but they mark the *Zeitgeist* in which he would start his intellectual development, namely the emergence of experimental psychology and its first encounter with 'disequilibrium' and 'restructuration'.

Wundt was trained, just like Piaget, in the life sciences, and more particularly in neurophysiology. After his degree in medicine, he worked for several years with Hermann Helmholtz (who later held a chair in physics in Berlin) in his famous lab for neurophysiology in Heidelberg. By that time Wundt had already tried to apply the methods of neurophysiological research to the study of the consciousness, then the most important psychological topic in philosophy. We know, for example, that in 1862 he gave private lessons in 'psychology as natural science' at his home in Heidelberg. What has remained best known from that period, of course, is his book *Grundzüge der physiologischen Psychologie*, the first edition of which he published in 1873. But then, after holding a chair of philosophy for one year (in 1874) in Zurich, he went to Leipzig and created his famous institute that we recognize in hindsight as the official beginning of the new science of experimental psychology in Europe.

Consciousness, neurophysiology, and psychology

It is an intriguing question why something that until then was investigated exclusively in philosophical terms, i.e., consciousness, was suddenly transformed into a topic of research within an existing branch of science, i.e., *neurophysiology*. In some of my earlier papers[3] on this question, I have attributed this step to the *logic of objectification* in natural sciences, which implies that the contribution of the researcher, namely the *method*, must be objectified and not confused with the phenomenon.

Astronomy is the first natural science that, in retrospect, we consider objective, capable of reflecting the constant properties of its object. After resolving the mathematical and physical problems of perspective, which arise from spatiotemporal variations of the earth, the next step was optics, the study of light and lenses. It is now clear that we see stars only because of light, but it takes time for light to reach us. It is also clear now that light is diverted by the lens. To maintain the constancy of the original object, i.e., the stars, we have to account for the influence these instruments of observation had in the formation of the new discipline of optics. The next step was the human lens, the eye, or the self-adapting telescope, then the study of the nerves, which led to neurophysiology, and finally, the psychological functions of the brain. These steps led Wundt to study apperception and to found *experimental psychology*.

Going beyond the initial confusion between the researcher and the object of study . . .

The step from one branch of science to the next has always been triggered by 'disturbances' – or observed variations in results – which the existing branch of science could not account for, because it vainly sought these variations in the objects of the study themselves, rather than in the *method* of research. In other words, according to the logic of objectification mentioned above, one learns step by step to see these variations as a result of the method used by the researcher and not as belonging to the object being studied. These 'disturbances' in the observation are generally due to the method of the researchers not having been objectified yet, and thus science is unable to describe the process at stake.

These progressive *regressions* from the more distant object (such as a star) to the closer object (such as the researcher and his method) constitute an object in itself, as I have tried to capture in *Ars artefactorum*[4] and have illustrated by the *step* from *general* to *social* psychology at the beginning of the last century. This step marks the transition from the individual to the social dimension of knowledge. It is obvious that all we know about stars (or any object) is, in the end, only a collective discourse coordinating different points of view of what has been observed.

. . . to recognize the social dimension of knowledge

It takes a long time before the new level of analysis is translated into a genuine ontology that comprises the principal terms that are necessary for that level of analysis. At first, the new discipline takes the form of a systematic description of the 'artefacts' that influence the original facts, rather than seeing that, in fact, they actually constitute them. That is why a new discipline begins to be methodologically the scientific branch from which it was born. After some time, researchers who were less attached to the original methods started to develop new methods, better adapted to the foreseen perspective. Finally, they took the most important step – a new ontology or a description, which is based on new principles. Thus, 'external disturbances' that are first seen as simple artefacts become in actual fact 'constitutive' elements of the object studied. In this way, neurophysiological psychology was replaced by psychology and that, in turn, by social psychology. Social psychology was originally an experimental demonstration of social influences, and it only recently became a social ontology of the intellect (as we shall see below).

But the question remains of how far we can regress in our objectifying process from the object to the knowing subject, including the relationship between such subjects. Can we go back infinitely and create a collective story that takes in the entire construction of knowledge, including the collective creation of stories? Clearly not. In 1931, the mathematician Kurt Gödel offered a compelling demonstration of the formal impossibility of complete self-knowledge (at that time, Piaget was 34 years old and fully engaged in the study of the growing consciousness of children, including the consciousness of the Self) by showing that any formal system, such as mathematics, must be based on principles that are from outside the system. The procedure Gödel followed was complex in its elaboration yet quite simple in principle: Transform meta-mathematical expressions into mathematical terms and one finds that some theorems contain contradictions, or expressions that are necessarily true and false at the same time, which means that the system is incomplete. This resembles the dilemma of Heidegger, who, in his philosophical lectures in Heidelberg (the city where Wundt started his physiological psychology), had to admit that it seemed impossible to purify language by means of language and hoped for the advent of better times in a log cabin in the mountains – in vain, of course. There are better methods, as we shall see later, but they require a crucial revision of the concepts of knowledge and of truth.

Piaget between Wundt and Freud

Piaget's transition from a philosophy of consciousness to experimental psychology was not, like Wundt's, embedded in the disturbances of neurophysiological research, but was due to his amazement over errors in another branch of a so-called objectification of consciousness, namely the differential study of the wrong answers of children on intelligence tests.

For Wundt and his contemporaries it seemed that children did not exist, or at least they seemed to have no place in psychological research. Wundt's conception of consciousness was that of a general disposition that could only be studied with articulate adults, i.e., people able to report their variable impressions resulting from experimentally manipulated stimuli. In effect, in psychology, it seems that children were considered as either hidden or taboo. They seemed to exist only in the form of sexually obsessed young people whom Freud discerned in the neurotic highbrow adults who were treated as patients with his 'talking cure'. Freud also talked a lot with adults from imperial Vienna. Financially strained to meet the costs of educating their children for specialized jobs in the new industrial society, and lacking effective means of contraception, these adults invented sexual repression. But energy that is repressed does not disappear, it may manifest itself in a different form: sublimation (as Joule, Mayer, and Helmholtz had demonstrated in physics). It is the same for the child whose repressed (sexual) energy drives him to becoming a sublimated adult, sometimes excessively, which leads to neuroses. Country people were not as afraid of sexuality, since offspring were an asset to the farm and to their parents' retirement. They were less inclined to turn into adults chattering about their repressed libido in the secret language that Freud read 'between the lines' through introspection.

Piaget was also trained for a while in this marvellous art of talking with the child through the secret language of the adult, during an internship in 1918 at the Bleuler psychiatric clinic in Zurich. However, it seems that he was put off by what psychoanalysis revealed to him about himself. He retained from this internship the technique of the clinical interview, which helped him later in speaking with children, when he finally met them. After moving from Zurich to Paris he had just such an occasion when offered a job with Théodore Simon, an early collaborator of Alfred Binet, to help standardize an intelligence test for children.

This approach to consciousness, using differential measures, was first developed by students working in Wundt's laboratory. It soon became obvious that not all subjects in the laboratory were identical and that the techniques used to study the general properties of consciousness could also be used to study their differences. This was, for example, what an American student of Wundt, James Cattell, tried to do. But by proceeding from a functionalist's perspective, Cattell did not look at *what* different subjects said, but, rather, at *how fast* their reaction time was; thus his research was essentially a study of different *speeds* of behaviour.

This notion of speed (rate of growth) is also typical for the differential definition of intelligence, as used by Cyril Burt in England and Binet in France. Their method was based on a comparison between chronological age and mental age, or IQ: those who can solve a problem at a younger age than the average age are more intelligent. Not surprisingly, this notion of rate is also present in so-called cognitive psychology, which considers the notion of intelligence in terms of processing of information, to which we shall turn our attention later in the chapter. The metaphor for this cognitive psychology is the computer, whose primary virtue, of course, is speed. But this virtue is at the same time an imperfection, since speed alone, as the processes of parallel treatment have shown, can never replace heuristics. It is ironic that this computer view of intelligence originated with a man also named Simon – Herbert Simon, the only psychologist ever to be awarded a Nobel Prize, in economics no less (for the notion of the necessary limitations in the human processing of information).

Speech and behaviour

At the time when Piaget discovered psychology using the technique of talking with children in Paris, experimental psychology elsewhere was already struggling with disequilibrium and some forms of accommodation. For example, Oswald Külpe in Wurtzburg affirmed that the consciousness of human beings should not be studied with a limited and controlled speech of adults under conditions of manipulated stimuli, but should be based on free conversations touching on all subjects. Külpe had discovered 'imageless' thinking. His colleague in the United States, Tichener, did the same, but without developing this imageless thinking. In 1913 John Broadus Watson had had enough of the 'psychobabble' and decided that one should not be working on a consciousness that was dependent on the analyst's conversational abilities. He proposed a surface psychology: Only the external world of behaviour is what psychologists should study.

Watson was only a prophet. B. F. Skinner was the true god of the new movement in psychology, which became known as *behaviourism*. In 1938 Skinner published his famous work *The Behaviour of Organisms*, and by *organisms* he meant all living beings capable of movement: not only adults but animals, as well as children. Wundt himself had never seen either an animal or a child in his laboratory and was familiar only with adults speaking in the name of a universal consciousness. Naturally Skinner had to recognize that speech also appears, in a sense, on the surface and thus is behaviour. As a result he published another book, perhaps his most famous one, in 1957, titled *Verbal Behaviour*. Language is described here as a repertoire of behaviours that we have within us, and not as a means of reflecting thought (which leads me to wonder whether I, myself, am correctly reflecting Skinner's thought! I hope so). His expression 'We have a poem', just as one says 'We have a baby', became famous. Like Piaget, Skinner also had babies, and he subjected them to the Skinner-box, to mould their intelligence (or rather, in behaviourist terminology, to give them intelligent behaviour). Piaget played with his own children in order to be able to describe the growth of the epistemic subject. The Piagetian subject, contrary to Wundt's consciousness, needed action and play to form its intelligence.

Part and whole

In his analytic approach to his newborn epistemological subject, Piaget often made use of some notions that he had pondered long before in his philosophical reflections, namely the binome of part and whole. This problem was crucial not only in the philosophical definition of meaning but also in biology, because exemplars are codified in categories. Let us remember that at the start of his career Piaget, the biologist, had classified molluscs.

However, other psychologists of the Wundt school, such as Wertheimer, Kofka, and Köhler, were also taken up with this fundamental notion of part and whole. According to them, certain products of consciousness – for example, a musical sentence – cannot be seen as a mere composition of discrete parts, but form units in themselves, or psychological Gestalts, which need to be studied as such: as primary data of consciousness (and not as sums of their parts). Regarding this conception of consciousness, Piaget wrote, 'If I had known at that time the work of Wertheimer and Köhler, I would have become a Gestaltist, but having only come across the writings of the French school . . .'[5] It would be difficult today to make such a remarkable affirmation without being discredited by the university – unless, of course, one were Piaget.

The question of part and whole also appeared in physics. In 1900 Max Planck resolved a classic problem in radiation by conceiving of energy as being discrete rather than continuous, as appearing only in intermittent leaps, called quanta. In 1905 Einstein in turn broke light up into particles: Waves became photons. A year later, Ludwig Boltzmann committed suicide, partly because his atomic interpretation of matter, expressed in his formula $S = k \log W$, had not (yet) been accepted by his colleagues.

Mechanics and energy

One can find other correspondence between concepts in physics and concepts in psychology during those years. In a sense, Wundt's stimulus version of consciousness is close to Newton's stimulus version of mechanics: Apply a stimulus to a given state of movement or mind, and it will change. But the medium of stimulation may be intangible, like the notion of ether, which disappears in order to be replaced by the notion of field according to Gestalt psychologists, especially Lewin. In all these examples, the intellect is still conceived as an instrument that passively records the external world.

Towards the mid-nineteenth century, the notion of energy in a closed container and transformed in directional movements led to the steam engine. This was the model that Freud used in his conception of man as a vessel of energy transformed in societal movement, in sublimated action. In a sense, it was also the model Piaget used to describe how action in the outer world forms the basis of intelligence, via the processes of internalization. The thinking child for Piaget was a living organism, given to moving and acting, and not a passive camera equipped with a brain, resting on a tripod, and registering stimuli from the outer world according to the laws of consciousness.

With the arrival of the metaphor of information processing and the computer, one sees again consciousness represented as immobile, not on a tripod, but as a machine that, virtually without energy, processes information at an incredible speed – but retrieves it with difficulty. It does not let itself be irritated by stimuli (unlike consciousness, according to Wundt), nor does it repress information (unlike the ego, according to Freud).

Artificial intelligence and cognitive psychology

Kamikaze pigeons

Skinner attempted to contribute to the technology of the Second World War with a remarkable strategy. He trained carrier pigeons to peck at the cabin of a flying bomb. When a signal announced the presence of the enemy, the pigeon would cause the bomb to explode on the enemy and on itself as well. The Japanese kamikaze pilots worked for the honour of the emperor; Skinner's pigeon did it for food, yet their reward was the same: eternal rest.

As far as I know, the Americans never used Skinner's organic war technology, but they did use a non-organic variant of the principle: a computer, nourished on (so to speak) feedback concerning deviations from the target. Up-to-date versions of this early technology were broadcast live on television during the Gulf War. In the meantime, computers have become capable of accomplishing tasks much more complex than guiding a bomb in a pigeon-like way. They are capable, among other things, of deriving mathematical theorems from axioms faster than Whitehead and Russell, and of reacting with Rogerian non-directive elegance to existential questions.

The history of artificial intelligence is long and complex, and this chapter is certainly not the place to explore it. Readers who want to know more about it should consult the brilliant book by Howard Gardner, *The Mind's New Science, A History of the Cognitive Revolution*, published in 1985 (New York: Basic Books). We learn there, among other things, that artificial intelligence, on both a hardware and a software level, made great strides forward around the time of the Second World War, the same period in which Piaget's epistemic subject came into its own and won over the world with great aplomb.

For somebody like myself who, in 1965, had to punch his own cards to merely calculate some simple correlations, but whose children now create worldwide networks of communication, 'artificial intelligence', in fact, does not seem artificial but appears, rather, as a very real 'genetic' phenomenon. On the emotional level, this 'genetic' aspect may resemble the fascination caused by the machine 'Johniac', created by John von Neumann, which has its own *internal* program in contrast to Turing's machine, which used an *external* punched program. It is interesting that in writing these lines on my PC, I am using a recent variant of this Johniac, Bill Gates's *Word* program.

The same John von Neumann, like so many of his brilliant contemporaries, also contributed to the development of the atomic bomb, in Los Alamos, during the Second World War, which transformed into concrete reality with a cataclysmic explosion the formula that had sent Ludwig Boltzmann to his grave. This was also part of the intellectual and technological scene in which Piaget studied the child's conception of physics, but without letting himself be distracted from his original goal: the genetic study of the epistemic subject that *internalizes its relationship with the external world*.

As fate would have it, the city that hosted the peaceful study of atomic energy after the Second World War is the same city in which Piaget founded his Centre for Genetic Epistemology – Geneva. I am speaking about the European Centre for Nuclear Research, CERN. This centre, like Los Alamos during the war, attracted the best minds from the international community and, with them, some of their children (one of whom would hold a chair previously held by Piaget).

A rapid brain

It was neither atomic fission nor fusion but the rapidity of the brain of the computer that became the leading metaphor for the description and analysis of the human mind after the war. The possibility of simulating certain human activities with a computer was reversed and translated into a concept according to which the human mind should resemble the computer. It seems that Piaget remained impervious to this revolution, for there is hardly any comparison to a computer in his genetic epistemology. It is difficult to overlook certain important differences. The Piagetian image of a subject that internalizes its operations on the world by structuring them, and attains ever higher levels of abstraction through disequilibrium and restructuration, cannot be easily translated in terms of the syntactic processing of information by a computer that does nothing else but that. The difference is obvious: The computer need not live or survive, and thus the form of intelligence of a computer does not reflect this relationship of adaptation to the world.

The psychology described with the computer metaphor is known today as cognitive psychology. According to George Miller, this psychology was introduced at a congress held at the Massachusetts Institute of Technology in 1956. Other participants at this congress were, besides George Miller (who claimed that the human brain was capable of dealing with five to nine elements simultaneously), Newell and Simon (who, as I mentioned above, had announced the concept of the limited capacity of human reasoning) and Noam Chomsky (for whom our understanding of language was founded on a genetic basis). James Watson and Francis Crick, researchers who had discovered the real bases of heredity at Cambridge in 1953, were not in attendance. Nor was Piaget, at least not personally, although his work was alive in the spirit of the participants.

Two centres of cognitive studies

This period of the cognitive revolution also saw the founding of two major centres. One is the above-mentioned Centre for Genetic Epistemology, founded by Piaget in Geneva in 1956, largely sponsored by the Rockefeller Foundation, and the other is the Centre for Cognitive Studies, founded by George Miller and Jerome Bruner at Harvard in 1960. Both centres defied the computer metaphor, for they had been primarily conceived as venues for interdisciplinary meetings, where knowledge would be constructed on the basis of communication, and not on the basis of individual processing of information. This brings me to the following aspect in this constructivist sketch of the *Zeitgeist* of Piaget's period, namely social constructivism, or the idea that knowledge is the fruit of social coordination rather than of an isolated subject, be it passive or active.

Can the epistemological subject think on its own?
Towards a socio-constructivism

Piaget's opening address to the World Congress of Psychology in Paris in 1976, at which he presided and, in spite of his advanced age, showed an alert interest in the development of his work, was followed by his young colleagues from Geneva – his intellectual children, so to speak – who demonstrated by way of classic experiments the notion of conservation to illustrate the social dimension of the development of the epistemic subject. The social dimension was none other than one of the signs of the new *Zeitgeist* in which Piaget would round out his career and that has become more and more apparent in the past two decades: the principally social (as opposed to individual) vision of the development of human knowledge and thinking.

'Social psychology' was not a social approach to thinking

One may suppose that this principally social epistemology of human thinking had already been present for some time in another branch of the social sciences, explicitly 'social psychology' (rather than genetic or cognitive psychology), but such a supposition would be a major error. In fact, social psychology (particularly experimental social psychology) as it existed then – and still exists in many universities – hardly ever used a social ontology of mind but started from the classic individual definition of mind, while never-theless recognizing the possibility of mutual influence of individual minds. Even the current term 'social cognition', which could suggest a social approach to cognition, is essentially 'individual cognition', but about social objects (human beings and not stars!). Social cognition tells us nothing about how cognition is produced, other than that it must be the product of the psychological functions in the cognitive apparatus of the individual subject. And even if it cannot be denied that cognition needs a brain (and brains are found in the heads of individuals), it is not the constituent condition for what we call meaning. In order to have meaning, there must be at least two human subjects who communicate and coordinate their activities.

Before describing this point of view in more detail, a possible misunder-standing must be eliminated, namely that Piaget denied the relation between the epistemic subject and the social world. He most certainly did recognize this relation, but in the sense of a parallelism,[6] and not in the principal and intrinsic role described here. Most of the works in which Piaget describes this parallelism have been re-edited in the volume that also contains the revised version of his autobiography – the special issue of the *Revue européenne des sciences sociales* (European review of the social sciences), edited by Busino in 1976 – which has already been cited repeatedly in this chapter. It is evident that for Piaget the progress of intelligence is accompanied by changes in the forms of social interaction, in morality, and in communication. But he never suggests a 'social' definition of knowledge, which remains essentially individual. This 'extrinsic' approach to the social factor is clear, albeit paradoxically, when he defends it as something that we must 'add' in an interdisciplinary way to psychology in order to understand language and communication correctly. According to Piaget, psychology can be intrinsically combined with one other discipline: epistemology. However, for him it is a matter of a transformation into intelligence of the relation between the subject and his environment, or to cite his autobiography: 'the relationship between intelligence and the real, that is between the subject and the object'.[7]

Social constructivism and its avatars

By contrast, social constructivism, strictly speaking, departs from a different axiom, one that is social. In this approach, 'meaning' (or 'signification') is seen not as a product of the subject–object relationship, but as a product of an 'intersubjective' relationship. Indeed, the phenomenon that we call 'meaning' or 'signification' emerges only when two (or more) subjects exchange signs and thereby coordinate their activities. The resulting meaning attributed to the object is the expression of this social coordination, and not something *prior*, like a pre-existing message transmitted by nature.

However – and here we touch upon the source of one of the most widely held misunderstandings in the history of psychology – it is obvious that the subjects, after having established these semantic social coordinations, can retain them in memory and reproduce them later in individual circumstances. When such a phenomenon occurs, and we actualize interiorized social coordinations on the individual level, we all have the impression that the meaning thus produced is individual and pre-existing, like a natural source of information that only needed (to take up once again the 'computer' metaphor) to be 'processed' by the cognitive functions of the individual subject.

To further complicate the situation, this illusion of individualism requires, by its very logic, communication, or some other form of social construction. However, this is a form of social construction that I shall call 'secondary' in order to make clear the fact that the concept of signification upon which it depends is not social but principally individual.

The logic that leads to this secondary social constructivism, based on the individualist definition of meaning, is the following: Clearly, if we define meaning as the individual subject's processing of information from nature, truth must be the correct match between the message transmitted by nature and the image produced by the subject. By consequence, it is also clear that all objective subjects and all subjects who hold the correct signification must have the same meaning. Suddenly then, the individualist–realist definition of truth offers us a social definition of truth: consensus! But this consensus arises from truth; it does not constitute it.

If subjects do not properly process the information that resides in nature – either because the information itself is insufficient (e.g., degraded stimuli) or because the cognitive ability of the subject is biased, incapable, or limited (and according to Herbert Simon, this is always the case to some extent) – they arrive occasionally at divergent meanings. Since *consensus* is an undeniable criterion of truth, they may 'then' try to restore consensus and, thereby, restore their psychological feeling of truth. But this psychological truth is not objective in the realist sense – a perfect pairing between information and image. It is quasi-truth or quasi-objectivity, or a 'social construction' in the secondary sense of the word. Needless to say, this search for consensus to compensate for a lack of objectivity requires language and communication.

It is exactly this way of considering social construction as secondary that we find in Leon Festinger, a contemporary of Piaget's and often credited as the inventor of the social dimension of human thought. According to Festinger,[8] the practical world is full of social constructions based on processes of communication, but these social constructions exist only to compensate for the lack of objective knowledge, which is possible in principle (in the realist sense) but often fails in reality (unclear situations, emotional or biased subjects, etc.). Thus, although Festinger seemed to introduce the aspect of the social in the concept of human cognition, in fact he reinforced the individual dimension. We might say that by dressing his Trojan horse in social clothes he smuggled the individualistic theory back into the city – a city that is not Troy but, rather, the Sparta of his behaviourist colleagues at Yale, such as Clark L. Hull and Kenneth Spence, who conceived of human cognition in terms of habits of thought.

Individualist epistemology and group psychology

With this secondary view of the role of the social in human thinking and perception, Festinger simply repeated the individual epistemology of the mind, which was present in experimental social psychology from the beginning. As mentioned above, experimental social psychology started early in the last century as a kind of systematic control of the social influences that seemed to create artefacts in the results of experiments on individual thinking and perception performed in laboratories. This is precisely what is meant by the title Floyd Allport used in the publication of his experiments on co-action, 'The Influence of the Group upon Association and Thought',[9] and by that which Muzafer Sherif used in his experiments in which subjects communicated their judgements about unclear stimuli: 'A Study of Some Social Factors in Perception'.[10] A year later, Sherif called the same experiments studies in 'social norms' (rather than artefacts),[11] but he was merely borrowing a term from his pre-scientific conception of society and using it to describe his experimental findings. This manner of proceeding led to new questions, inspired by what he already knew about norms (instead of artefacts). The same happened with Walther Moede when he called his experiments on co-action (very similar to those of Allport) *Experimentelle Massenpsychologie*.[12] In the introduction he wrote that this was a new, experimental sociology. Of course, Moede was not studying masses but, rather, the difference between experimental tasks performed by subjects acting alone and by subjects acting together (co-acting). In fact, he thought that this difference would show up in different results, which was not supposed to happen in the classic individualistic interpretation of experimental results. The sociologists were then studying ordered institutions, or, in other words, human technology applied to a society constructed by, with, and for humans (a technology that we might also call a social construction, but in yet another sense that we have used above). At that time they were quite caught up with research on the masses, considered as a kind of natural chaotic condition from which one must start to create institutions, and to which they seem to return, if not taken care of properly, in a process like that of entropy of physical mechanisms. Moede, not finding a more adequate term in the laboratory of general psychology, simply borrowed the dominant term from sociology at the time: 'masses'.

Everybody understood what he meant: He did not mean a social artefact of thinking and perception, but something we had known about for a long time. It was the same for conformity, obedience, consensus, power, mentality of groups, rejection, deviance, etc., known sociological terms that were taken over to describe research paradigms in which the social seemed to influence the individual. But it was Wundt himself, the founding father of experimental psychology, who claimed that in order to study the social (in the sense of the societal) one should look at society itself – the norms, rituals, myths, and languages of peoples. He devoted 20 years of his life to editing an immense volume on *Völkerpsychologie*.[13]

Attempts to study social influences appear not only in the general study of human thinking and perception, but also in the differential study of intelligence, to which I have already referred. For example, Alfred Binet (whose assistant, Théodore Simon, later inspired Piaget's work on children) was also concerned with the question of the possible influence of other children to the responses on the test. Together with V. Henri, Binet did a number of experiments on conformity where the subject has to judge the length of lines while listening to the wrong answers of other subjects.[14] These experiments greatly resembled those of Solomon Asch,[15] and are nowadays considered the prototype of the process of conformity studies. But just as in the mainstream of experimental psychology, which was born shortly thereafter, the social was not presented as the fundamental condition required for meaningful reaction. The social was considered an extrinsic factor, but one that could certainly be systematically observed thanks to the experimental paradigms of so-called social psychology, even though it lacked a *social ontology* of thought.

Vygotsky and Piaget

Vygotsky is a different case. The well-known Russian psychologist and contemporary of Piaget defined thinking primarily in social terms, as an internalization (privatization) of a collective action. This view was doubtless influenced by Marxism, according to which economic exchange is seen as the source of ideology and not the converse. It may seem strange that Piaget, who had many contacts with Vygotsky's thought,[16] was not truly inspired by this social definition. However, on closer inspection it is not so surprising. As I have explained above, an individualist approach to thinking leads automatically to a social dimension, even if it is only to the second degree. This is why it is so difficult to escape from an individualist concept, once it has been adopted. In effect, one can always claim to have kept account of speech, of communication, and the evident practical possibility of social constructions (even if one has not made a rule of the matter). But it is not that type of social constructions that is meant in the principally social definition of the intellect.

Socio-genetic constructivism and social constructivism

The above definition has gained a lot of territory in the past 20 years. But – aside from the epistemological obstacles mentioned above – it would have been highly unlikely that Piaget would renounce his individualist approach. Approaching the end of his career and his life, Piaget would probably have found it difficult to make such a radical existential change.

It is striking, and perhaps even symptomatic of the dialectic forces in the social construction of science, that one of the most important contributions to a principally social constructivism was developed in the department of psychology in Geneva, where Piaget had worked on his solitary epistemic subject; it was further developed in the city where he was born and studied, Neuchâtel. I am thinking here of genetic constructivism, a term I used at the beginning of this chapter with reference to the claims of superior realism by painters like Picasso and Braque. It is now used to refer to a *socio*-genetic constructivism, a term that clearly indicates the principally social dimension. Those researchers who developed the basic concepts of Piaget in this direction are well known: Doise,[17] Mugny,[18] Perret-Clermont.[19] By working with numerous other researchers worldwide, including myself, an indirect collaboration with Piaget has been established – a collaboration with a constructive critical attitude that perhaps best serves his intellectual heritage. An emblematic image comes to mind when I think of this kind of research: Two children are supposed to share equal amounts of juice in two unequal glasses and, in fulfilling the task, make unexpected giant leaps in understanding the notion of conservation.

This socio-genetic approach to social construction focuses on what we might call the molecular aspect of thinking, that is, concepts – and particularly formal concepts – among children. Of course, the world also consists of adults who also coordinate their activities and create worlds of meaning, not only at the conceptual level but also in sentences (long, sometimes too long), stories, and entire communities of discourse. And as with children, conflicts of coordination can emerge, which may lead to new perspectives but also (and too often) to abandoning cooperation and to clinging stubbornly to original positions. Why should we not follow the example of children? Ought we not make sure, just as the experimenter does in experiments with children, that cooperation does not stop, and that the socio-cognitive conflict among adults leads to new perspectives (which does not mean without a fight!)? The contradictions appear only as formal differences of what otherwise is the same, and, therefore, objects of potential social exchange. Piaget must have hoped for just such an outcome because he believed in the beneficial effects of interdisciplinary work and reflection with his colleagues at the Centre for Genetic Epistemology. This conviction was perhaps latent when he defined his role as director of the International Bureau of Education: 'This affair has certainly taken up a great amount of time, which I could have better used in concentrating on child research, but it has taught me a lot about adult psychology.'[20]

Social constructivism emphasizes the more global aspects of speech and communication, as well as the corresponding discursive constructions. Piaget's basic epistemology is no different from that in socio-genetic constructivism, but social constructivism differs in what is stressed and what is developed.[21] Kenneth Gergen has most vehemently defended and developed this form of social constructivism in the past couple of decades. His monumental works in this field contain several reflections on social epistemology, such as it is.[22] These works present numerous propositions concerning the professional practice of psychologists, such as organizational psychology[23] and psychotherapy.[24] Note that the value of this social approach, as advocated by its supporters, is particularly apparent when collaborators work directly together and thus are able to resolve contradictions as they arise.

Epilogue

It is difficult to bid farewell to a person like Piaget – if only to finish a chapter – without musing for a while on his style, or personality, or method, if you wish, and without putting one last drop of ink on my constructivist sketch of his *Zeitgeist*. I made several remarks on the characteristics of Piaget's work at the beginning of this chapter. I have discussed how he managed to combine life sciences and philosophy, to talk in a specific way with children, his taste for interdisciplinary work, etc. But let us look now at some of these characteristics with a little more apprehension instead of apperception (to paraphrase a classic distinction in the Wundtian analysis of consciousness).

Why not, once again, take Wundt as the starting point for my interpretation of Piaget? After all, both of them were founding fathers, one of experimental psychology and the other of genetic epistemology. Both were clearly interested in philosophy, an interest – I think it is fair to say – derived from religious considerations. Wundt's father was a pastor; Piaget, as he admits in his autobiography, became interested in philosophy after reading a book on religion that his father had offered him. In spite of these interests in philosophy and religion, both men pursued scientific studies, Wundt in neurophysiology and Piaget in biology. They made use of this training to transform their philosophical concerns about the soul (a variant of the word 'consciousness', which I feel free to use here, because 'soul' is etymologically present in the word 'psychology') into an empirical science. Both arduously undertook this endeavour and wrote more books and articles than one would normally produce in the course of academic studies. Both were, at the end of their careers, broadly engaged in interdisciplinary work in which anthropology played a major role: Wundt with *Völkerpsychologie*, and Piaget with his interdisciplinary symposia at the Centre for Genetic Epistemology. Both also had something of a paradoxical attachment to their homelands, which meant the world would come to them rather than the other way round.

Both had immense influence: Wundt, it seems, had around 200 doctoral students and 20,000 other students. I do not know the exact numbers in the case of Piaget, but his students must have been numerous. Furthermore, each was able to write and publish in his own language. As trivial as that remark may seem, it is hard to imagine either of them obliged to write in English and then wait for peer reviews, sometimes for months or even years, because of delays in publication. Wundt founded his own journal, and Piaget published his own books.

Most remarkably, it seemed that they both knew the answers before they were confirmed by facts. A sentence in Piaget's autobiography struck me in this regard: 'Lacking a laboratory and advice (there was no experimental psychology in Neuchâtel, even at the university), the only thing I could do was theory and writing . . . and I have never believed in a system under precise experimental control.'[25] That seems paradoxical. What did he mean by 'precise experimental control'? If we compare what he did with what was traditionally considered 'experimentation' (two groups of subjects, placed in different conditions, and then compared to see if there was a significant difference between them), then we must conclude that Piaget never did any psychological experimenting at all. Of course, that is not what Piaget meant by 'experiment'. For him, the empirical basis of ideas was demonstration. He did collect thousands of interviews or observations of children, but he has analysed them only case by case. It is striking how much he resembles Skinner in that regard. In fact, the father of behaviourism is often seen as the proto-type of a 'hard' experimental scientist, but Skinner never did any experiments in the statistical sense of the word, and he was even explicitly against this type of procedure. For him, as for Piaget, if a phenomenon made sense, it would work in isolated cases. In fact, on careful inspection, that kind of rigour seems to be the hallmark of the great scientific minds that transformed our image of the world. Nevertheless, the lack of a laboratory at the time of his studies is not the reason why Piaget did not obtain a graduate degree in psychology. If such a 'degree' were necessary, it could be said that it was conferred by his students. This reversal of custom led him to remark with characteristic irony that 'As a result I shall die without a valid degree, taking with me the secret of the gaps in my training.'[26] And what a secret!

Notes

1 J. Piaget (1976) Autobiographie. *Cahiers Vilfredo Pareto–Revue européenne des sciences sociales, XIV*, 1–43.
2 In his autobiography, Piaget ironically evokes his appointment as professor of sociology; ibid., p. 19.
3 J. Rijsman (1973) *Ars artefactorum*. Louvain: Acco; (1988) Les échanges symboliques, in A.-N. Perret-Clermont & M. Nicolet (Eds.) *Interagir et connaître* (pp. 123–137). Cousset (Fribourg): Delval; (1990) How European is social psychology in Europe?, in P. Drenth, J. Sergeant, & R. Takens (Eds.) *European Perspectives in Psychology*. Chichester, UK: Wiley; (1990) Sociale Psychologie. *Grondvragen van der Psychologie*. Assen, The Netherlands: Van Gorcum.
4 Rijsman, *Ars artefactorum*, op. cit.
5 Piaget, op. cit., p. 7.
6 W. Doise & J. Rijsman (1981) Piaget en het experimenteel onderzoek naar de sociale dimensie van de cognitieve ontwikkeling. *Neederlands tijdeschrift voor de psychologie en haar grensgebieden, 36*, 583–603.
7 Piaget, op. cit., p. 31.
8 L. Festinger (1950) Informal social communication. *Psychological Review, 57*, 271–282; (1954) A theory of social comparison processes. *Human Relations, 7*, 117–140; (1957) *A Theory of Cognitive Dissonance*. Stanford, CA: Stanford University Press.
9 F. H. Allport (1920) The influence of the group upon association and thought. *Journal of Experimental Psychology, 3*, 159–182.
10 M. Sherif (1935) A study of some social factors in perception. *Archives of Psychology, 27*, 187.
11 M. Sherif (1936) *The Psychology of Social Norms*. New York: Harper & Row.
12 W. Moede (1920) *Experimentelle Massenpsychologie*. Leibzig, Germany: Hirzel.
13 W. Wundt (1920) *Völkerpsychologie* (10 vols.). Leipzig: Engelman.
14 A. Binet & V. Henri (1884) De la suggestibilité naturelle chez les enfants. *Revue philosophique, 10*, 337–347.
15 S. Asch (1948) The doctrine of suggestion, prestige and imitation in social psychology. *Psychological Review, 55*, 250–276; (1956) Studies in independence and conformity. A minority of one against a unanimous majority. *Psychology Monographs, 70*, no. 416.
16 See Chapter 14 of this volume.
17 W. Doise & G. Mugny (1981) *Le développement social de l'intelligence*. Paris: InterEditions.
18 G. Mugny (1985) *Psychologie sociale du développement cognitive*. Berne: Peter Lang.
19 A.-N. Perret-Clermont (1979) *La construction de l'intelligence dans l'interaction sociale*. Berne: Peter Lang [English translation: *Social Interaction and Cognitive Development in Children*. London: Academic Press, 1980]; A.-N. Perret-Clermont & M. Nicolet (Eds.) (1988) *Interagir et connaître*. Cousset (Fribourg): Delval.

20 Piaget, op. cit., p. 17.
21 For a comparison between these two types of constructivism in the context of other social versions, see for example J. Rijsman & W. Stroebe (Eds.) (1989) Controversies in the social explanation of psychological behaviour. *European Journal of Social Psychology*, *19*, special issue.
22 K. Gergen (1985) The social constructionist movement in modern psychology. *American Psychologist*, *40*, 266–275. See also: (1995) *Realities and Social Construction*. Cambridge, MA: Harvard University Press.
23 K. Gergen (1992) Organization theory in the postmodern era. In M. Reed & M. Hughes (Eds.), *Rethinking Organization* (pp. 207–226). London: Sage.
24 S. McNamee & K. Gergen (1992) *Therapy as Social Construction*. London: Sage.
25 Piaget, op. cit., p. 6.
26 Ibid., p. 43.

12 The new education

Jürgen Oelkers

Geneva, Neuchâtel, and the new education

It was not without reason that in 1949 Henri Grandjean called Geneva the 'city of education'. Since the beginning of the twentieth century, Geneva had become an international centre of the 'new education', the same as in New York, London, and Brussels.[1] In October 1912, Edouard Claparède founded the Jean-Jacques Rousseau Institute in Geneva; in January 1922, Adolphe Ferrière started a major review of the new education, *Pour l'ère nouvelle;*[2] the International School of Geneva was founded in 1924;[3] in December 1925 Pierre Bovet was appointed the first director of the International Bureau of Education; and in 1921 Jean Piaget became junior associate professor of the Jean-Jacques Rousseau Institute.

The essential driving force for establishing the new education spread from Geneva to other French-speaking regions. Like other European nations, Germany also came under the influence of Claparède and Ferrière, and, thanks to Piaget, the audience for this pedagogical approach became international. However, in isolating Geneva as the seat of the new education, Grandjean overlooked the city of Neuchâtel, which was also significantly involved in the movement.

Pierre Bovet, a Neuchâtelois like Piaget, is a central figure in the theory of the new education. Professor at the Academy (which became the University) of Neuchâtel from 1903 to 1912,[4] Bovet not only revealed the pragmatism of William James[5] but also opened the way to John Dewey; it is to Bovet that one owes the central concept of the 'active school'.[6] He had the idea of applying Henri Bergson's theory of the 'creative impulse'[7] to the theory of child development. In addition to all of this, Claparède contributed to the psychology of development, as well as the tradition of the 'new education' according to the pedagogy of Rousseau. Ferrière established the connection between the theories of the active school and the movements aimed at reforming practices. This, then, was the theoretical framework that Piaget found upon arriving in Geneva, not just a simple institute enlivened by a certain enthusiasm for the new education.

From the new education to child psychology

What was meant by 'new education' at this time? After 1870, new ideas about education and, in particular, the idea of reforming school began to appear nearly everywhere.[8] Paul-Edmond Dreyfus-Brisac was probably the first to speak of the new education. His ideas were centred on the comparative development of school and on innovative methods of teaching.[9] This was followed by a shift in interest from new education to child-study[10] and child psychology. In 1914, for the newly published German-language journal *Archiv für Pädagogik*, Edouard Claparède described this decisive development. In this article, the author stated that Alfred Binet was, strictly speaking, the founder of experimental child psychology. Binet drew attention to the individual pupil and made central the theme of intelligence, which was at last measurable. Gabriel Compayre, at the same time as Binet, advanced developmental psychology and introduced Stanley Hall in France. Pedagogy, ensconced until then in abstractions and ideals, only embraced the new education once it became aware of child psychology. This new education came to light on *psychological* and *practical* bases, taking as important premises the concepts of the *elementary school* of John Dewey at the University of Chicago,[11] of schoolhouses throughout rural Europe, of kindergartens, of Maria Montessori's *Casa dei bambini*, of open-air schools,[12] of holiday camps, of the Scouts, and finally of initial psychological tenets for school reform.[13]

The arrival of Jean Piaget

This was more or less the panorama of the new education that Piaget had to take into consideration as of 1921. He did so successfully, for in 1929 he became the first director of the International Bureau of Education, which was then a worldwide organization. Piaget represented the bureau at the international conferences of the New Education Fellowship[14] and established contacts with the various movements of the new education, which he actively promoted. In 1932 he became co-director, along with Bovet and Claparède, of the Jean-Jacques Rousseau Institute, which was by then a first-rate research centre. In 1939 Piaget published two decisive articles on the 'new methods' for the 15th volume of the *Encyclopédie française* (French encyclopaedia),[15] which dealt with aspects of the new education. At this time, though, he did not belong to the group of 'founders' of this movement,[16] which centred on the writings of Ferrière[17] and especially the canons of Claparède in 1941. It seems that Piaget was only marginally involved in this movement.

In 1926 Bovet described 'the unity of contemporary pedagogy'. His starting point was a critique of the associative psychology of the eighteenth century, which had had – thanks to Johann Friedrich Herbart – an influence on training for teaching school. According to Bovet, the psychology of association had neglected two elements: the development of children and their spontaneous activities. These two conditions – William James is once again cited[18] – emerged favourably into a new point of view: that of 'the view of the child as very *active*'.[19] The unity of the new education developed from this central concept,[20] which proved itself repeatedly through practice. Bovet mentioned yet again the new 'laboratory school' of Dewey in Chicago, as well as the open-air school (*Oldenwaldschule*) of Paul Geheeb; Helen Parkhurst and the 'Dalton system';[21] the reforms of school books; methods centred on independent learning activity; the concept of the school city;[22] Montessori classes;[23] methods for project teaching; and Piaget. By then, Piaget was thoroughly integrated into the movement.

Bovet referred to Piaget's work, *Le jugement et le raisonnement chez l'enfant*[24] The results opened the way for new responsibility and a precise mission for future teachers:

> The task of tomorrow's normal school will be . . . twofold. It will have to give the teacher an understanding of a child's *spontaneous life*: experimental psychology . . . is in this respect a great prize. . . . The normal school will also have to stimulate the *teacher himself* spontaneously to doing both manual and intellectual activities, thus keeping him lively and alert, capable of astonishment and curiosity in the throes of problems to be resolved instead of rigidly adhering to pre-packaged sciences.[25]

The alternative psychology

The following, in Bovet's eyes, was the limitation of Piaget's approach: Piaget is exclusively associated with experimental psychology (Bovet called it 'quite simply psychology with all the procedures of observation and induction to which it has access'[26]). Yet there is also *another* kind of psychology related to the child's spontaneous life that ought to be taken into account: 'The educative psychology with the revelations it gives us about the hidden power of instincts, with their ability to transform and sublimate could also be of great service.'[27]

In one of his first articles on child psychology, Piaget did an analysis of psychoanalysis. After describing, not unsympathetically, the doctrines of Freud, of Adler, and of the Zurich school, Piaget reached a critical conclusion. The merit of psychoanalysis was to have added new themes to the theory of affects, and the need to consider its implications for moral teaching, but all of that does not suffice to make up for its deficiencies: a simplistic theoretical construction, an 'excessively brutal' opposition between the conscious and the unconscious, and fundamental concepts riddled with ambiguity.[28] But above all, psychoanalysis does not explain the origins of reason,[29] a vital theme for Piaget. His co-disciple and elder, Pierre Bovet, had published in 1920 an analysis of the relation between psychoanalysis and education which was much closer to the tendency of the new education. The unconscious, and not the development of intelligence, was at the centre of

Bovet's analysis, which was Freudian in spirit. His interpretation of psycho-analysis was similar to that of Théodore Flournoy,[30] which led to a religious conception of pedagogy,[31] the last being the only true link with 'the soul of the educator'.[32]

The reception of the new sciences of the psyche affected the international new education after the First World War, particularly *outside* research insti-tutes and state-run teacher-training centres. If one looks at the documents of the world congresses of the New Education Fellowship, it is clear that experimental psychology had been replaced by depth psychology, which seemed better suited to so-called *creative expression*,[33] or 'the development of the child's creative abilities'.[34]

The sense of development and Christian pedagogy

The principal problem for Piaget was the sense one needed to give to repre-sentation and to development,[35] without expecting the descriptions – such as those of a child's reality or causality – to be connected to an aesthetic unity of the *image* 'of the child'. What was fundamental for Piaget was the genetic logic of thought – which is neither that of feeling nor that of perception – an idea he had taken from J. M. Baldwin:[36] 'A child's thought proceeds simul-taneously: 1. from realism to objectivity; 2. from realism to reciprocity; and 3. from realism to relativity.'[37] Development goes through stages; the unity of the person is only a genetic presupposition that does not tally with the mysterious reality which is the child himself.

The logic of development has important consequences for the theory of the child: Early *forms* of a child's thinking, especially when pertaining to causal hypotheses, differ fundamentally from that of adults.[38] It is necessary to overcome the difference, but at the same time the process reveals a para-dox: 'The child is at once closer to, yet farther away from, things than we are, and, in evolving towards an adult mentality, he grows more distant yet nearer to the real.'[39]

The new education never conceives of child development as *paradoxical*. It considers two other relations as much more important: on the one hand, a linear and harmonious development of the child's 'disposition' and 'poten-tial'; on the other, disturbances in this development. Children develop accord-ing to their natures, but a deprived environment or educational errors can compromise or repress that development. This point of view is *non*-paradoxical, and its unequivocal clarity dominates the *moral* of the new education: It is good when it allows for an organic and unified development. Any other theory is by consequence wrong. It is not only the child's point of view that is 'unified', but that of the new education itself. However, that is plausible only if empirical differences have been eschewed. The model of thought from a pedagogical standpoint founded on the Christian soul pre-dominates: 'A soul is formed only by contact with another soul, where through self-forgetting and through love one soul unites with another.'[40]

Such adaptations of Christian pedagogy are widespread in the new education. For the American observer Martha Gruening,[41] the novelty of the new education was the spirit, *the spirit of education*. 'Spirit' is a term Ferrière borrowed from Martin Buber, and the new education is defined as essentially a spiritual renewal. 'The religious homage', as Ferrière wrote on 1 January 1905 in the *Journal de Genève* (Journal of Geneva), is a decisive criterion in evaluating the success of the 'new schools'. Later, school itself was expected to offer a renewal by way of an evolution 'towards spiritual equilibration', 'a fervent effort towards the truth', and to be directed 'towards the triumph of the Spirit over the material'.[42] According to Bovet, who drew on Pestalozzi as much as on Bergson, education is not merely 'development'; the child is seen as a unified being – spiritual and corporal – headed towards eternity.

Cooperation and social progress

The New Education Fellowship welcomed many aspects of pedagogical currents based on a transcendent view: theosophical or depth psychology concepts, Christian ideas. Early in his career Piaget showed an interest in the psychology of religious values,[43] and he never lost sight of the connection between education and transcendence. This was evident in his pedagogical discourse. In one of the most important papers read at the congress of the New Education Fellowship held in Nice on 1 August 1932, Piaget asked how the new education could contribute to social progress. In his talk he also examined the theory of egocentrism and explained the connection between limits and freedom in modern society. According to Piaget, the new society ought to be a form of community or a cooperative group organized according to the 'method of reciprocity'. Reciprocity develops spontaneously in the child. Thus Piaget's conclusion was once again in accord with the aspirations of the new education:

> We see that the child, different from the adult and often different at school, creates a *social life with his peers*; and especially we notice that, in measure to the degree to which he mixes with his peers, he reaches, intellectually speaking, both a critical spirit and a sense of reflection. On the moral level, this social world fosters a sense of nuances and of intentions beyond blind obedience. Yet, why is this *tendency towards cooperation* that we observe in children more likely to be crushed rather than used and developed by education?[44]

Pierre Bovet drew a connection between the genius of Baden-Powell and the pedagogical exploitation of a child's natural sociability. Ferrière adhered in this respect to the thesis Dewey defended in *Democracy and Education*.[45] Cousinet's 'free work' was founded on similar hypotheses. In 1932 Piaget expressed a consensus, equally applicable to the child and to the tasks set for the new education: 'This spirit of cooperation has not yet entirely penetrated society. Why not? Because of education.'[46]

Here, Piaget contradicted a thesis of Emile Durkheim,[47] according to which the master ought to represent the *authority* in society in order to make possible moral (lay) education:

> Such an image of the schoolmaster incarnating the limits of the group in order to impose them on future generations neglects precisely this treasure of cooperation that there is in the human soul and in the soul of the child, which the new methods allow to develop.[48]

Piaget had already remarked in 1914 that a Christian reading of Bergson's concept of creative *evolution* was possible, in the manner of Sabatier.[49] According to Piaget, social progress is hardly possible without a basis in social values, but that cannot be artificially grafted on to education: Such a value-based society is naturally given when one takes account of the social behaviour of *children*. What Piaget called 'new methods' refers to the presupposition that active, lively children construct a social order among themselves and acquire at the same time a moral education. It is necessary to adapt these methods to a process characterized by an understanding reached without constraint and without calling on the authority of the society. If one wants to change society, it is necessary to have a 'community in miniature'.[50] This was a central promise Piaget made for the new education:

> The new methods, the active methods, insist . . . on the relation between children. Group work, shared research, self-government, etc., imply cooperation in all intellectual and moral areas. That is where the solution lies. *Only a pedagogy founded on the social relations* witnessed in adult relationships will lead to the development of healthy moral and international attitudes and will let the child go beyond us.[51]

Piaget made self-government and teamwork areas of study, and in 1934 and 1935 he published articles on these subjects in two collections for the International Bureau of Education. Like other publications of the bureau, these articles show that the new education should not be either a political or an ideological affair, but, rather, should be a matter of true child psychology. According to Piaget, one should not inculcate into children political or economic ideas, and the new education should not aim at very exact social goals:

> All that should be provided is simply a method, a psychological instrument based on reciprocity and cooperation. The *only* way to do such is the new education. *Only* the new education, which puts into practice these realities and is not satisfied with extraneous talk, is able to transform the child.[52]

The limits of spontaneity

However, reciprocity and cooperation are not only physical gifts but also social ideals, one founded on the other. Talk about the new education shows very clearly that the development of *institutions* is not simply the result of cooperation between children. Even when the child-centred education[53] was at its peak, the 'new schools' always remained schools with a training mission of a particular type. They could not be simply founded on spontaneity, as Ferrière had said,[54] but required also a 'minimum programme'[55] that could not be reduced to reciprocity and cooperation. The experimental school offered a curriculum[56] that was not merely synonymous with methods of learning social behaviour.

The two aspects (the priority of reciprocity and cooperation on the one hand, and the need to follow a set curriculum on the other) are in conflict: Either Piaget transfers the psychological concepts of 'reciprocity' and 'cooperation' into social ideals that can be used as one wants, or these concepts exclude certain social models of the new education. If reciprocity and cooperation grow out of the natural community of children, they do not specify the kind of adult society they are leaning towards. This is also true for didactics: A school cannot be simply a society of children. The fact of there being reciprocity and cooperation in social behaviour is not sufficient for defining the curriculum that the school must set.

New education and Piagetian theory: Interdependency

Piaget's theory was central for the aspirations of the new education. At the end of his 'Examination of the New Methods', Piaget wrote: 'The unity of these techniques is the child.'[57] In fact, Piaget developed for the new education a theory of the child that had been lacking in 1921. This theory differed profoundly from the premises aimed at the practical application of experimental psychology, as established by Binet and N. Vaschide[58] in 1898. It is not a matter of psychological laws projected onto the pupil but, rather, that the school and its methods should be organized in function with the development and, finally, the nature of children. By replacing experimental psychology with child-centred education,[59] Piaget made a decisive change in the theory. Binet had already encouraged the passage from the laboratory to real life, but he did not have a real theory of the *development* of the child. Piaget was the first to present such a theory to the new education, encouraged by the milieu of Geneva.[60] The observation of children in natural situations was a means of verifying the central intuition of the new education about the autonomy of growth. In this sense, Piaget *confirmed* the theories of the new education, and in equal measure his theory *depended* on the new education.

The new education may be part of the past but it also has a bearing on the present; the cardinal question of its future is to know whether the Piagetian child truly exists. The religious bases of Piaget's thought have not yet been thoroughly studied, nor has the influence of his social background and of the lengthy work put into the new education been adequately examined. One can suppose that the idea of the active child, the *élan vital* of personal development, was decisive in forming Piaget's theory. This theory tries – in contrast to Freud's – to render justice to children, to listen to them, and to observe them with interest while attributing independence to them, which is exactly the position of the new education from Montessori to Decroly. The child may construct his *own* world, but there still remains the question of knowing up to what point he needs to be educated and what are the limits of 'education'. Piaget was unequivocal on the relations between psychology and pedagogy: 'Pedagogy' is the methodological practice of child psychology. But if one looks at the religious background – inspired particularly by Bovet – of hopes placed in the new education, one can easily reverse the relationship: Without either the image that the new education had of the child or the environment that confirmed that image, this theory would never have been developed; the 'inspiration', which Bovet[61] had taken up from Bergson, would have been missing.

Notes

1 These centres were all university institutes: Teachers' College in New York, the London Day Training College, which became the London Institute of Education, as well as the Haute Ecole de Pédagogie attached to the University of Brussels in 1919. These three centres had remarkable professors: Dewey, Thorndike, and Kilpatrick; Percy Nunn and his students; and Tobie Jonckheere, Ovide Decroly, and others in Brussels.

2 *Pour l'ère nouvelle* (1922–1940, 1946–1954) was the first French-language journal of the 'new education' (or of the 'reforming pedagogy') to appear on the international scene, in parallel and in exchange with the English journal, *The New Era* (1920–1971), for which Béatrice Ensor was the first publisher and Alexander Neill the editor-in-chief for the first two years. The German-language journal *Das werdende Zeitalter* (1922–1932) was edited by Elisabeth Rotten and Karl Wikler.

3 The technical adviser of this school was Adolphe Ferrière. The institution was founded first for the employees of the League of Nations on property belonging to Ferrière in Florissant, near Geneva. Ferrière left the school in 1926. See A. Ferrière (1929). *La pratique de l'école active. Expériences et directives*. Geneva: Forum.

4 Pierre Bovet defended his doctoral thesis in philosophy at Geneva in 1902: *Le dieu de Platon d'après la chronologie des dialogues*. In 1903 he began teaching philosophy at the cantonal college in Neuchâtel, at the Ecole supérieure for young women, and at the Academy of Neuchâtel where he founded the collection 'Actualités pédagogiques' (1909). Published by Editions Delachaux and Niestlé, this series was the most influential in bringing the changing pedagogy to French-speaking milieus. In 1912 Bovet was invited by Claparède to become director of the Ecole des sciences de l'éducation at the Institut Jean-Jacques Rousseau, which was a private institution at the time. Bovet held this post until his retirement in 1944. In 1919 Bovet turned down a chair at the University of Basle, but then became professor of educational sciences and experimental pedagogy at the University of Geneva. From 1925 to 1929, Bovet was the director of the International Bureau of Education. See: Pierre Bovet et l'école active, *Cahiers de l'Institut neuchâtelois*, Neuchâtel, 1978.

5 P. Bovet (1910). *William James psychologue – L'intérêt de son oeuvre pour les éducateurs.* Saint-Blaise-Neuchâtel: Foyer solidariste. This brochure is related to the studies in the psychology of thought that led to Bovet's principal work: *L'Instinct combatif. Psychologie, éducation.* Neuchâtel; Delachaux & Niestlé, 1917.

6 It was Bovet and not Ferrière who coined this phrase. See P. Bovet (1919). La tâche nouvelle de l'école. *L'intermédiaire des éducateurs,* pp. 71–73, 9–10. Ferrière's work, *L'école active,* made use of the basic idea in creating an explicit theory of the school. Ferrière formally recognized Bovet's prior use of the term (see *Cahiers de l'Institut neuchâtelois,* op. cit., pp. 23ff., and D. Hameline, A. Jornod, & M. Belkaid (1995). *L'école active: Textes fondateurs.* Paris: Presses Universitaires de France.

7 Bovet introduced the philosophy of Bergson to the Geneva public in October 1911. P. Bovet (1911). La philosophie de Bergson. *La semaine littéraire, 927–928,* 469–471, 481–483.

8 H. Marion (1889). *Le mouvement des idées pédagogiques en France depuis 1870.* Paris: Imprimerie nationale. Marion (1846–1896) defended a double thesis in philosophy. He was active in teacher training. From 1883 he held a chair in the faculty of arts at the University of Paris and was lecturer in the 'science of education' treated from a philosophical standpoint. In 1887 Marion was appointed professor. His *Leçons de psychologie appliquée à l'éducation* (1881) is an exemplary treatment of pedagogical subject-matter *prior to* child-study and developmental psychology.

9 Paul-Edmond Dreyfus-Brisac studied at Strasbourg and at Paris. He was one of the first to graduate from the Ecole libre des sciences politiques with a major in comparative studies in the area of training. From 1881 to 1897 he was editor of the important journal *Revue internationale de l'enseignement.* His comparative studies of the new education were published in three series between 1882 and 1897.

10 The term was coined by Stanley Hall (1893). Child-study. The basis of exact education. *Forum,* December. In Boston in 1881, Hall, who had studied in Germany, gave the first course on research into children, and later, as rector of Clark University, organized research into the domain. 'Child-study' was not psychological experimentation in a laboratory but was practical research carried out with quantifiable procedures.

11 Edouard Claparède translated the project, and the description of the experiment of Dewey, *School and Society,* 1889, was published in 'L'école et l'enfant' in 1913 with an important introduction by Claparède in Bovet's collection of 'Actualités pédagogiques'. Claparède's introduction had a decisive effect on the reception of Dewey's ideas in the French-speaking world.

12 The French movement for open-air schools was not greatly studied; it was, rather, the German *Waldschulen* that played a significant role in school reform in Berlin in the 1920s. See J. Nydahl (Ed.) (1928). *Das Berliner Schulwesen.* Berlin: Wiegand u. Grieben.

13 E. Claparède (1914). Die französische psychologisch-pädagogische Bewegung (Frankreich und die französische Schweiz). *Archiv für Pädagogik, II,* 241–258.

14 For the first time in 1929, as director of the bureau, at the Helsigör conference, whose proceedings were published by W. Boyd (1930). *Towards a New Education.* New York: Knopf.

15 Piaget begins tracing the history of the 'new methods' by referring to precursors such as Rousseau and Pestalozzi, considered as references in the 'Selbsthistorisierung der Reformpädagogik' (The self-historization of reforming pedagogy). Then he describes the psychological basis that, according to him, leads to the thesis that the empirical intuitions of its precursors were only then able to be made evident, to present a few isolated approaches such as Montessori and Decroly. The description finishes with the social ideal of the new education: J. Piaget (1939). Examen des méthodes nouvelles. *Encyclopédie française, IV,* Paris, 1–13.

16 A. Millot (1938). *Les grandes tendances de la pédagogie contemporaine*. Paris: Alcan; Albert Ehm (1933). *L'éducation nouvelle. Ses principes, son évolution historique, son expansion mondiale*. Paris: Alsatia.

17 A. Renard (1941). *La pédagogie et la philosophie de l'école nouvelle d'après l'oeuvre d'Adolphe Ferrière*. Paris: Ecole et collège.

18 One of Bovet's sources is 'Talks to Teachers', a lecture course in 1892 at Harvard University and published in 1899. The German translation appeared the following year.

19 P. Bovet (1926). L'unité de la pédagogie contemporaine. *Schweizerische Pädagogische Zeitschrift*, *4*, April, 97–103.

20 Though Bovet's idea of 'active being' referred to Bergson, in 1899 Dewey compared this to a Copernicus-like change of attitude towards the child.

21 Bovet (1926), op. cit., p. 99.

22 In the contemporary literature, the concept of the school city is almost always attributed to essays by Wilson Gill in New York, dating from 1897 and intended to achieve the principles of self-government. The two terms, school city and self-government, formed the basis of an international discussion taken up especially by Friedrich Foerster. It is not accidental that the translation of *Schule und Charakter* (1908) comes from Pierre Bovet, who had published *L'école et le caractère* in 1908, in Neuchâtel. See A. Ehm (1937). *F.W. Foerster. Sa pédagogie morale*, thesis submitted to the Faculty of Arts at the University of Paris. Paris: Alsatia.

23 The 'Maison des petits' at the Jean-Jacques Rousseau Institute was directed according to the Montessori method. See P. Bovet (1932). *Vingt ans de vie. L'Institut J.-J. Rousseau de 1912 à 1932*. Neuchâtel & Paris: Delachaux & Niestlé.

24 J. Piaget (1924). *Le jugement et le raisonnement chez l'enfant*, Neuchâtel & Paris: Delachaux & Niestlé. [English translation: *Judgement and Reasoning in the Child*. Totowa, NJ: Littlefield Adams, 1969.]

25 Bovet (1926), op. cit., p. 102.

26 Ibid.

27 Ibid.

28 J. Piaget (1920). La psychanalyse dans ses rapports avec la psychologie de l'enfant. *Bulletin de la Société Alfred Binet*, January, 18–58.

29 Ibid.

30 Théodore Flournoy (1854–1920) was a student of Wilhelm Wundt and as of 1891 held the first chair of psychology at the University of Geneva. In 1901 Flournoy founded with Claparède the *Archives de psychologie*; this, along with Binet's *L'Année psychologique*, would be the most important journal of experimental psychology for French-speaking regions before 1914.

31 P. Bovet (1920). La psychanalyse et l'éducation. *Annuaire de l'Instruction publique en Suisse*, *11*, 9–38.

32 P. Bovet (1930). L'âme de l'éducateur. *L'éducateur*, *LXVI*, October, 289–293.

33 G. Hartmann & A. Schumaker (1926). *Creative Expression. The Development of Children in Art, Music, Literature and Dramatics*. Washington, DC: Progressive Education Association.

34 E. Roten (ed.) (1926). *Die Entfaltung der schöpferischen Kräfte im Kinde. Bericht der Dritten Internationalen Pädagogischen Konferenz des Internationalen Arbeitskreises für Erneuerung der Erziehung in Heidelberg*, Gotha, Germany, 1926.

35 J. Piaget with the collaboration of 17 co-workers (1927). *La causalité physique chez l'enfant* (pp. 267ff.). Neuchâtel & Paris: Alcan. [English translation: *The child's conception of physical causality*. London: Routledge & Kegan Paul, 1970.]

36 The French translation of Baldwin's book on the child's mental development was published in 1897. Baldwin's influence on developmental psychology (and on Piaget) has not been thoroughly examined. Repeated references to Baldwin are to be found in Piaget's writings, particularly the early work.

37 Piaget (1927), op. cit., p. 273.
38 Ibid., p. 306.
39 Ibid., p. 288.
40 E. Rolland (1933). Réflexions pédagogiques. *La vie intellectuelle*, Paris, April, 324–342.
41 The expression comes from a regional conference of the New Education Fellowship, which was held in Territet in summer 1923.
42 Ferrière, op. cit.
43 J. Piaget (1922). *La psychologie et les valeurs religieuses* (pp. 28–82). Sainte-Croix and Lausanne: Association chrétienne d'étudiants de la Suisse romande.
44 J. Piaget (1932). L'évolution sociale et la pédagogie nouvelle. *Pour l'ère nouvelle*, December, 311.
45 A. Ferrière (1926). La démocratie et l'éducation selon John Dewey. *L'Education*, October–November, 274–280.
46 Piaget (1932), op. cit., p. 312.
47 The articles of Durkheim concerning pedagogy and moral education were made available only as of the 1920s ('Education et sociologie', 1922; 'L'éducation morale', 1925). The concept of the social mechanic and of the group moral were among the ideas of education that Piaget challenged most vehemently.
48 Ibid.
49 J. Piaget (1914). Bergson et Sabatier. *Revue chrétienne*, March, 92–200.
50 Ferrière (1926), op. cit., p. 279.
51 Piaget (1932), op. cit., p. 312.
52 Ibid.
53 H. Rugg & A. Schumaker (1928). *The child-centered school. An appraisal of the new education*, Yonkers-on-Hudson, NY & Chicago, IL: World Book Company.
54 Ferrière (1929), op. cit., p. 138.
55 P. Bovet (1932). Les trois buts de l'enseignement. *L'Educateur*, Paris, January, 37.
56 O. Decroly (1921). Abbozzo di un programma applicato in una scuola sperimentale. *Rivista di psicologia*, Bologna, 2–22.
57 Piaget (1939), op. cit., pp. 1–13.
58 A. Binet & N. Vaschide (1898). La psychologie à l'école primaire. *L'Année psychologique*, Paris, 1–14.
59 V. Walderkine (1984). Developmental psychology and the child-centred pedagogy: The insertion of Piaget into early education. In J. Henriques (Ed.), *Changing the subject: Psychology, social regulation and subjectivity* (pp. 153–202). London & New York: Methuen.
60 'The city, its traditions and education have developed a critical attitude', Bovet wrote in homage to his friend Claparède: Souvenir d'Edouard Claparède (1873–1940), *Action et pensée*, 1950, December, 100. He cites a phrase of Claparède that can also be applied to Piaget, his successor: 'I unite in my spirit liberalism, pragmatism and Protestantism which are to politics, philosophy and religion what the experimental method is to science.'
61 P. Bovet (1932). Bergson et le problème de l'éducation. *L'Educateur*, January, Paris, 171.

13 The intellectual journey after the Neuchâtel period

Jean-Jacques Ducret

When in 1920–21 Piaget carried out his initial research in genetic psychology with the idea of testing a conception of life, of thought, and of existence developed during his adolescence, he could not have foreseen either the extraordinary fecundity or the extent of the empirical[1] and theoretical results that the field of study thereby discovered was going to bring him. A considerable work, which dealt with four major disciplines, was born in fact from the initial querying of the learned philosopher and from the answers that he could give thanks to the research procedures created for this purpose. The following pages can only give a very general and schematic glimpse of the immensity of the work, of the great number of insights that it was able to bring to many – and often the most fundamental – aspects of biological, psychological (intellectual and moral), and social life. I will try to retrace here the major steps in the construction of the work and of its parts and show how its organic character reflects the author's theses.

1920–1935: The discovery of the fields of research

Recherche, written in 1916–17 and published in 1918, set out the four or five principal areas in which Piaget would from then on be involved scientifically: biology, psychology, the social and moral sciences, and finally logic and epistemology. *Recherche* contained, furthermore, the two scientific problems that would be the organizing centre of the work: that of the origin of biological forms and that of the origin of the forms of intellectual and moral thinking, two problems intimately linked to the philosophical questions on life. Piaget also proposed an initial solution that represents a kind of original synthesis of concepts in biology, in psychology, in sociology, and in epistemology taken from the sciences and from philosophy at the beginning of the century, areas in which he was knowledgeable. However, reading the early work shows that, except perhaps for the first experimental works designed to prove a neo-Lamarckian thesis on the evolution of living forms, it was only as of the 1920s that the author began establishing and adopting research procedures capable of grounding empirically the intuitions of his youth and of developing them.

The most important discovery made in the 1920s is without doubt that of genetic psychology. However, its importance cannot be understood without knowing the general context in which the concept was developed, in particular the construction of the entire conceptual framework connected to work carried out in biology, in logic, in the human sciences in general, and in epistemology (or the philosophy of science).

Biology

In 1920, aged 24, Piaget already had ten years of research in natural science behind him. He had numerous contacts with those working in malacology. Their work made him aware of one of the two fundamental problems of biology, with the origins of life: the problem of the origin of species. He was familiar with the two major opposing theses on this question, those of Darwin and of Lamarck, and was able to distance himself from the fixism (or creationism) held by his first teachers (Paul Godet in particular). Thanks to Bergson and the biologist Le Dantec, and through his own research and reflection, Piaget knew the stakes hidden behind the choice of a solution in favour of one or the other theory. The work dating from the 1910s may remarkably foreshadow the development of his newer work, but it was not until the 1920s that the wide-ranging experimental and theoretical study on 'L'adaptation de la *Limnaea stagnalis* aux milieux lacustres de la Suisse romande' (1929) was realized. This study includes two complementary aspects that will structure research in psychology and genetic epistemology. The first aspect is the interactionist solution the author favoured to explain the origins of living forms, a solution he sought to prove by observing the adaptation of lake-dwelling limnaea. The new forms that the observed limnaea take on in different habitats were the final step in the process the organisms undergo in adapting to a given environment.[2]

The second aspect of this work established a first classification of possible general solutions to the problem of the origin of living forms. Four solutions were presented, to which Piaget later added and which he extended to questions about the psychology of intelligence (the problem of behavioural adaptation) and about epistemology (the problem of objective knowledge). The original solutions were Lamarckism (adaptation by direct effect of the environment on the organism), Darwinism (spontaneous production of arbitrary varieties, followed by selection of the best ones), preformism (existing forms that will emerge when corresponding environments appear for which these forms are pre-adapted), and finally a kind of synthesis between the first and the second solutions. This synthesis prefigured the ultimate theory – constructivism – that would develop from studying the origins of forms and intellectual norms.

Thus emerges the method by which Piaget approached and treated the question of the origin of biological forms, and upon which he developed his study on the origins of intellectual forms.

Logic

At the beginning of the 1920s, when Piaget discovered genetic psychology, which was to become his principal area of research for at least 30 years, he did not limit himself to studies in psychology. Already schooled in biology, he was able to broaden his approach to an extensive range of disciplines that his years of study at Neuchâtel had exposed him to. These disciplines included general psychology (including psychoanalysis), of course, as well as sociology, ethnology, the philosophy and history of science, and also logic. Given the initial similarity in the early stages of these disciplines in focusing on life, humanity, and society as objects of enquiry, one readily understands how Piaget's first work in genetic psychology integrates the notions and concepts specific to each discipline. At first it may seem strange that this work takes up notions and concepts coming from the philosophy of science and logic, but this was the result of the intellectual process the young Piaget originally followed before psychology. In particular, the question of the origin of the forms of intellectual and moral thought became the centre of his interest. His curiosity for logic, which became apparent during his studies in Paris, was the direct result of his studying under A. Reymond at grammar school and later at the University of Neuchâtel. His interest in logic grew out of the classical concept, which reigned until the nineteenth century, that held logic not only as the key to truth and to the conditions for truth but also as the doorway to thinking, including the classical sense (true thinking is by nature logical, so logic is thinking). Being aware of these two aspects meant for Piaget that research on thought implied to do and to use psychology *and* logic.

In the 1920s Piaget was basically a beginner in logic. Logic had become a complex science, related to mathematics in the largest sense. It was now a matter of learning not merely about syllogistic but also about the algebraic logic of Giuseppe Peano and especially of Alfred Whitehead and Bertrand Russell. It is not surprising, then, that between 1920 and 1935 Piaget did not produce work on logic itself, even though he was productive in psychology of logical thinking and in epistemology. It was only as of 1935, once he had a firm grasp of mathematical logic and an understanding of its usefulness as a tool in analysing thinking, that Piaget began using and even contributing to this science, which he saw as a tool necessary to resolve fundamental problems about the origins of forms of thinking. Even if logic as a 'modelizing' tool did not appear in the initial drafts of the theory about the intellectual and moral thinking of children, it was nevertheless present as a guiding force in Piaget's psychological enquiries. Indeed, his initial research in genetic psychology relates to child's logic (such as the child's ability to perform 'logical multiplication').

Genetic psychology

From the beginning, works in genetic psychology approached psychology in an original way. Armed with what knowledge he had acquired in mathematical logic and fortified with the conceptual knowledge gleaned from reading texts on cognitive psychology and on the philosophy of science, Piaget took the opportunity to adapt a French version of an English intelligence test to develop a method of research and to draft an empirically founded theory describing how a child and an adolescent think. Faithful to a habit acquired in working in malacology, Piaget quickly published articles and then books on the results of his analysis of the thinking process of children engaged in working out logical and elementary mathematical problems. The quality and promise of these early writings attracted the world-renowned psychologist Edouard Claparède, to welcome the young author as early as 1921 to the Rousseau Institute, where he was appointed lecturer, and to the University of Geneva, where he lectured on child psychology. From then on Piaget's impressive intellectual activities developed successively, like pieces of a large puzzle falling into place over the next decades. In 1923 and 1924 Piaget published two works, one on the language and thought of the child,[3] the other on judgement and reasoning,[4] which coincided with the current research in psychology itself and in the human sciences at the beginning of the century (authors such as Charles Blondel tried to show the determining importance of language, and more generally the social factors, on genesis of reason). These books are nevertheless profoundly original in that the theses advanced continue – by adapting and by reformulating in light of the first facts developed – the theoretical framework set out in *Recherche*, which already contained logical, psychological, and biological notions (assimilation, accommodation, organization, etc).

Two new books were published at the end of the 1920s, one on the child's representation of the world,[5] the other on the child's understanding of physical causality.[6] As their titles indicate, the subject matter of these publications is no longer essentially the logical tools by which the world is conceived, but the way a child thinks of the world. The works drew on the anthropological theses of Lévy-Bruhl and the philosophy of science and knowledge, such as that practised by Brunschvicg. The first works showed that the child should learn to decentralize his self-centred vision of the world and that he should learn to express logically the contents of his thinking. The new works showed that like mythological thinking, children begin by giving animist or artificial explanations of physical reality before using mechanical explanations. Finally, research was also undertaken at that time on the forms and characteristics of the moral thinking and moral behaviour of children. In the work on moral judgement, which came out of this research and was published in 1932, we see once again how Piaget made use of concepts found in sociology and law, such as objective responsibility and heteronomy, and in turn clarified them.

The above remarks show that the principal work in psychology achieved by Piaget between 1920 and 1935 had to do with the distinctive characteristics of the thoughts of a child compared to those of an adult. However, one finds from the beginning a preference for an explanation based on a form of structuralism rather than on distinctive traits. Thus one can discover in *Le jugement et le raisonnement chez l'enfant*[7] an attempt to explain the traits of thinking of the child by its inability to recognize logical connections. Although Piaget already had an inkling of what the explanation might be, it was not until the mid-1930s, while he was working in logic, that the key would be found. We shall return to this question later, but for the moment it is necessary to see what was at the core of Piaget's interests: questions about the foundations of intellectual and moral thought, and particularly the question of epistemology. Note that the births of Jacqueline, Lucienne, and Laurent Piaget between 1925 and 1931 gave the young psychologist the possibility of carrying out research based on 'the logic of action' (intelligence before language); meanwhile, nearly a dozen years would pass before a complete theory of sensorimotor intelligence could be drawn from the observations of his children (a theory of such richness that it is still relevant to cognitive sciences).

The philosophy of science and epistemology

Although from 1920 to 1935 Piaget's work seemed to be concentrated primarily on genetic psychology, he was still partly engaged, as we have seen, in working in biology and in epistemology, as well as in moral philosophy and the philosophy of science. He was particularly interested in reflections on values and how they are anchored in reality.

The manner in which Piaget formulated his questions about the nature of cognitive life reflected his training both in the philosophy of science and in epistemology. Here he was faced with a delicate question. The goal he had fixed for himself in 1918 had been to construct a scientific epistemology. Yet the epistemology he had already learned in the French school of the philosophy of science was still considered a branch of philosophy, in spite of the use of the historical method. His principal concern then in the 1920s was to show through his own work in genetic psychology, and from examples of this school, that epistemology was indeed a science as it uses scientific methods and as its problems correspond to similar problems found in genetic psychology and biology. His first two works on epistemology defended the view that it was a science in the strictest sense. The first was a critical review of a book by Brunschvicg on physical causality;[8] the second was the text of the inaugural lecture Piaget delivered on being appointed to the chair of philosophy of science and psychology at the University of Neuchâtel in 1925.[9] Lecturing on the philosophy of science allowed him to accelerate considerably his own training in epistemology. Furthermore, it allowed him to participate actively in the area by way of discovering and proposing some ideas that would be fundamental in genetic epistemology. One of these ideas, which he defended for the first time in 1929, posits the view of two distinct directions in scientific thought: One is oriented towards mathematics and the subject; the other towards physical explanations and exterior reality. But with Piaget there is never the question of an absolute beginning, or of a definite end. The origin of this essential thesis, which would be considerably enlarged upon and refined in later works in epistemology (namely, in the studies of awareness done in the 1970s), is to be found in the circularity of the sciences and the subject/object circle shown by Piaget in *Recherche*. The difference is that at the end of the 1920s the author had a much better knowledge of contemporary sciences, of their problems, of their object of study, and of their conceptual framework. That which had been a rude intuition became 'empirically' founded knowledge. The fact remains, however, that in light of what would emerge in the 1940s, the epistemological writings of the 1920s appear as prologues or drafts.

Moral and philosophical reflections

In the 1920s and at the beginning of the 1930s, Piaget's work, though original, was not yet a moving force in psychological research, as it would later become once its scope and value found world recognition. This work was still similar to what was being done in the human sciences, i.e., a broad rather than a specific approach to the subject. This approach required the researcher, whether in psychology or sociology, etc., to have a passing familiarity with neighbouring fields. Furthermore, Piaget shared with contemporary intellectuals the disquiet generated by the first forms of the globalization of geopolitical problems, as well as by the rise in sciences, such as biology and psychoanalysis, that called traditional ethical and religious values into question. This disquiet, coupled with his interdisciplinary curiosity, drove the author to look for answers to these ethical and religious problems from the scientific knowledge he had acquired both in biology and in psychology. Piaget's interest in a variety of subjects as well as in science and ethics can be seen in some of his articles. In 1923, for example, he published the text of a lecture on 'La psychologie et les valeurs religieuses' given at Sainte-Croix the preceding year. He found in psychology facts that he could use to support religious values such as love, but not necessarily faith. He especially wrote articles at the beginning of the 1930s that drew from psychology and epistemology to defend, while modifying by way of the principle of the circle of sciences, a solution inspired by the immanent philosophy of Brunschvicg, the philosopher who certainly had the strongest influence on his final choice of a philosophical, religious, and ethical stance. Lastly, *The Moral Judgement of the Child*,[10] which applies the type of enquiry carried out on the level of speculative judgement and reasoning, shows that this way of articulating philosophical reflection and scientific method is effective for moral matters as well as for cognitive ones.

1935–1955: The discovery of the structures of intelligence and the consequences for epistemology

The stage we are about to discuss is doubtless that in which Piaget had the greatest effect on the twentieth century. His major role in the important years of psychology that marked the last century would have been amply assured by the work of this period, which can be divided into four principal sections complemented by ancillary studies. The four sections begin with studies in logic, followed by research on the development of sensorimotor intelligence, then research on the operational structure of thought, and lastly, the link between these psychological studies and studies in genetic epistemology. The ancillary work focused mainly on the psychology of perception. With the exception of writings on the epistemology of sociology and of biology, and marginal writings on pedagogy, we notice the almost total absence of work on subjects other than psychology and genetic epistemology, as well as logic, the last treated not only as an object of study for the psychology of thought but also as an instrument for modelling intellectual structures.

Logic

As of the 1970s and perhaps even earlier, if one had asked Piaget whether he had worked in the field of scientific logic, he would have probably said no.[11] But if one looks at the work dating from the 1930s and 1940s and the historical and intellectual context of the time, it is clear that at the beginning, at least, the author considered this work to fall within his field. In 1935, at the time of doing psychological research on the child's development of logical operations, Piaget discovered in logic groups of operations that, though similar to numerical groups, only partially adhered to arithmetical laws.

The reasons for his interest in the operational structures of logical thinking, which was the starting point for his discoveries in logic as science, are evident. First, as a biologist, the study of forms or structures and their origins is naturally at the heart of one's enquiries. Then, thanks to his lectures and to his friends in mathematics and physics, he was aware of the concept of structure in mathematics and in physics that was then on the rise. This concept was becoming central both as the formative core of the mathematical edifice (according to the thesis of basic principles of 'Nicolas Bourbaki') and as the fundamental element of physical explanation.

Piaget had been fortunate in choosing to study the forms of logico-mathematical thinking (as well as the forms of moral thinking) and their sources in action, and he knew how to benefit from this choice. An outstanding scientific breakthrough, in a way comparable to Einstein's discovery of the theories of special relativity and of general relativity in physics, consisted of three ingredients: an object having a structure, a method adequate to examine it, and finally the growing awareness of this sense of structure in mathematics and in physics. Piaget had the genius to bring it all together. In order to do that he had to overcome a sizeable hurdle: Totally occupied by the problem of the foundations of mathematics and the need to formalize them, logicians in the 1930s showed absolutely no interest in seeking logical structures, even though the work at the end of the nineteenth and the beginning of the twentieth centuries should have put them on this track; whereas, while studying the functioning of operational logic in a child in parallel to studying functioning of arithmetical operations, Piaget could not help but see the need to use the tools of structural modelling, given how close the result of the first analysis of these phenomena was to the goal required by an explanation of this kind.[12]

The only problem was that there were no structural models that could be usefully applied to the structures of groupings of logical operations studied by the psychologist. There were no such mathematical entities. They had to be created, which might have appeared to Piaget as a trivial task, because the structures of logical thinking were evidently close to the existing structures of numerical thinking for which models had already been created by mathematicians. Sensing the value and importance of this connection, Piaget could not help but pursue this end. However, what he most certainly did not realize was that this would take him nearly 15 years (to reach a sufficiently acceptable result, at least provisionally for the psychologist, if not for the professional logician). Three books and numerous articles show the effort Piaget put into this modelling work in mathematical logic, which allowed him to uncover and to analyse better how a child and an adolescent think. The first work,[13] published in 1942, describes by way of comparison the mathematical structures underlying classification operations and for drawing logical relation as well as doing arithmetical calculations, operations of which the groupings produce the equilibrium and the reversibility of logical thinking (equilibrium and reversibility had already been established as fundamental characteristics of such thinking in the 1910s and 1920s). The second work is the famous *Traité de logique*,[14] strongly criticized, sometimes positively but more often negatively, by professional logicians. Few have been able to understand the motives that led Piaget to work so many years in a field foreign to his own. Finally, the third work deals with the *256 opérations ternaires de la logique bivalente des propositions*.[15]

The effort this took may seem strange to today's psychologists, but in order to understand it, one must remember that Piaget had been influenced by the empirical/mathematical model prescribed by the highly demanding and advanced science of the day: physics.[16] Judged from this perspective there is little doubt that still today, thanks to this effort, the genetic psychology of the logico-mathematical operations of thought can pride itself on being the only area of psychology that tries to meet the requirements of the rational, and not merely empirical, science of nature. The considerable time spent by Piaget on logic ought not to be minimized. Logic makes up one of the two or three essential aspects of this author's scientific work. It remains now to recall how, equipped with these specifically developed logical tools, Piaget clarified the hidden nature of our intellectual abilities.

Genetic psychology

Between 1935 and 1955 there were two sub-stages in genetic psychology. Piaget's backgrounds in biology and in logic influenced the first step, which deals principally with sensorimotor intelligence and its further development in representational thinking as well as with the construction of the real closely connected to this form of intelligence. The second sub-stage owes its source to the systematic study of the development of universal categories of thinking (time, space, number, chance, etc.) and intellectual operations that underlie them (temporal, spatial, numeric, etc.) in the child and the adolescent. This became the best-known aspect of Piaget's work (although this is often merely a superficial acquaintance with the theory that requires a good knowledge of biological, logical, epistemological, and philosophical aspects of his work in order to be fully understood).

Works as important as *La naissance de l'intelligence*,[17] *La construction du réel*,[18] and *La formation du symbole chez l'enfant*[19] cannot be summarized. Let it be said that the study of sensorimotor intelligence shows how a baby begins building up more and more complex behaviour based on his inherited ability to accommodate and assimilate (i.e. mechanisms of adaptation). Going from habits to the first steps in intelligent behaviour (i.e. coordination of means to reach a goal), the child then accedes in the course of the second year of age to elementary forms of comprehensive intelligence (viz., a primary understanding of how things work and how actions have to be coordinated to reach a goal). With the maturing neurophysiological process and the stimulation of the physical and social world, the baby builds an ever more complex and organized network of behavioural schemas with logic. This network of schemas, including its cognitive elements, forms the groundwork on which thinking will rise, thanks to the use of symbols and icons ('motivated signifiers') and then signs ('conventional signifiers'). However, this twofold development of symbol and sign, connected with sensorimotor intelligence, requires the simultaneous development of a sense of space and of time as well as a sense of an object. The second of the three psychological works by Piaget, which is about the child's conception of reality, is the most biological of the series in its description and analysis of the processes of assimilation and accommodation within the baby's sensorimotor grasp of the world. The second ancillary stage of the work in genetic psychology carried out between 1935 and 1955 is distinct from the first in that the functioning of the intelligence and of thinking – the 'teleonomic' schematic coordination – is no longer, with their genesis and 'anatomy', one of the three privileged objects of psychology. The genetic psychologist is indeed constantly concerned with studying and analysing the logico-mathematical operations of thinking and the mathematical structures and properties of their groupings. This does not mean that intuition, not only mathematical but also biological (in the widest sense of the term), which had been a guiding force for sensorimotor intelligence, was now lost from sight. This mathematical and biological intuition continues to underlie the use of mathematical concepts and is also apparent on the most abstract level to justify the property of reversibility seen in mature thinking, i.e., a thought capable, when necessary, of articulating in a rational way its manner of coping with an object. But now, whether it is a matter of a child's conception of space or of time or a question of arithmetic or of logic, genetic psychological enquiry primarily draws attention to the stages of intellectual growth proper to the child's ability, then of that of the adolescent, to conceive in an operational way realities that go beyond and integrate the world of perception and action. In all these areas, the structural intuition and mathematical knowledge of structures (from Evariste Galois and Felix Klein to Bourbaki) is a tool to reach – in the thought of the child and of the adolescent – partial or complete groupings of operations pertaining to temporal, spatial, or numerical concepts. Complete grouping appears thanks to operational identities such as physical conservation of quantities (substance, weight, volume), or conservation of numbers. Genetic psychological enquiry shows further the two major stages of the constitution of knowledge and operational competences. The first step is a concrete mastery of spatial, temporal, and logico-mathematical operations and notions during their use to grasp the external world. The second step is formal mastery within the thinking process itself (requiring the grouping of superior-type operations) of previously acquired operations with respect to concrete thinking.

If one takes into consideration the studies on the origins of sensorimotor intelligence and the construction of the real that corresponds to it, i.e., the discovery of the organization of sensorimotor actions that also are subject to the laws of structure, one sees that much of the research between 1935 and 1955 led to fundamental results. The first established the three major steps in the development of human intelligence, namely the practical structures of sensorimotor intelligence that lead to a primary mastery of the living reality, then the structures of concrete intelligence allowing a mastery relative to concrete reality, and finally the structures of abstract intelligence used in acts of reflection, which are also themselves relative to the conditions of application, of thinking itself. The second fundamental result demonstrates the integration of groupings of inferior operations into groupings of superior ones. These results, reported in numerous works known to psychologists in the field of intelligence,[20] were of considerable importance not only for psychology but also for epistemology, and in some cases for philosophy as well. They are the basis of the conceptual constructivism that Piaget developed in the last stages of his work, and they offer the first complete empirically founded explanation of the origin and universal value of theoretical reason, of practical reason, and of rational science (this explanation contains the first attempts to solve the problem of the origins of rational forms that had been suggested by the American psychologist James Baldwin and the French philosopher Brunschvicg).

Genetic epistemology

At this point in our summary, we have reached what is probably the heart of Piaget's work: the first and most complete presentation, founded on psychological enquiry and studies in science, of the thesis of genetic epistemology. How is science possible? To this Kantian question, Piaget – influenced by the

intuitions and knowledge gained from the history of science and other informative ideas – would reply that it is due to the place humans occupy in reality,
to the nature of human intelligence, to the mechanisms that allow humans to
construct their intelligence, and to the nature of the science itself. A human is,
above all, a living creature, i.e., a complex entity that not only is self-contained
(self-preserving and self-creating, or in the current idiom 'autopoïetique') but
also is an organism interacting with his environment. This we know from
biology. But a human is likewise a psychological creature, gifted with an
intellect, which is the outgrowth of the human biological form. The genetic
characteristics of the intellect are the same as those of the living creature:
self-contained yet environmentally interactive. Both the biological organism
and the intellect are fed by the very world to which they give form and from
which they arose (the former directly, the latter by way of the former). As
suggested by the sciences of life and of thought, neither of these forms can be
accidentally constructed. Both the human organism and intellect exist only to
the extent that they are subject or inclined to be subject to a universal constraint of a balance between whole and parts. In accord with these constraints
and with the constitutive mechanisms of intelligence, universally applicable
forms and ideas are thereby constructed. Building on this, these forms and
ideas conform to the general mathematical structure of biological reality,
which is the source and the basis of psychological life that gives shape to the
reality to which the intellect and its forms apply. Science, finally, as its history
shows and as results of psychology demonstrate, has not fallen out of some
sort of platonic sky (platonic epistemology is probably the only one apart
from constructivism to provide an acceptable interpretation, however 'extra-
scientific', of the origin of rational forms). Science, like the representative
intelligence of the child and then of the adolescent, is the fruit of human
thinking, first drawing support from it and then in turn nourishing it.
Furthermore, science also has the two characteristics found in living creatures: internal cohesion and external openness. The mathematical thinking of
mathematicians is essentially fuelled, as with the child, by its own cohesion.
The tools and ways of its progress are found within its own structure. Coherence is also the guiding principle of physical thinking (in the widest sense
of the term 'physical'), a major part of which is logico-mathematical thinking. The second characteristic of openness in the external world comes
from its biological structure. In order to be more than exclusively a logico-
mathematical thought there needs to be a connection with the world: a
reciprocal connection built on the 'information' obtained from the world and
from the sense it makes of that information. The *Introduction à l'épistemologie génétique*[21] aims at highlighting the circles and the processes of adjustment
that connect the biological organism and physical reality, thought and reality.
These circles and adjustments explain or clarify how rational sciences are
possible, and how they depend on one another with regard to their specific
objectives and to the fundamental problems they seek to resolve.

The author concentrated on the epistemology of mathematics in the first part of this work, on physical knowledge in the second, and on biological, psychological, and sociological knowledge in the third, all of which bear witness to the exchanges Piaget had maintained with scientists of the first half of the last century. One understands without difficulty that, given the reputation Piaget had already established in the psychology of intelligence, this work was classed among the major undertakings of its day and was readily received by well-known fellow researchers in philosophy, mathematics, logic, biology, psychology, and sociology, who contributed to it either in the short or in the long term. In the last decades this work proved to be more and more a collective effort by a wide range of researchers. Before describing the work of the International Centre of Genetic Epistemology, where this collaboration took place, it is necessary to remember all that Piaget accomplished in the years between 1945 and 1955. Not only did he achieve the goal he had set for himself as an adolescent and on which he had focused in the 1920s, he also turned to new ground and, with the help of colleagues, undertook a study in the mechanisms of perception.

The psychology of perception

If one can justify all the research done on the origins of cognitive and moral ideas and thinking, one may find the time spent on the mechanisms of perception more difficult to explain. However, the results gained here shed light on the specificity of the structures of intelligence compared with those of perception, which are neither as stable nor as 'compositional' as the former. Two fundamental reasons governed this side enquiry. First there was Gestalt psychology, psychology of forms, which was a different concept from that of Piaget's yet had been equally empirically and theoretically founded. Gestalt psychology sees the forms of thinking against the background of the theory of perception that it had formulated as a result of studies on sight, hearing, etc. Intelligence, like perception, emerges from a non-historical organization of the contents of perception or of thought, processes obeying field laws. This theory is relatively close to that of Piaget and those working in genetic psychology, so it was important for Piaget to show the difference between the structures of perception and those of thought. The second reason comes from epistemology, not psychology: Perception was at the centre of empiricist explanations of knowledge. Knowledge thus became little more than a reflection of the external world, produced by the senses of sight, hearing, etc., whereas one of the principal tenets of genetic psychology is to show that the key player in forming intelligence is action and not perception (with 'perceptive activities' included in what we mean by action). The genetic psychological approach provided researchers in 'the mechanism of perception' with a rebuttal of the empiricist and Gestalt theses by showing the importance of 'perceptive activities' in the constitution of perceiving itself and by demonstrating the effect of the development of intelligence on perception. That being said, let us now briefly look at the penultimate stage in the evolution of Piaget's work, which can be characterized as being principally an extension and a confirmation of the results achieved between 1935 and 1955.

1955–1965: The consolidation and extension of genetic psychology and epistemology

The International Centre for Genetic Epistemology (ICGE) was founded in Geneva in 1955–56. From that time on, Piaget placed genetic epistemology at the centre of his research. Genetic psychological methods that had served him till then in developing genetic psychology and in resolving epistemological problems would now essentially serve in the epistemological work. However, that does not mean that Piaget had now lost interest in psychology. On the contrary, he gave a lot of time to it, but it was Vinh-Bang and especially Bärbel Inhelder that, while collaborating with Piaget, led research in this field (Vinh-Bang continued the work on perception; Inhelder carried out research on image, then memory, on mental functions whose psycho-genetical analysis would demonstrate their relations with intelligence). On the other hand, if the studies undertaken at the ICGE served above all to resolve epistemological problems, their results had no less value for psychology because they also shed light on certain conceptions and intellectual competences of the child and the adolescent. Even if these conceptions and competencies are examined in very particular contexts, they manifest themselves in common activities of daily life.

From the point of view of the evolution of Piaget's work, the collaborative effort, and not only the result, is perhaps the most interesting aspect. Besides confirming and complementing earlier results, such collaborative work allowed Piaget to stay abreast of new ideas in the various sciences included in his work in genetic epistemology. These sciences, of course, were useful sources for better understanding the intellectual reality of the child and the adolescent who were being studied at the ICGE. During these years, Piaget became aware of the first works in artificial intelligence, which opened a new field of study for Inhelder, Cellérier, and their collaborators at the centre in Geneva in the 1960s. It was also thanks to the visitors at ICGE that Piaget revived the earlier view, as much biological (functional) as mathematical, of psychological reality, and that, perhaps, he returned to his earlier studies in biology of the adaptation of various limnaea in lakes. The revival of this latter work was doubtless an attempt to confront once again the Darwinian problem of the transformation of species (i.e., establishing a primordial place for ontogenetic biological adaptation in the explanation of the origins of new species). The presence of logicians among the guests at ICGE was an impetus to form questions about the models of forms of thinking that precede operational competences, using for this endeavour original tools delivered by new forms of logic. Finally, having philosophers and psychologists at hand defending different, even opposing, theses to that of Piaget's, which, following Brunschvicg, accorded a privileged place to the subject in the constitution of knowledge, inspired originality in research and occasioned fellow researchers at the centre to refine their respective arguments – even to come to agreement on genetic epistemological theses.[22]

If the epistemological work done between 1955 and 1965 attests above all to the value of collective work in making genetic epistemology a science in the fullest sense of the term, the research carried out and added to work done previously on the development of the major categories of thought, such as time, was of equal importance. Moreover, the research done with Inhelder on the image and the memory, or the thesis of H. Sinclair (a close collaborator of Piaget's) on the development of language, both completed and challenged the observations made on the relations between perception and intelligence. In other words, if image, memory (in the narrowest sense of the term), and language are necessary tools for the functioning of representational intelligence, and can by that fact contribute through their own properties to the subject's cognitive functioning, their characteristics, their mode of functioning, are likewise partially determined by the level of development of that intelligence. One can see that, apart from the contributions made by logic and cybernetics to the relationship and the development of cognitive structure, there are no truly new ideas in the general way of conceiving intelligence and knowledge. Things would change in 1965, inasmuch as new research programmes would be undertaken that aimed less this time at confirming and making known the psychological and epistemological solutions reached already between 1935 and 1955, and more at resolving either new problems or those left hanging from earlier research.

1965–1980: The study of physical causality, broadening of the theoretical framework, and researches on mechanisms of constructing biological and psychological forms

Three major paths of research were pursued in Piaget's last period. The first concerns the broadening of the logical and mathematical framework on which were based epistemological problems relative to mathematical thinking and to children's intellectual competence. This enlarged framework enriched the way in which one looks on a child's intellectual life. Combinatorial logic, intentional logic, and the mathematical theory of categories were thus implicated in better identifying the logico-mathematical forms of thinking, particularly in the steps preceding the acquisition of specific operational competence of concrete thinking. The second path led towards the study of physical causality, a study that, in the three preceding decades, had been somewhat neglected to the benefit of that of the categories of logico-mathematical thinking, or 'mixed' categories (substance, weight, volume, time, space, movement, chance). Numerous enquiries, psychological as much as historical, promoted the thesis according to which causal explanation is the result of an attribution to physical reality of the transformative power of logico-mathematical operations (a thesis that takes up and enriches the philosopher

Emile Meyerson's opposition to positivism). Finally, the third path – the study of the 'mechanisms of growth' – was the newest in that it was the object of concern that had changed. Here the researcher's primary interest was no longer focused on the categories and operations of thought but, rather, on the mechanisms by which the categories and operations were built. This third area of study was also part of the epistemological thesis Piaget defended: epistemological constructivism. Considerable effort was made at this time to lend support to a basic solution of this thesis with respect to evolutionary biology. Furthermore, this period was also one in which exemplary care was taken to show the connection between biology and knowledge. Philosophically, Piaget was distancing himself from scientific philosophy in order to accord to philosophy the highest place among the functions of intellectual activity: the search for wisdom, i.e., a determination and a value choice that give sense to human life and guide action.

It is hardly possible to recount here the very rich collection of solutions that came out of these three directions of research. I shall settle for evoking the study of the mechanisms of construction of what is new. In fact, while in earlier stages the universality of knowledge (as well as the universality of moral forms) had been researched more from the perspective of the genesis of 'constituted reason' than from that of the processes of 'constituting reason', in the last two decades Piaget would search above all else in the mechanisms of construction to explain why reason is one and universal.

Constructivism

Towards the end of the 1940s and at the beginning of the 1950s, while Piaget was formulating a primary general synthesis of the results achieved in genetic psychology and the problems raised by genetic epistemology, two notions struck him as capable of explaining the origins of structured and structuring organizations of action and then of thought: 'regulation' and 'abstraction'. The first, which was to see a remarkable boom thanks to the development of cybernetics, seems to characterize the steps leading up to operational competence, in other words, the 'intermediary stages'. During these stages, the child appears to waver between opposing answers when faced with questions requiring access to operations to have complete resolution. 'There is more water in this vase because it is taller; or no, there is more water in this one because it is wider . . .', etc. The second notion, already mentioned by philosophers like Brunschvicg, comes from the way in which logico-mathematical knowledge at one stage of development seems to grow out of knowledge acquired at an earlier stage. More precisely, what is key here is the way thinking operations appear to depend on prior competences acquired on the level of action (e.g., the groupings of concrete operations abstracted from the groupings of sensorimotor actions). The notion of abstraction, next to that of generalization, had long been used in the tradition of empiricist explanations of the origins and genesis of knowledge. But what psychological facts about the development of logico-mathematical intelligence reveal is a different form of abstraction. In this case, abstraction does not have to do with the physical properties of the object 'given' to perception; rather, it has to do with the organization of actions, of which the origin is internal to the subject, and which finds its roots in the biological organization.

Until about 1960 Piaget seemed satisfied with the mass, non-differentiated view of the notions of regulation and abstraction inasmuch as it was a matter of the genesis of the forms of thought. As of the end of the 1960s and the beginning of the 1970s, though, his attention – like that of his collaborators – was ever more drawn to a closer analysis of what is involved in the passage from one stage to another in intellectual development and in the building of knowledge. This shift in attention from the product to the mechanisms of production, so to speak, had a number of consequences. First of all, the notions of regulation and abstraction were no longer considered as responses but as problems. The application of the method of genetic psychology to the examination of processes of regulation and, especially, of abstraction allows one to differentiate regulations at different levels and shows how an abstraction beginning with the order contained in the action is an abstraction that reflects; i.e., that the organization at the end stage reflects on the organization at the outset of the process and is the result of a process of thinking (or of biological and psychological activities at the origin of thought) – a process that brings about a new organization that is more powerful than that at the start. Thanks to the greater attention given to the notion of abstraction, it seems that there is or there could be mutual support between reflecting abstraction and empirical abstraction (founded on empiricist epistemology and associative psychology, redefined within the framework of the constructivist concept). Finally, it seems that the process of reflecting abstraction operates on a more local level, already discernible in structural progress in the development of sensorimotor intelligence (and perhaps even earlier, at the level of biological adaptation, as Piaget suggested in his last biological texts). Complementary studies[23] added to these results by showing how reflecting abstraction works with the processes of 'synthetic generalization' and 'completing generalization', the study of which points out how they produce new cognitive forms, which have the particularity of being simultaneously (1) greater in extension (like the 'empiricist generalization' of empiricist epistemologies, they refer to classes of objects that are more extended than the forms about which they are built), and (2) greater in 'comprehension' (i.e., their operatory power and the way they can transform reality are more powerful than those of the cognitive forms on which they are built). These studies on 'reflecting abstraction' and on 'constructive generalization', as well as other research bearing on the inherent characteristics of the construction of ever more powerful cognitive structures (as, for example, openness towards the new possibilities – in French: 'nouveaux possibles' – proper to each stage of development of human intelligence in the child, and also in science), allowed Piaget to formulate a new 'theory' about the equilibration of structures that explains the constitution and the progression of thought and natural sciences, as well as that of thought and logico-mathematics.

Conclusion

The reader might find the preceding remarks (and the most recent writings of Piaget himself) rather abstract. Nevertheless, it is important to see that for the author of the new theory of the equilibration of cognitive structures, such abstraction is not for nothing. Not only is it the result of reflections and experiments performed at the ICGE in the 1970s, but it also comes from the quasi-totality of intuitions forged, theses suggested, and results obtained during the five preceding decades, to which one must add certain empirical results, intuitions, and theses achieved in the 1910s. In reality, Piaget's thought is neither formal nor abstract. In its manner of proceeding it is eminently concrete thinking that patiently and obstinately starts from biological, psychological, and epistemological observations, both spontaneous and induced. These observations were then classed according to underlying forms, highlighting their relationships, in order to study with an almost equal patience (almost, for the time was recorded) the passage of one form, biological or cognitive, to another, and to construct, when that seemed necessary, logico-mathematical tools able to model forms observed in nature. This manner of proceeding, in a large measure comparable to that practised by the great naturalists of the nineteenth century (Darwin included), which is reflected both in the title and in the sense of one of the last works published (*Morphismes et catégories*[24]), led the author to a theory, itself organic, of intelligence and knowledge. In order to be understood, this theory requires that one should have an idea of the whole in which the individual parts of the work provide mutual support for (and are in resonance with) one another. United they give sense to the ways by which intelligence and science create a universe and logico-mathematical instruments, ever more sophisticated and synthetic, for an intersubjective, objective, and universal explanation and understanding of the physical, biological, psychological, and social world, as well as creating the necessary intellectual competence to construct a universally shared ethic. The researcher and thinker of the 1970s retained the inquisitive spirit of the adolescent and young man of the 1910s. That means that there was not only a certain continuity in the manner of studying realities, but also a permanent 'religious' concern, in the sense that the adolescent had set for himself the requirement of finding a unifying concept of life and of thought, a concept able to unite beings in a community of spirit and existence without denying them their individuality. Briefly, finding the 'reason of reason' with the aim of answering theoretical and practical questions was perhaps the deep-seated motive that drove Piaget, from his youth to his venerable old age, to follow the path of research of which science and philosophy are, in the end, the only judges.

Notes

1 Henceforth, the term 'empirical' will be used in a general manner to refer to empirical research that either proves or disproves a judgement or a concept about the nature or the properties of an object or a reality. The term 'experimental' will be used when empirically corroborating or invalidating is part of the experimental method, understood in the narrowest sense (control of variables, etc.).

2 This solution, revised and clarified, will strongly be reasserted four decades later in the book significantly entitled *Le comportement moteur de l'évolution*, Paris: Gallimard, 1976. [English translation: *Behaviour and evolution*. New York: Pantheon Books, 1978.]

3 J. Piaget (1926). *The language and thought of the child*. London: Routledge & Kegan Paul.

4 J. Piaget (1924). *Le jugement et le raisonnement chez l'enfant*. Neuchâtel & Paris: Delachaux & Niestlé. [English translation: *Judgment and reasoning in the child*. Totowa, NJ: Littlefield Adams, 1969.]

5 J. Piaget (1972). *The child's conception of the world*. Totowa, NJ: Littlefield Adams.

6 J. Piaget (1927). *La causalité physique chez l'enfant*. Paris: Alcan. [English translation: *The child's conception of physical causality*. Totowa, NJ: Littlefield Adams, 1972.]

7 Piaget (1924), op. cit.

8 J. Piaget (1924). Etude critique: L'expérience humaine et la causalité physique de L. Brunschvicg. *Journal de psychologie normale et pathologique, 21*, 273–304.

9 J. Piaget (1925). Psychologie et critique de la connaissance. *Archives de psychologie, 19*, 193–220.

10 J. Piaget (1932). *The moral judgement of the child*. London: Routledge & Kegan Paul.

11 Cf. Preface to the 1972 edition of *Traité de logique* of 1949.

12 The reader is advised to consult the convincing article on this point: Les relations d'égalité résultant de l'addition et de la soustraction logiques constituent-elles un groupe? *L'enseignement mathématique*, 1937, *36*, 99–108.

13 J. Piaget (1942). *Classes, relations et nombres: Essai sur les groupements de la logistique et sur la réversibilité de la pensée*. Paris: J. Vrin.

14 J. Piaget (1949). *Traité de logique: Essai de logique opératoire*. Paris: Armon & Colin.

15 J. Piaget (1952). *Essai sur les transformations des opérations logiques: les 256 opérations ternaires de la logique bivalente des propositions*. Paris: Presses Universitaires de France. In the preface of this work is to be found an explicit comparison of modelling work in logic for psychologists (i.e., 'logistique opératoire') with modelling work done in mathematical physics.

16 This similarity between, on the one hand, mathematics and knowledge of physical objects, and, on the other, mathematics and knowledge of psychological reality, seems to be corroborated by a similar capacity of mathematics to anticipate, on one side, the discovery of physical structures, and, on the other, the discovery of psychological structures. For example, in psychology, the purely formal work of Piaget in the science of logic has to theoretically discover the formal mathematical structure of the INRC group, before the empirical discovery of INRC structure in the propositional thought of adolescents!

17 J. Piaget (1936). *La naissance de l'intelligence chez l'enfant*. Neuchâtel & Paris. Delachaux & Niestlé. [English translation: *The origins of intelligence in children*. New York: International Universities Press, 1952.]

18 J. Piaget (1937). *La construction du réel chez l'enfant*. Neuchâtel & Paris: Delachaux & Niestlé. [English translation: *The construction of reality in the child*. London: Routledge & Kegan Paul, 1955.]

19 J. Piaget (1945). *La formation du symbole chez l'enfant.* Neuchâtel & Paris: Delachaux & Niestlé. [English translation: *Play, dreams and imitation in childhood.* New York: W.W. Norton.]

20 See, for example, *Le développement des quantités physiques chez l'enfant.* Neuchâtel & Paris: Delachaux & Niestlé, 1941 [English translation: *The child's construction of quantities: Conservation and atomism.* London: Routledge & Kegan Paul, 1974]; and *La genèse du nombre chez l'enfant.* Neuchâtel & Paris: Delachaux & Niestlé, 1941 [English translation: *The child's conception of number.* London: Routledge & Kegan Paul, 1952]. The first of these was co-authored with Bärbel Inhelder, the second with Aline Szeminska. These books show how Piaget's work was greatly supported by a number of collaborators, in particular Inhelder and Szeminska.

21 J. Piaget (1950). *Introduction à l'épistemologie génétique* (3 vols.). Paris: Presses Universitaires de France. [English translation: *Genetic epistemology.* New York & London: Columbia University Press, 1970.]

22 The work co-authored by Piaget and the logician Evert W. Beth, or the collective writings on the apprenticeship and the development of logical mathematic structures, to which authors such as the empiricist psychologist D. E. Berlyne contributed, are revelatory of the effort at coordinating points of view and at theoretical clarification practised at ICGE, an effort conforming to the Piagetian theory of intelligence.

23 See Ducret for the list in order of completion [cf. J. Piaget (2006). Reason (translation and commentary by Leslie Smith). *New Ideas in Psychology, 24,* 1–29.]: J. J. Ducret (2000). *Jean Piaget 1968–1979: Une décennie de recherches sur les mécanismes de construction cognitive.* Geneva: Service de la recherche en éducation, Cahier 7.

24 J. Piaget, G. Henriques, & E. Ascher (1990). *Morphismes et catégories.* Neuchâtel & Paris: Delachaux & Niestlé, 1990. [English translation: *Morphisms and categories, comparing and transforming.* Hillsdale, NJ: Lawrence Erlbaum Associates, Inc., 1992.]. Since the French version of this chapter, a new book has been published [G. Henriques (2004). *La formation des raisons.* Brussels: Mardaga, 2004] that presents the results of the last research launched by Piaget in 1979.

14 The reception of Piaget's early ideas in the Soviet Union

René van der Veer

In his preface to the combined Russian edition of *The Language and Thought of the Child* and *Judgement and Reasoning in the Child*, Piaget[1] wrote that he was grateful to his Soviet colleagues for their willingness to organize 'a series of investigations which aim to complement and correct the work we succeeded to carry out in Geneva'. He added that the work of his Soviet colleagues would be useful to tease apart the respective influences of individual and social factors in child development. As he himself had been forced to work in only one social milieu, Piaget writes, he had not been able to solve this methodological question.

> That is why it is such a great pleasure for me to have such skilled colleagues, such as several Soviet psychologists, who study children in a social environment which is entirely different from the one I myself studied. Nothing can be more useful for science than this rapprochement of the investigations of Russian psychologists with the work done in other countries.[2]

When Piaget wrote his preface, he probably did not know that his Soviet colleagues had set themselves a much more ambitious goal than the one he suggested. For a number of years they had been replicating Piaget's studies not merely with the aim of 'complementing and correcting' his work and studying the contribution of a different social environment in child development, but in order to refute Piaget's theoretical interpretation of the facts, his methodology, and his epistemology. The results of this research were little known in the West,[3] and Piaget's hope that his Soviet colleagues would join forces in the development of a new child psychology was entirely justified, although perhaps slightly naive. He could not know that countless attempts were being undertaken by his Soviet colleagues to undermine his whole conception of the child's mind; that he had become – at least in writing – their principal theoretical opponent; and that ideological developments would make any future rapprochement between Russian and Western science impossible. The reception of Jean Piaget's writings in the Soviet Union was destined to proceed along the lines of ideological categories such as 'bourgeois science', 'cosmopolitism', and 'capitalism'. Rather than, or in addition to, giving us a picture of the role of the social environment in child development, the Soviet scientists provided us with a picture of the role of the social environment in the production of scientific knowledge.

In order to be able to get a fair impression of the reception of Jean Piaget's early works in the Soviet Union, we would do well to distinguish between, on the one hand, the assessment of his writings in the scientific press in the form of reviews, critical essays, etc., and, on the other, the factual use made of his work. In the former Soviet Union the evaluation of psychological theories in scientific journals was always to a greater or lesser extent dictated by ideological motives, and Piaget's work forms no exception to this rule. In fact, it has been shown[4] that in the 1930s Piaget came to be seen as one of the many decadent bourgeois psychologists whose work needed to be ignored, and that as recently as 1949 his work was branded as 'a militant attempt to depict child intelligence in an absolutely distorted form'. However, explicit condemnations of a researcher's views in the scientific and public press might well go hand in glove with abundant use of this very researcher's ideas in scientific practice, and in the case of Piaget it can be convincingly argued that researchers such as Blonsky, Vygotsky, Zankov, and various members of the Kharkov school of psychology[5] made ample and fruitful use of many of Piaget's seminal ideas.[6] Let us proceed, then, to an overview of the way Piaget's works were received in the written press both in the 1920s and 1930s and in our time.

The assessment of Piaget's early ideas: Recent views

Until quite recently Russian books on the history or theory of psychology presented a picture of Jean Piaget's work that was rather one-sided and uniform, and it may be instructive to have a brief look at several of these views set forth by leading Russian psychologists. Incidentally, not all of the potentially relevant authors consider it necessary to deal with Piaget's views in any detail; Petrovsky,[7] for example, in his book on the history of psychology, makes no mention of Piaget at all. However, it is fair to say that the majority of the leading Russian psychologists one way or another reflected on the meaning of Piaget's work. In so doing, they naturally built on each other's ideas and, as mentioned above, could hardly neglect the prevailing ideological views.

Among the more recent Soviet reactions to Piaget's work we should definitely single out the critique voiced by Pyotr Gal'perin and Daniil El'konin, two of the leading representatives of the cultural–historical school founded by Vygotsky. In their afterword to the Russian translation of Flavell's *The Developmental Psychology of Jean Piaget*,[8] Gal'perin and El'konin presented one of the most thoughtful and extensive Soviet criticisms of Piaget's early and later views. The authors express their happiness with a number of Piaget's ideas (e.g., the idea that external objective actions are the basis of cognitive development, the distinction between the moving forces and the

structures of thinking, the obviously dialectical picture given of child development) and claim they feel very close to some of Piaget's conceptions, but
they add that because of this very affinity they are saddened and surprised by
several of his concepts which in their view explain nothing and lead him and
his readers into 'scholastic debris'.[9] Gal'perin and El'konin are particularly
dissatisfied with the concepts of adaptation, accommodation, assimilation,
and equilibration, which they find utterly vague and empty. In their view,
such terms are only applicable in a very broad sense, but exactly then they
become rather empty, mere truisms in fact, and can hardly explain anything.
They also reject the use of a biological concept such as adaptation for
explanatory purposes because it disregards a difference between human
beings and animals that they regard as fundamental. The difference is, very
broadly speaking, that humans adjust the environment to themselves by
making use of tools whereas animals are forced to adapt to the environment.
Here the authors are, on the one hand, merely restating a fundamental tenet
of Marxist anthropology that contributed to turning Russian psychology
into Soviet psychology. However, it should not be overlooked on the other
hand that Gal'perin himself developed a theory in which the differences
between animal and human mental functioning are conceptualized in very
subtle ways.[10]

For similar reasons Gal'perin and El'konin criticize the concept of equilibrium. In their view, the concept of equilibrium is not applicable to human
cognition. It is a physical term that has meaning only when one is talking
about physical forces. However, in the case of human cognition we are talking about persons who satisfy certain needs. The satisfaction of a certain
need (such as curiosity) can temporarily end the child's investigative process,
but the state then reached is in no way comparable to that of a physical
equilibrium. One obvious difference, the authors argue, is that in human
cognition we cannot talk about forces of equal strength that balance each
other. Rather, what happens is that certain forces (such as curiosity) lose
strength or even temporarily disappear. Gal'perin and El'konin argue that
the use of such physical concepts is unfortunate as they remain mere
metaphors without explanatory power, which might lead us to accept a
mechanistic model of mind. Fortunately, as the authors say, in his concrete
psychological investigations Piaget followed his 'amazing feeling for psychological reality'.

The authors regard Piaget's logical characterizations of the developmental
stages as hardly more satisfactory. In their view, logic cannot be the ultimate
criterion of thinking, nor can the level of formal–operational thought be
the highest level attainable. What is important in thinking, Gal'perin and
El'konin argue, is organized knowledge of the subject area and the ability to
orient in the task conditions. The formal–operational thinking of adolescents
is still far from that level and, consequently, formal operations cannot be the
ideal end level nor the sole criterion to judge thought acts. In this connection,
they raise the issue of wisdom as a level of thinking that is broader and higher
than mere formal–logical thinking.

Piaget's formal–logical characterization of intellectual development is even less suitable to explain the transition from one stage to the next. Gal'perin and El'konin argue that no intrinsic, quasi-logical laws can fully account for the development of thinking. What propels the child's intellectual development is instruction – intellectual demands put on the child. Gal'perin and El'konin point out that two factors are relevant in this context. First, the child's attempts to acquaint himself with the surrounding world proceed via the adult. Second, the child's orienting activity is controlled by the satisfaction or reinforcement of his needs. Reinforcement being a conservative force, one must ask what changes the direction of the child's orienting activity. One way or another every child eventually learns about the difference between volume and height in Piaget's jar problem. According to Gal'perin and El'konin, this happens because outside the laboratory other people will implicitly or explicitly explain what the matter is. This fact is denied by Piaget, who claims that education can do no more than follow development. But this pedagogical pessimism is based on the imperfect form of instruction we know now. Against this position, Gal'perin and El'konin argue that intellectual development is not predetermined by some intrinsic laws but called into life and guided by the requirements of the milieu. The child is, consequently, in need of active guidance; he has to be taught how to think. But this whole process of teaching remains behind the curtains of Piaget's experiments. Why the child suddenly begins to take more dimensions or perspectives into account remains unclear. According to the authors, this was partly due to the cross-sectional approach adopted by Piaget. The shortcomings of this approach (i.e., its inability to lay bare the genuine longitudinal development of the child's capacities) were already pointed out by Vygotsky. What also played a negative role was that researchers often did no more than vary the form of pedagogical influence and then registered the results, which they subsequently explained in terms of the pupils' alleged (in)attention, (dis)-interest, and (lack of) capabilities. According to Gal'perin and El'konin, terms such as interest and attention explain nothing and are merely means to hide our ignorance. Even Vygotsky's concept of the zone of proximal development, which was one way of conceptualizing what happens in the process of instruction, remained vague about its actual mechanism. Piaget's negative attitude towards instruction, then, was based on the inadequate teaching methods of his contemporary schooling. Incidentally, when Piaget met Gal'perin in Moscow he told him that his own view of the role of education in development was based on real, actual education whereas Gal'perin's theory merely dealt with education as it is theoretically possible in some imaginary world. Gal'perin is said to have replied to this that what is actual is merely a particular case of what is possible.

The authors then proceed to present Gal'perin's well-known method of the stepwise formation of mental acts[11] as a viable alternative for present-day teaching methods; they claim that this lays bare the mechanism of the internalization of new mental acts in the process of instruction. They fulminate against allowing the method of trial and error to be used by the pupil in the school setting as this approach results from insufficient orientation in the task conditions, from the lack of a plan of action. They claim that using Gal'perin's method they managed to teach six- to seven-year-old children to solve tasks that were on the adolescent level. Moreover, development was not merely speeded up but the children actually skipped levels of development – a claim that is not, however, substantiated in their essay.[12] Of course, the authors admit, this does not mean that in their view development *coincides* with instruction, but it does mean that instruction leads to development. It does mean, or so the authors argue, that development is possible only if learning and teaching take place. Humans develop only when they learn. The conditions for the transition from pre-operational thought to concrete operational thought are that new demands be put on the child, that he be confronted with new tasks, provided with new instruments. The child learns that he cannot trust his own perception, that he must measure, must make use of all sorts of measuring devices. But all these methods, devices, and tools come from social experience. It is social experience that equips the schoolchild with tools with which to solve the new tasks. They are societal entities, and the step to their use is the step to the objective–societal viewpoint in the assessment of reality. Thus the driving force of the transition to new stages of development is not logic, and the criterion of truth is not the coherence of various viewpoints, but correspondence with reality.[13]

Gal'perin and El'konin argue that Piaget has become the captive of logic because he regards intellect as a system of operations, not as the knowledge of things. For Piaget experience is no more than fuel for the inner logic of development. But if he is right – if intellect is about the logic of operations – what then remains as the subject for psychology? Is psychology mere logic? The authors regard Piaget's endeavour as just one of various attempts to reduce the psychic to the nonpsychic,[14] attempts that are rooted in a mistaken understanding of the subject of psychology. In their opinion the real subject of psychology is orienting activity. And intellectual development involves the alteration of the content or givens of a situation, the use of social means of which logic is only one means. It is new tasks that lead the child to the mastery of new means of activity. Depending on the organization of instruction this will more or less slowly cause the change of his structures of thinking.

Gal'perin's and El'konin's afterword follows a pattern that was by then well known in Soviet psychology. There is unanimous praise for his emphasis on the qualitatively distinctive nature of childhood cognition and for his ingenuity in establishing the peculiarities of children's thinking. At the same time, Piaget's interpretation of the facts is contested, the alleged limitations of his approach are pointed out, and attempts are made to lay bare the philosophical roots of his thinking. It is probably fair to say that Gal'perin's and El'konin's criticism is partly in line with Western criticism[15] and partly has a distinctive flavour of its own. Typical for Soviet psychology is the emphasis on the human–animal distinction (based on Marxist anthropology) and the subsequent rejection of general biological concepts as being insufficiently specific. The Soviet emphasis on human tool-use and sign-use does not necessarily seem to be in conflict with Piaget's ideas. The Soviet psychologists had always argued that the subject (child) can never directly interact with either the social or the physical world but must necessarily make use of social means, signs, words, categories, etc. The world as perceived by the child is a socially constructed world. But in itself such a view is not contradictory to Piaget's view of the epistemic subject, for he always defended a Kantian view of knowledge in which the subject is only aware of reality through intervening cognitive structures such as schemes, categories, and concepts.[16] What distinguishes the two viewpoints, perhaps, is the Soviet emphasis on the social – in the sense of interpersonal – origin of these intervening structures, which they oppose to the Piagetian subject who is allegedly operating in a social vacuum.

Ljudmila Obukhova, in her interesting *The Conception of Jean Piaget: Pro and Con* (1981),[17] basically addressed the same themes as the previous authors and arrived at similar conclusions. Hers is the first Russian book that attempts to present an unbiased view of Piaget's system in its entirety and of the origin and development of his ideas. In her discussion of such basic themes as children's egocentrism, the relationship between instruction and development, and internalization, she constantly compares the views of Piaget and those of Vygotsky and his school and, almost invariably, comes to the conclusion that the cultural–historical views are to be preferred. This should come as no surprise as Obukhova is a student of Gal'perin and as such belongs to the cultural–historical tradition in Soviet psychology. The interest of her book lies in the matter-of-fact presentation of Piaget's ideas and in the presentation of countless Soviet replications of Piaget's experiments that show how deeply the Soviet psychologists studied Piaget and how eagerly they tried to refute his interpretations of the facts. Most important in Obukhova's book, perhaps, is her discussion of Piaget's and Vygotsky's respective theories of internalization or interiorization. However, this is a topic that is still very far from solved and the discussion of which would require a separate chapter. Suffice it to say that Obukhova promotes the theory of her teacher Gal'perin[18] as a viable and powerful alternative to Piaget's account of internalization.[19]

Mikhail Jaroshevsky is one of the very few Russian psychologists of the first post-revolutionary generation who is still alive and active. He is one of the major historians of psychology and philosophers of science of the Soviet period. In his interesting *The History of Psychology*,[20] Jaroshevsky argues that Piaget was a dualist because he opposed the individual and the social world, conceived, after Durkheim, as the totality of collective representations. In his first works he emphasized the child's transition from his own egocentric viewpoints to socialized thought under the influence of social interaction; in his later works he emphasized the transition to logico-mathematical structures. Following the criticisms of Wallon,[21] Jaroshevsky[22] discerns three vulnerable points in Piaget's thinking, as follows.

1   The object of analysis is not the whole psychophysiological being but the cognizing mind whose development is pictured in isolation from biological factors such as the maturation of the nervous system.
2   Piaget deals with intellect as such, without paying attention to the motivational, emotional factors connected with it.
3   In Piaget's conception the child finds itself in a world of objects, devoid of other persons, whereas in reality, as Jaroshevsky remarks, even in the artificial conditions of the experiment there is also a social other present. Piaget's mistake is that he proceeded from the two-factor conception of adaptation in which a subject (the child) interacts with an object (the physical world). What is missing here is the third factor of social signs and tools created by man in the course of history, which come between the subject and object. Taking this third factor (discovered by Marxism) into account allows one to overcome Piaget's individualistic approach.

As we will see below, Jaroshevsky's criticisms were not entirely new in Soviet psychology. The accusation that Piaget was some sort of a dualist who mixed psychoanalytic ideas with those of the French sociological school had already been voiced by Rubinstein (see below) and Vygotsky. What is interesting is that Jaroshevsky draws on the ideas of Henri Wallon, the French Marxist contemporary and lifelong opponent of Piaget, to counter the ideas of the Swiss psychologist. As is well known, Wallon entertained very friendly relationships with leading Soviet psychologists such as Leont'ev, and one could find no better proof of his status in Soviet psychology than this passage in a major textbook.[23]

The reactions to Piaget's ideas discussed above definitely belong to the more recent Soviet appraisals of his work. The case of the theorist we wish to discuss now, Sergej Rubinstein, is slightly different. Rubinstein's monumental *Foundations of General Psychology* was first published in 1940, had various re-editions, and the latest edition was published posthumously in 1989. Over the years, Rubinstein kept polishing the text of his *magnum opus* – partly because of the heavy ideological pressure exerted on him – but his assessment of Piaget's ideas seems to have changed very little. We may regard him, then, as a figure standing between the more recent Soviet views discussed above and the genuinely historical views to be discussed below.

Rubinstein, regarded by many as one of the leading theoretical psychologists in Russian psychological history, in the various editions of *Foundations of General Psychology*[24] argued that the early Piaget's conception of the child was due to a curious combination of psychoanalytic thinking on the one hand, and ideas from the French sociological school on the other.[25] In his view, Piaget proceeded from the concept of autistic thinking and defines egocentric thought as an intermediate link between autistic and rational thought. Autistic thought is characterized by the fact that it is not subjected to the principle of reality, egocentric thought by the fact that it is not subjected to the principle of sociality, i.e., it is not communicable. According to Piaget, says Rubinstein, rational thought is socialized thought, meant to be communicated, whereas autistic thought is by its nature individual and not communicable. Here Piaget mingles psychoanalytic thought about the primordial autistic nature of the child with the ideas of Durkheim's sociological school, according to which objectivity is the same as socially organized and conventional experience. The originally biologically autistic child becomes socialized under continuing pressure from the outside social environment, which gradually forces the child to relinquish his egocentrism and to adapt to the thinking of those surrounding him, i.e., to the collective representations of his culture. The result is that the child in Piaget's conception is opposed to the adult, that when Piaget created a child–adult dichotomy he created a dichotomy between the individual and the social. Philosophically speaking, Piaget created an idealistic, conventionalist system because in claiming that the child's thought becomes rational in the process of its socialization, he neglected the role of objective reality.

Rubinstein's succinct description contains a good deal of debatable points that cannot be fully discussed in the context of this chapter. The argument that Piaget's early viewpoint of egocentrism resulted from his involvement in psychoanalytic thinking is, of course, well known, and Piaget did not hide his knowledge of psychoanalysis.[26] Much more interesting is Rubinstein's claim that Piaget somehow adopted the theoretical framework of the Durkheim school in French sociology, a claim that at the time when Rubinstein first voiced it carried the meaning of an accusation or condemnation. It is an interesting point for at least two reasons.

First, modern research has noted the influence of Durkheim's thinking on Piaget but has not yet reached agreement about the direction of this influence. Ducret,[27] for example, prefers to sidestep the whole issue of Durkheim's influence on Piaget as he regards his knowledge of Durkheim's writings to be insufficient. Kitchener[28] boldly declares that Durkheim 'strongly influenced Piaget' but fails to point out in what this influence consists. Vidal,[29] in his superb *Piaget before Piaget*, remarks that Piaget 'was always much closer to Tarde[30] than to Durkheim'. Finally, Piaget[31] himself declared that he was 'deeply influenced by the social psychology of Blondel', who clearly was a follower of Durkheim and Lévy-Bruhl.[32] It seems then that the question of the strength and direction of the influence of the French sociological school on Piaget's thinking still awaits a definite answer and that the Soviet claims were at any rate not totally absurd.

Second, in the history of Soviet psychology Piaget was not the first or the last to be 'accused' of undergoing Durkheim's influence. Exactly the same accusation was levelled at Piaget's theoretical opponent, Vygotsky, in 1934 by a certain Razmyslov, who claimed that Vygotsky's view that individuals appropriate the ideas of the collective of which they form part reminded him very much of the ideas of the 'neopositivist' Durkheim.[33] Ironically, then, in the context of Soviet psychology, the ideas of Durkheim served to discredit both Piaget and Vygotsky, who would have been, had they known the quoted writings, *bien étonnés de se trouver ensemble* (surprised to find themselves together).

The assessment of Piaget's early ideas: Historical views

The assessment of Piaget's views so far encountered partly follow a pattern that has its roots in Soviet psychological history. In the present section we wish to show that many of the critical remarks levelled against Piaget's ideas were originally voiced by the founder of the cultural–historical school in Soviet psychology, Lev Vygotsky, and – to a much lesser extent – by his contemporary, Pavel Blonsky. A broader analysis of the Soviet reception of Piaget's ideas in the 1920s and 1930s, like the one that Parrat-Dayan[34] is carrying out on the reception of Piaget's early ideas in the French and English scientific press on the basis of book reviews etc., is unfortunately impossible due to the scarcity of available writings.

Pavel Blonsky, one of the leading Russian pedagogues and educationists of his time, never formulated an extensive criticism of Piaget's writings, but it is clear that he knew his work well and that he replicated several of Piaget's findings. The influence of Piaget's investigations on the later work of Blonsky is unmistakable. In one of his major books, *The Development of the Thinking of the Schoolchild*, Blonsky[35] devotes a paragraph to children's explanations that shows clear traces of Piaget's approach.

Blonsky begins his exposition of the nature of children's explanations by explaining that the subject of young children's stories is people's actions – above all, one's own actions. At first, the child gradually acquires knowledge about the specific actions of various agents. After that, he becomes capable of inferring the agent of the actions – in other words, of indicating the cause of the phenomenon. This is easiest for the child when the cause is a person (in particular, when the person and the child are the same) and most difficult when the agent is little known or little like him and other persons. That is why, says Blonsky, causal explanations involving a non-living agent are most difficult. As a result, the child's early causal explanations are not the result of thinking but of memory: The child simply remembers whose action it was. It is only towards 12 years of age, according to Blonsky, that the child begins not to remember but to actively seek the real causes of events.

Blonsky arrived at his conclusions by conducting interviews with children in the spirit of Piaget's clinical method; i.e., he asked children of various ages questions such as 'Why is it cold?', 'Why are you small?', 'Why does it snow?', and followed up their initial answers with new questions in order to probe into the child's understanding. Blonsky's student Belkina asked preschoolers (during the winter) why there is wind. She obtained the following categories of answers:

1   teleological explanations referring to some alleged intended purpose of the event to be explained ('it is necessary'; 'to clean up the streets')
2   finalistic explanations referring to the result of the event to be explained ('it is cold')
3   explanations via some characteristic feature or action ('it is blowing')
4   explanations via contiguity in time ('it is winter'; 'the sky is red')
5   genuinely causal explanations ('by the branches'; 'because the trees move').

Blonsky remarks that the last category of answers may seem finalistic at first sight, but for the child they are really causal explanations as the child has witnessed many cases when moving objects cause wind (so that for the child it is entirely logical to think that the moving branches of a tree *cause* the wind). Most of the pre-schoolers' causal explanations, however, are about human action. The young child can answer the question 'Who did it?' and has a tendency to regard objects as the result of human action. Blonsky argues that this tendency explains the wealth of artificialistic and anthropomorphic explanations found in Piaget.[36]

In order to investigate the thinking of the young school child, Blonsky employed an interesting methodological device: He confronted second-grade pupils with the explanations given by three-year-olds and asked whether these were correct. Blonsky relates that explanations by contiguity in time and explanations via some characteristic feature were generally met with laughter. It was different, however, with finalistic and teleological explanations. Second-grade children might object to teleological explanations by simply giving another action that leads to the same result (e.g., the answer of a pre-schooler to the question 'Why is there wind?' is 'To clean up the street', to which the second-grade pupil objects that 'A woman can clean up the street.' In itself such an objection shows that young school children still see no problem in pointing out several causes of the same phenomenon. It is schooling, with its emphasis on the one and only correct answer to questions, Blonsky[37] argues, that forces the child to adopt the 'one cause–one result' schema. However, the influence of schooling does not tell us the whole story. Blonsky[38] argues that the child's growing understanding of temporal relations (before–after, earlier–later) is a prerequisite for the understanding of cause–result relationships. The child only develops such an understanding at school age, and first with respect to those human actions that are well known to the child from his own personal experience.

It is probably fair to say that Blonsky's analysis of children's explanations did not differ radically from Piaget's original approach. Like Piaget, Blonsky was interested in the origin of causal thinking, like Piaget he used some sort of clinical method, and like Piaget he established several 'stages' in the child's thinking. What is interesting is that he established a sort of 'gap' between the child's causal inferences about human practical actions well known from the child's personal experience and causal inferences about events that are not caused by human action and are, consequently, more remote from the child's own private life. What is also interesting is that Blonsky pointed to the role of schooling in promoting the (erroneous) idea that events have but a single cause. From the methodological point of view, his method of confronting older children with the answers of younger ones is not without interest. Although there is no doubt[39] that Blonsky was critical about several of Piaget's methods and conclusions, we may conclude that his work was in the spirit of 'complementing and correcting' Piaget's work that Piaget hoped for in his preface mentioned above.

This brings us to the work of the founding father of Russian cultural–historical psychology, Lev Vygotsky. It is not an exaggeration to say that Vygotsky was profoundly influenced by the early writings of his Swiss colleague. Like several of his contemporaries, Vygotsky immediately recognized Piaget as a major innovative thinker who radically changed the outlook of developmental psychology. It was Vygotsky who organized the translation into Russian of Piaget's first two psychology books; it was Vygotsky who staged a series of conceptual and exact replications of Piaget's studies; and it was Vygotsky who referred time and again to Piaget's writings.[40] It is significant that in the six volumes of Vygotsky's *Collected Works* (published in Russian), which represent about half of his writings, Piaget is by far the most frequently cited author.[41]

When I say that Vygotsky was profoundly influenced by the work of Piaget I do not mean to say that Vygotsky accepted very many of Piaget's ideas. As is well known, Vygotsky was one of Piaget's theoretical opponents who tried to prove that Piaget's views were basically mistaken. What I do mean to say is that Vygotsky recognized Piaget as a major new voice in science whose work had to be studied in great detail, had to be mastered, and had to be refuted in order for science to be able to make any progress. In other words, Vygotsky immediately grasped that it was only by standing on Piaget's shoulders, by going beyond Piaget's ideas, that developmental psychologists could advance their understanding of the child's thinking.

In the context of this chapter it is not possible to review the approximately 180 references to Piaget that Vygotsky makes in his *Collected Works* in order to show which of Piaget's ideas Vygotsky rejected and which he accepted, and to trace a possible development in his assessment of Piaget's work. We will restrict ourselves to Vygotsky's mature writings and notably to his lengthy preface to a work by Piaget.[42]

Vygotsky's preface has been characterized by Joravsky[43] as a deliberate caricature of Piaget's views, and we surely must ask ourselves to what extent Vygotsky was sincere in his evaluation of Piaget's early writings and to what extent he merely followed the prescribed views. But quite apart from this historical question, the preface is of interest in itself as it so clearly formed the model after which much of the later criticism of Piaget's work was written (see below), and as it stimulated many empirical investigations that improved our understanding of the child's thinking.

Quoting extensively (about fifty times) from Piaget's[44] early books, Vygotsky attempted to lay bare the philosophical presuppositions of Piaget's early writings. Vygotsky begins by criticizing Piaget's concept of childhood ego-centrism, which he sees (together with modern experts, e.g., Flavell[45]) as the fundamental concept uniting Piaget's first four books. As is well known, Piaget claimed that a characteristic of the young child's thought is ego-centrism, i.e., the inability to take the other person's point of view. Piaget claimed that it is a form of thought that stands halfway between autistic and rational thought; but in fact, Vygotsky argues, when we read Piaget it becomes clear that egocentric thought in his view comes much closer to autis-tic than to rational thought. According to Piaget's books, egocentric thought emerges as being functionally, structurally, and genetically the opposite of rational thought. Its function is to satisfy the child's desires and needs, whereas rational thought aims to adapt to reality. Structurally, it is incoher-ent, unconscious, and abbreviated, whereas rational thought is coherent, con-scious, and explicit. Genetically, egocentric thought comes before rational thought (this follows Freud's claim that the *Lustprinzip* is prior to the *Realitätsprinzip*). The resulting picture is that of a child who is originally, primordially asocial and who needs to be socialized. However, argued Piaget, this socializing influence exerted by adults on the child is distorted (assimi-lated) by the child, and in some sense the younger child is thus 'untouched by the experiences'.[46] It is only at seven to eight years of age that the child manages to overcome his general egocentric thinking, which, however, remains present in the domain of abstract verbal thought. What are we to think of this picture of the development of children's thinking?

Vygotsky's first step is to argue, with Bleuler, that primitive (autistic) thought is not functionally, structurally, nor genetically what Piaget held it to be. He quotes Bleuler[47] to argue that children cannot be primordially autistic: that is, it is true that infants satisfy their needs but this satisfaction is not in any way imaginary but very real and adapted to reality. In Bleuler's words, infants prefer real apples to imaginary ones. To assume, with psychoanalysis, that infants first go through a stage of autistic need satisfaction and sub-sequently adapt to reality is to create a dichotomy that does not make sense from the factual point of view and would violate the principle of evolution. Against this view, Bleuler argues – and Vygotsky quotes him approvingly – that it is only with the advent of speech that children can indulge in unrealistic fantasies and day-dreaming. Bleuler also argues that autistic thought need not be unconscious and that it can be aimed at reality. This would mean that the concept of childhood autism as used by Freud and Piaget is basically wrong and that autistic thought is not what Piaget thought it to be.

Vygotsky's next step is an attempt to undermine Piaget's factual basis for his claim that children think egocentrically. Here he mainly focuses on Piaget's finding regarding egocentric speech, and his ultimate conclusion is that the presence of 'egocentric' speech does not necessarily imply that children are *thinking* egocentrically. Vygotsky's argument is well known and has stimulated much fruitful research, so there is no need to give more than its bare outlines here. On the basis of both empirical research[48] and theoretical arguments, Vygotsky hypothesizes that Piaget's conception of egocentric speech was mistaken. Egocentric speech is not, as Piaget thought, without a function; its fate is not to fade away, and it is not an intermediate stage between autistic and socialized thought or speech. On the basis of his own (very vaguely described) empirical research, Vygotsky hypothesizes that egocentric speech has (or at least can have) a planning function and gradually gets transformed into inner speech as the child grows older. This would mean that Piaget's sequence from individual, autistic, to socialized speech would have to be replaced by the sequence from social to individual speech. According to Vygotsky, individual speech could either be communicative or egocentric. The latter form foreboded the inner speech of adults and served to plan the child's actions. This would mean that Piaget's interpretation of the function and fate of egocentric speech was erroneous and that the phenomenon of 'egocentric' speech does not indicate egocentric thought.

Vygotsky then dives deeper into Piaget's notion of the role of the individual and of the social in child development. He quotes Piaget's preface where Piaget says that the dominating idea of his first books is that:

The child's thinking cannot be deduced solely from innate psycho-biological factors and from the influence of the physical environment, but must be understood also and primarily from those relationships which are established between the child and the social environment that surrounds him. By that I do not simply wish to say that the child reflects the opinions and ideas of those who surround him; that would be banal. The structure itself of the child's thinking depends upon the social environment. When the individual thinks only for himself, thinks egocentrically (which is exactly typical of the child), then his thought finds itself in the power of his fantasy, wishes and personality, and then it has a number of properties which are completely different from those properties which characterize rational thinking. When the individual undergoes the systematic influence from some specific social environment (for example, when the child experiences the influence of the authority of adults), his thought takes shape in accordance with certain external rules ... as individuals jointly cooperate with each other, the rules of this cooperation will develop as well, will communicate discipline to their thinking which forms the intellect in both its aspects – the theoretical and the practical. Egocentrism, coercion and cooperation – these are the three currents between which the developing thinking of the child constantly wavers and with which to a greater or lesser extent the thinking of the adult is connected, dependent on whether it remains autistic or grows into one or the other type of social organization.[49]

This quote would seem to imply, says Vygotsky, that Piaget acknowledges the full importance for child development of the social (and physical) environment, but does he? What essentially does Piaget mean when he talks about socialization? Vygotsky argues that for Piaget socialization is equivalent to social coercion or constraint. The (autistic) child resists this constraint but must eventually yield to the pressure exerted by the social environment because this social environment is the only source of rational, logical thought. But, says Vygotsky, this is equivalent to saying that everything that is truly child-like is individual/biological, whereas everything that is rational or logical comes from the environment. The child is, as it were, living in two worlds – his own world of fantasy and day-dreaming and the adult world of reason and logic – and the adult's task is to force the child out of his own world. This means that cognitive development becomes equivalent to repressing the child's original, true nature, to overcome/replace his primordial autism. According to Vygotsky, the implications of such a view are twofold.

First, in and by himself the child can never arrive at logical, rational thought. Vygotsky quotes Piaget as saying that:

> These things are not sufficient in themselves to make the mind feel any need for verification, since things themselves have been made by the mind. . . . If there were not other people, the disappointments of experience would lead to over-compensation and dementia. We are constantly hatching an enormous number of false ideas, conceits, Utopias, mystical explanations, suspicions, and megalomaniacal fantasies, which disappear when brought into contact with other people.[50]

Vygotsky cannot accept this viewpoint, as it seems to imply that external, objective reality plays the decisive role in the origin of rational, logical thinking neither in the case of children nor in the case of the 'primitive' man. Piaget seems to eschew a realistic epistemology and clearly implies that the need for logical thinking and the knowledge of truth emerges from the interaction of the child's mind with other minds. To Vygotsky this was anathema, and he emphatically exclaims that such a conventionalist theory of knowledge 'resembles very much the philosophical character of the doctrine of Durkheim and other sociologists who deduce both space, time, and all objective reality from man's social life'.[51]

For Piaget, says Vygotsky, it is not the mastery of objective reality that leads both primitive man and the Western child to develop rational thought but the pure interaction with other minds. This whole perspective was borrowed from the work of Lévy-Bruhl, and it has the same shortcoming: The activity of both primitive man and child can be pre-logical or autistic or *imperméable à l'expérience* only to a very limited extent, because both primitive man and the child are constantly interacting with objective reality and are thus *forced* to adopt a rational, logical perspective. For the early Piaget the interaction with the objective world of things plays only a limited role in the development of rational thought.

Second, development is conceptualized not as some sort of synthesis of the social and the individual factors but as a replacement of the primordial autistic thought by social rational thought. The child eventually yields to the constant pressure exerted by his peers and adults. But this means, says Vygotsky, that the whole concept of (autonomous) development disappears and that social others dictate the various stages of thought.

The least one can say of Vygotsky's analysis is that it is a powerful piece of rhetoric and that it set the pattern for the Soviet criticism to come. The idea that Piaget's theory was an unhappy mixture of psychoanalysis and Durkheimian ideas,[52] the argument that his findings are valid only for subjects that lie outside the child's immediate sphere of practical interests,[53] the argument that the criterion of truth cannot be the coherence of various viewpoints,[54] among other arguments, were all first voiced by Vygotsky. In the subsequent years he still followed Piaget's work attentively but did not substantially change his evaluation of Piaget's views. Thus, in an essay written several years later, Vygotsky dealt with Piaget's concept of spontaneous and non-spontaneous concept, and he concluded that:

For Piaget, a child's intellectual development comprises a process of gradual displacement of the peculiar qualities and characteristics of childish thinking by the more powerful and vigorous adult thinking process. The starting point of this development is described by Piaget as the solipsism characteristic of infantile consciousness which, as the child adapts to the adult way of thinking, gives way to the egocentrism of childish thinking, which is a compromise between the peculiar features inherent in a child's consciousness and the characteristics of mature thinking. The signs of egocentrism are more pronounced in the youngest children. The characteristics of children's thinking decline with age, as they are forced out from one sphere after another, until such time as they disappear altogether. The process of development is seen not as an uninterrupted emergence of new characteristics which are higher, more complicated and closer to developed thought, out of more basic and primary forms of thinking, but as gradual and uninterrupted replacement of one group of forms by another. The socialization of thinking is viewed like an external, mechanical replacement of individual features of a child's thinking process. From this point of view, the developmental process is quite like the process of displacing one liquid already present in a container by forcing another into it from the outside. In the process of development, everything new comes from the outside. The child's own peculiar characteristics do not play any constructive, positive, progressive or shaping role in the history of his intellectual development. They are in no way responsible for creating any of the higher forms of thinking. These higher forms simply take the place of the former ones. According

to Piaget, this is the only law which applies to the intellectual development in children.[55]

We may conclude, then, that Vygotsky stuck to his original criticism of
Piaget's ideas until his untimely death in 1934. It must be considered a great
pity and a loss for the development of child psychology that Piaget waited
until 1962[56] to give his comments on Vygotsky's critique. He surely knew the
critique earlier, if not from the reading of Vygotsky's (1932) preface to the
Russian edition of his own writings or from Vygotsky's and Luria's (1930)
paper on the function and fate of egocentric speech, then surely from the later
writings and communications by Luria to which Piaget[57] himself refers in
the third edition of *The Language and Thought of the Child*. By remaining
silent Piaget robbed himself of the opportunity to correct those of the Soviet
views of his work that he considered incorrect, and robbed developmental
psychology of a theoretical debate that perhaps would not have led to a
'rapprochement' of the different views but surely would have enhanced our
understanding in this difficult field of science.

Conclusions

Good criticisms of scientific theories can be informative for two reasons. In
the first place, they may highlight the strong and weak points of the theory
discussed and, at best, reveal its inner logic, its hidden assumptions, and its
roots in the scientific and social discourse of the time. In the second place, a
good critique may reveal the hobby horses or obsessions of the critic, what he
or she regards as relevant and important in scientific theories, and what is 'not
done' in the social reference group of the critic. The Soviet criticisms of
Piaget's ideas form no exception to this rule. On the one hand, they provide
us with a plethora of arguments raised against Piaget's several ideas and their
theoretical and ideological background. On the other hand, they provide us
with an interesting picture of what Soviet psychology over the past five or six
decades found important in developmental science. Soviet criticism of
Piaget's ideas fits in with the abundant contemporary Western literature critical of Piaget;[58] its voice will perhaps not go unnoticed, nor will it be dissonant
in this huge choir to which it is historically and theoretically interconnected.

Finally, we should like to repeat that Soviet criticisms of Piaget's writings
were often theoretical, or *de jure*, so to speak. The critics pointed out what
they saw as the vulnerable points of Piaget's theoretical ideas. However, this
critique did not prevent them from using many of Piaget's insights in their
own scientific practice and theory. In practice, or *de facto*, therefore, many
Soviet researchers were always pleased to use Piaget's methods and techniques and his particular ways to analyse the data. One might even argue, as I
have done elsewhere,[59] that the important Kharkov school of psychology –
seen by many as the natural heir to Vygotsky's cultural–historical school – has
been very much influenced by Piaget's writings. As in the case of much of

Vygotsky's own later research, many of their investigations can be seen as exact or conceptual replications[60] of Piaget's seminal work. The early and later work by Piaget changed the landscape of international developmental psychology, and, fortunately, no ideological or legal boundaries could safeguard Soviet psychology from undergoing the influence of Piaget's 'militant attempt' to change our picture of the nature, origin, and development of human intelligence.

Notes

1 J. Piaget (1932) *Rech i myshlenie rebenka* (p. 55). Moscow & Leningrad: Uchpedgiz.

2 Ibid., p. 56.

3 L. S. Vygotsky & A.R. Luria (1930) The function and fate of egocentric speech. *Ninth International Congress of Psychology. Proceedings and Papers* (pp. 464–470). Princeton, NJ: Psychological Review Company.

4 A. Kozulin (1984) *Psychology in Utopia* (pp. 25–28). Cambridge, MA: MIT Press.

5 R. van der Veer & J. Valsiner (Eds.) (1991) *Understanding Vygotsky: A quest for synthesis*. Oxford: Blackwell.

6 M. Gulutsan (1967) Jean Piaget in Soviet psychology. *Alberta Journal of Educational Research*, *13*, 239–247; A. Kozulin, op. cit.

7 A. V. Petrovsky (1984) *Voprosy istorii i teorii psikhologii* [Problems in the history and theory of psychology]. Moscow: Pedagogika.

8 P. Ya Gal'perin & D. B. El'konin (1967) Posleslovia. Zh. Piazhe. K analizu teorii o razvitii detskogo myshlenija [Afterword. J. Piaget. Towards the analysis of a theory about the development of children's thinking] (pp. 596–621). In J. Flavell (Ed.), *Geneticheskaja psikhologija Jean'a Piazhe* [The developmental psychology of Jean Piaget]. Moscow: Prosveshchenie.

9 Ibid., p. 597.

10 I. M. Arievitch & R. van der Veer (1995) Furthering the internalization debate: Gal'perin's contribution. *Human Development*, *38*, 113–126.

11 J. Haenen (1995) *Pyotr Gal'perin: Psychologist in Vygotsky's footsteps*. Commack, NY: Nova Science.

12 Gal'perin & El'konin, op. cit., p. 612.

13 Ibid., p. 618.

14 Ibid., p. 619.

15 M. H. van IJzendoorn & R. Van der Veer (1984) *Main currents of critical psychology: Vygotsky, Holzkamp, Riegel*. New York: Irvington.

16 R. F. Kitchener (1986) *Piaget's theory of knowledge: Genetic epistemology and scientific reason* (pp. 104–111). New Haven, CT: Yale University Press.

17 L. F. Obukhova (1981) *Kontseptsiya Zhana Piazhe. Za I protiv* [The conception of Jean Piaget: Pro and con]. Moscow: Izdatel'stvo Moskovskogo Universiteta.

18 Haenen, op. cit.

19 Arievitch & van der Veer, op. cit.

20 M. G. Jaroshevsky (1985) *Istorija psikhologii*. Moscow: Mysl'.

21 H. Wallon (1942/1970) *De l'acte à la pensée*. Paris: Flammarion.

22 Jaroshevsky, op. cit.

23 O. M. Tutundzhan (1966) *Evolutsija psikhologicheskaja kontseptsija Anri Vallona* [The psychological conception of Henri Wallon]. Erevan, Armenia: Ajastan. Evolutsija psikhologicheskoj Konseptsija Anri Vallona [The evolution of the psychological conception of Henri Wallon]. *Voprosy Psikhologii*, 161–167.

24 S. L. Rubinstein. *Osnovvy obhchei psikhologii. Tom I* [The foundations of general

psychology, Vol. 1]. Moscow: Pedagogika, 1940, 1946, 1989; id., Vol. 2. Moscow: Pedagogika, 1989.

25 Ibid., 1989, pp. 434–435, 207–208.

26 J. Piaget (1926a/1959) *The language and thought of the child* (p. 43). London: Routledge & Kegan Paul.

27 J.-J. Ducret (1984) *Jean Piaget: Savant et philosophe* (Vol. 1, p. 236, note 17), Geneva: Droz.

28 Kitchener, op. cit., p. 12.

29 F. Vidal (1994) *Piaget before Piaget* (p. 241). Cambridge, MA: Harvard University Press.

30 Durkheim's theoretical opponent.

31 Piaget, *The language and thought of the child*, op. cit., pp. xx–xxi.

32 L. Mucchielli (1994) Sociologie et psychologie en France, l'appel à un territoire commun: vers une psychologie collective (1890–1940). *Revue de synthèse, 3–4*, 445–483.

33 R. van der Veer, M. H. van IJzendoorn, & J. Valsiner (Eds.) (1991) *Reconstructing the mind: Replicability in research on human development* (pp. 381–382). Norwood, NJ: Ablex.

34 S. Parrat-Dayan (1993) Le texte et ses voix. Piaget lu par ses pairs dans le milieu psychologique des années 1920–1930. *Archives de psychologie, 61*, 125–155; (1993) La réception de l'oeuvre de Piaget dans le milieu pédagogique des années 1920–1930. *Revue française de pédagogie, 104*, 73–83.

35 P. P. Blonsky (1935) Razvitie myshlenie shkol'nika [The development of the thinking of the schoolchild]. In M. G. Danil'chenko & A. A. Nikol'skaya (Eds.), *P.P. Blonsky, Izbrannye pedagogicheskie i psikhologicheskie sochinenija, Vol. 2* [P. P. Blonsky, Selected pedagogical and psychological writings, Vol. 2]. Moscow: Prosvescenie.

36 J. Piaget (1926b) *La représentation du monde chez l'enfant*. Paris: Alcan. [English translation: *The child's conception of the world*: London: Routledge & Kegan Paul, 1929.]

37 Blonsky, op. cit., p. 50.

38 Ibid., p. 51.

39 Ibid., p. 368.

40 J. Piaget (1921) Une forme verbale de la comparaison chez l'enfant. *Archives de psychologie, 18*, 141–172; (1923) *Le langage et la pensée chez l'enfant*. Neuchâtel: Delachaux & Niestlé [*The language and thought of the child*. London: Routledge & Kegan Paul, 1926]; (1924) *Le jugement et le raisonnement chez l'enfant*. Neuchâtel: Delachaux & Niestlé [*Judgement and reasoning in the child*. Totowa, NJ: Littlefield Adams, 1969]; (1927) *La causalité physique chez l'enfant*: Paris: Alcan [*The child's conception of physical causality*. London: Routledge & Kegan Paul, 1970]; (1927) La première année de l'enfant, *British Journal of Psychology, 18*, 97–120; (1932) *Le jugement moral chez l'enfant*. Paris: Alcan [*The moral judgement of the child*. London: Routledge & Kegan Paul, 1932]; (1933) Psychologie de l'enfant et l'enseignement de l'histoire, *Bulletin trimestriel de la Conférence Internationale pour l'enseignement de l'histoire, 2*, 8–13; J. Piaget & P. Rossello (1921) Notes sur les types de description d'images chez l'enfant. *Archives de Psychologie, 18*, 208–234.

41 R. van der Veer (1985) Vygotsky's interpsychology. Proceedings of the meeting *Lectures croisées dans les sciences de l'homme*, 22–25 May, Moscow.

42 L. S. Vygotsky (1932) Predislovie [Foreword]. In J. Piaget, *Rech i myshlenie rebenka* [The speech and thinking of the child] (pp. 3–54). Moscow & Leningrad: Uchpedigiz.

43 D. Joravsky (1989) *Russian psychology: A critical history* (p. 362). Oxford: Blackwell.

44 Piaget, op. cit., 1923, 1924, 1926a, 1926b, 1927.
45 J. H. Flavell (1963) *The developmental psychology of Jean Piaget.* New York: D. Van Nostrand.
46 Piaget (1924), op. cit. p. 264.
47 E. Bleuler (1912) Das autistische Denken. In E. Bleuler, S. Freud, & C. G. Jung (Eds.), *Jahrbuch für psychoanalytische und psychopathologische Forschungen,* Vol. 4 (pp. 26–29). Leipzig & Vienna: Wien Franz Deuticke.
48 Vygotsky & Luria, op. cit.
49 Piaget (1932), op. cit, p. 55.
50 Piaget (1924), op. cit., pp. 265–266.
51 L. S. Vygotsky (1934/1994) *Myshlenie i rech'. Psikhologicheskie issledovanija* [Thinking and speech. Psychological investigations] (p. 59). Moscow & Leningrad: Gosudarstvennoe social'no Ekonomicheskoe Izdatel'stvo.
52 Rubinstein, op. cit.; Jaroshevsky, op. cit., notes 24 and 43.
53 Blonsky, op. cit.
54 Gal'perin & El'konin, op. cit.
55 L.S. Vygotsky, *Myshlenie i rech'*, op. cit., pp. 362–363.
56 J. Piaget (1962) Comments on Vygotsky's critical remarks concerning the language and thought of the child, and judgement and reasoning in the child. In L. S. Vygotsky (1962) *Thought and Language.* Cambridge, MA: MIT Press. See also the new annotated translation by Leslie Smith: J. Piaget (2000) Commentary on Vygotsky's criticisms of 'Language and thought of the child' and 'Judgment and reasoning in the child'. *New Ideas in Psychology, 18,* 241–259.
57 Piaget (1923), op. cit., p. 263.
58 Parrat-Dayan, op. cit.
59 R. van der Veer (1984) Omgang en handelen [Social interaction and conduct]. *Psychologie en Maatschappij, 28,* 338–351.
60 Van der Veer et al., op. cit.

15 The great images of Jean Piaget [1]

Daniel Hameline

The image of a person is neither the person himself nor his character. Talking about an image, in any event, is a way of defining space, where the object and its contours are laid out, where the limits of the *ad intra* and the *ad extra* are set in an inexpressible relation. An 'image' emerges invariably in the midst of other objects. One speaks of the 'image' as something that sets even itself 'apart'. That means, as one knows, two things: that there is a 'shape' against a 'background' and that one is not mistaken for the other. Yet without the background, the shape itself is insignificant.

An image is the manner by which an agent gives himself or is given a social surface. Others might call it a 'relief'. Whatever the metaphor, the point is that it becomes – or is made – visible. But 'visible', when talking about a person, is never merely an exercise in perception, except to specify that, as is widely agreed, there is no perception that is 'simply that' and not something else.

To give the perception of an image – to *see someone as an image* – is a matter of giving 'something else to see', rather as Le Lorrain arranged 'factories' in his landscapes. An image is always the intention of an artefact, for it is meant to be seen. While people may commonly make themselves seen inadvertently, nothing is less inadvertent than the act of creating an image. One always *makes* either a 'good' or a 'bad' image, as the saying goes.

Ordinary language is, on this point as on many others, a good teacher: To make an image is to endow value on something. For example, one may be described as 'looking nice' or as 'looking shady', and thus a scale of values is erected. And if we look at *brave* in French we can talk about the *brave garçon* who is respected as a 'decent chap', which has nothing to do with another meaning of 'brave', i.e., courageous.

Our heroic figures

Brave, of course, can also mean valour. 'Image' then becomes more than the ordinary psycho-moral description and takes on exemplary heroic virtues attributed to 'great figures'. It is no longer a question of 'making a good or bad image' in life. The exemplary figure emerges against the background of his time during which he has achieved memorable status among his fellow men. History is filled with our heroic figures.

Let us return to the age of Plutarch, when he wrote *Bioi paralleloi* [Parallel Lives]. Contemporary historians – though as early as 1840 Thomas Carlyle[2] was critical of the practice – have made no bones about protesting against the tradition of marking history through great figures: The masses make history; those who remain anonymous are the ones who are interesting, and factors determine actors. *Exit* the great figure, which he may do by the back door but only to return later through the front door.

Whether exiting or returning, the great figures are always there, like wary sentinels held fast in the collective memory. They form a gallery of sainted creatures, worshipped and scorned. As saints they are viewed as suspect and banal, worn by routine. Yet it is the routine itself that exculpates them because historical truth lies between two routines: the routine of suspicion and that of adhesion. One is as naïve as the other because reason, as much as enthusiasm, will dissuade fear.

But if Plutarch is dated, what can be said of Carlyle in this day and age? Have his lectures on heroes, hero-worship, and the heroic in history lost meaning?[3] Universal history, read like a saga, is commensurately interesting and unbelievable, yet it is full of the tales of *real* great figures. They are the ones who embody the wisdom and heroic virtues of the anonymous crowd. The consolation for the latter, according to Carlyle, is that the great figures, however they are seen, are good company.[4] In his *Préliminaires à la mythologie*,[5] Alain comments that, 'Great men are larger than life in memory. What we see in them is what is best in them and what is best in ourselves.'

Is there shame in being a mythologist? Great figures make history. Even during their lifetimes, if they are given the chance, they become part of history.

Can one trust an image?

Piaget is one of the great figures whom we look at suspiciously but at the same time trustingly. Faced with the image of such a person, the appropriate attitude to take is one of trust [the French text uses the term *fiance*, adapted from Montaigne to create a noun form for the verb *se fier*]. An image can most certainly be more or less truthful, or accurate. But more than an object of 'verification', the image is an object either of a *bene*-diction or of a *male*-diction, a blessing or a curse. That is to say that the person of whom we make an image acts within a society, whether it be traditional or popular, local or global, which prescribes (*dictum* – diction) what is worthwhile and what is not for the present, the past, and the future. The exemplary figure is always prophetic, announcing for better or for worse what is to come, and as such it is impossible for such a figure to be indifferent.

The heroic figure is always legendary, but certainly not in a fairy-tale sense. The 'legendary' is something to be read, the same as image is something to be seen. The word tells us 'to take up and read', to seize upon the matter yet at the same time understand it as something to be feared. The legendary inspires the reverential fear one feels before the sublime and the bizarre, or even simply before the exceptional. Reading, which instils such feelings of wonder, is a call to appropriation through interpretation as well as an appeal to distancing one's self. The subjective is at its height while the individual yields to the general, the particular to the universal.[6]

The person achieves the status of 'being talked about' only if he is also legendary, i.e., if he fits a 'type' identifiable with preceding heroic figures or by exceeding them even in the heroic hierarchy.

The images of Piaget come to us after a long absence of the person himself. We know him only through these images, which are something other than the real man. The 'type' has been reduced to the image, but it is the only means by which the reader comes in contact with the man. But the truth is that reducing a person to types that illustrate his image is inadequate because it goes against the common man's wisdom to avoid premature labelling. Yet a wise man's wisdom differs from it only by a more refined manner of expression. What is certain is that heroic figures belong in their own category.

There is nothing to be done: The best and most venerable tales are told in bold words.

Self-portrait of the artist

Piaget sketched his own image by writing his autobiography, and many other biographies contribute to a series of portraits. The point of departure is doubtless the place where Piaget himself wished one to start.

In the first part of his authoritative thesis, Fernando Vidal[7] presents and comments on this autobiography, which was first published in 1952 in English before it appeared, revised and updated, in French in 1966 and again in 1976. This worthy study has been a significant source of inspiration in writing this chapter.

The biographers had the habit of stressing the aspect of 'trust' and downplaying that of 'mistrust' with regard to the autobiography, and until this recent thesis, an authentic historiography of Piaget had been neglected. Historiography is, in fact, to articulate with unwavering force an indispensable confidence in the autobiography and with equal vigour a necessary mistrust of it.

The autobiographic process has found credibility over the past several years as one of the ways of approaching human phenomena. Everyone is master of his own easel, of sorts, in a 'clinical' examination of himself, not introspectively or alone, but retrospectively and in dialogue. It is not without significance that 'life stories' are seen by some,[8] like Dominicé, Josso, or Pineau and Le Grand, as part of a training process. The tale of one's self is a manner of seizing one's self that is not a documentary but, rather, a way of 'giving sense' to the trodden path. The content is 'instructional', not feedback; it 'forewarns'.

The autobiographer is not, in a sense, a historian. He cannot be accused of being an impostor even if he does 'embellish the facts', so to speak. In reality, as there are no facts, there is nothing to embellish. No facts? Is there only an imaginary reconstruction without control where each is free to tell his version? Things are not so dramatically antagonistic.

An autobiography is, first of all, an act. If we take 'act' in the sense of 'putting into action', an autobiography offers a way out of an impasse when one seeks to put into writing something revelatory. It is revelatory for oneself, above all. There is an intention, but not the sort that one can declare as such, that one can clearly sketch out. The intention is *nachträglich* – after the fact – and puts preceding events into perspective. The intention becomes manifest by the 'account', in the sense of resolution.[9]

The moment of deciding to act is not without importance. Perhaps there are autobiographic moments in everyone's life. In 1952 Piaget was invited to participate in the fourth edition of a gallery of self-portraits, which had been inaugurated in 1930: *A History of Psychology in Autobiography*. Other great figures had preceded him, particularly Edouard Claparède, the founder of the Rousseau Institute, who had introduced Piaget to this institute in 1921.

The commission was apparently of a didactic nature. Boring and his collaborators explained it in the preface to the 1952 volume (see Note 10): Readers, particularly the young, can learn from their great predecessors what it meant to pursue a scientific career; their motives, reactions, choices, and finally justifications.

Piaget seized on the occasion to give the image of an eminent intellectual eager to give coherence to his development, in spite of successive conversions and changes. Could it be that this 'acting out' is a 'rationalization' that traps even its author?

'Rationalizing' has become impregnated in ordinary language with psychoanalytic nuances, suggesting obscure intentions to cover up incoherence as a way of suggesting the contrary. But here, in this discussion among peers, the rationalizing achieved in the autobiography is a means of giving an explanation of events in such a way that a desired sense of unity emerges, as it does in any good drama. Thus, the author pursues his account with resolute steadfastness.

However, in his autobiographical writing, steadfastness for Jean Piaget was seasoned with some suspicions towards oneself. The proof lies in the rhetorical practice of prolepsis as a way of exordium. The art of anticipating objection – which is what prolepsis means – is a twofold craft: Disarm the eventual adversary by recognizing beforehand his well-founded reserve. It is a matter of covering up imprudence with prudence and vice versa. The tactic shows both authenticity and duplicity in the same step, which rhetorically go hand in hand.

An autobiography is never objective, writes Piaget at the beginning of his autobiography, and it is naturally up to the reader to adjust the sense according to impersonal truth. It (the autobiography) offers a certain insight into what the author wanted to do and how he understands himself.[10]

Thus Piaget wrote a story that cast a coherent image, but one with lacunae. One can then ask if the image is coherent *because of* the lacunae.

The autobiography of Jean Piaget is, first of all, the presentation of a scientific career by a scientist. That is certainly what the publisher expected, and it is the genre imposed by the preceding autobiographies. But the scientist was already present in childhood, in his youthful experiences with the Club of the Friends of Nature, and in the precocious malacologist.[11]

The publisher's instructions to limit the text to the 'scientific' aspect of his life allowed Piaget to skim over the young social Christian philosopher who in 1915 had penned *La mission de l'idée*, and even more so over the romantic believer caught up in the 'mysteries of divine suffering' pathetically expressed in a prayer published in *L'Essor* in 1916.[12] If one refers to *Recherche*, an autobiographical novel in which Piaget casts himself as the character Sébastien, one finds among the 'juvenile and somewhat naïve' considerations, which had been 'completely forgotten', a foreshadowing of ideas on equilibration that he would develop 30 years later.

The anxious young man

This retrospective is certainly not inaccurate. However, *Recherche* is anything but a step in a scientific development that led the youthful entomologist in a straight line to becoming a mature epistemologist. In Chapter 13 of the present work, Jean-Jacques Ducret shatters this beautifully drawn blueprint. He casts another image, equally unified, but which an autobiography of the 'scientist' would not take into account. And that image is one of a 'restless young man'.

Restlessness must be understood not as some kind of neurotic state but, rather, as the existential quest that is a secularized echo of the Augustinian apostrophe: *inquietum est cor nostrum donec requiescat in te* (our hearts are restless until they rest in you). In the course of life such disquiet is not limited to a single 'age', but is a sign of youth that continues to stir a soul that refuses to wither with time.

But might the appeal of such spiritual states not cast a doubt on the image of a would-be scientist? Piaget's autobiography leaves out this phase of his life as well as the determining philosophical significance it had for him. He also leaves out the ethical aspects of his work that touches upon moral judgement in children.[13] Piaget did not see the work done by his students at the Rousseau Institute in the late 1920s as a contribution to the ethical debate on the autonomy of moral consciousness. He preferred to interpret this work as a further step in the process of a unified 'idea' which had preceded his years at the Institute: the intention to construct an 'experimental and objective knowledge of the elementary structures of intelligence' and to attack the 'problem of thought in general' by developing a 'psychological and biological epistemology'.

Vidal summarizes very well the characteristics of the autobiographical account that Piaget rendered, which conformed to the letter of the received canons espoused by his community of intellectuals:[14]

> The presentation that Piaget gave of himself is typical of the scientific tradition of autobiography.[15] By conforming to the scientific canons, he leaves out displays of the self, and gives preference to objectivity over sincerity. He relates a career rather than telling the story of a life.

The effacement of 'the great pedagogue'

This self-revelation of Piaget's conforms to the agreement he had tacitly accepted with commissioners and readers. To that extent there is no quarrel. Yet the same data can lead to another description of the same person which is not limited to this image of the famed, precocious scientist. However true that may be, it is not the only unifying thread running through his life.

But what is striking in the autobiography as well as in the opening chapter on his adolescence in *Sagesse et illusion de la philosophie*, published in 1965, and again in interviews with Evans (1973)[16] and with Bringuier (1977)[17], is the absence of *pedagogically* related ideas. Education certainly would appear to be a matter of resolute indifference to this epistemology.

The age of childhood doubtless interested Piaget and was even his preferred subject. But this interest was not due to some particular liking for children, nor was he seeking to say something original about the way they ought to be brought up. He did not beat about the bush on this question. For him it was a matter of describing how intelligence is constructed, and the child happens to be the most spectacular example of this in the different stages of its development. In spite of the timing of his work, which appeared in the throes of the 'century of the child', Piaget seemed not to wish to associate his work with the sing-song chorus celebrating the happy dreaminess of childhood.

Let me insert a personal recollection at this point. Arriving in Geneva in 1977, I was struck by the nearly unanimous view of Piaget that held sway in the halls of the university. There were two 'truths' that circulated about the man. The first was that Piaget was not interested in pedagogy. The second was a warning not to try to apply his theses in a practical context: Piaget's theses on the stages of intelligence were not to be transposed word for word to the classroom.

This view shared by the Piagetians, and the consequences it can have on shaping an image of the great man, have been well summed up by Hermine Sinclair in a collective work edited by M. Schwebel and J. Raph, published in English in 1973 and in French in 1976:

Is it not surprising that a theory which clearly takes as its aim the study of the modifications in human knowledge through the ages and that of the development of knowledge in the child had relatively little effect on teaching? However, once one is a little familiar with the problems that Piaget studied, one sees that their application to teaching is not immediately evident.[18]

This account of a very close colleague of Piaget's is echoed in the title of the famous article by Rémy Droz in 1980: 'De la nécessité et de l'impossibilité d'exploiter les travaux de Piaget en pédagogie' ('On the necessity and impossibility of exploiting the works of Piaget in education').[19] This witty title is obviously more serious than it seems. It expresses with humour the glaring contradiction and gives the lie to two reputed and strictly observed beliefs falsely attributed to Piaget.

The first fact is that as director for 30 years of the International Bureau of Education, Piaget had written extensively on education. Some of this writing was annual reports of the activities of the bureau, but there were also two contributions to the *Encyclopédie française* (French encyclopaedia),[20] which will be discussed below.

The second fact is a simple observation. One was regularly warned about the danger of over-applying the thesis of genetic epistemology in the classroom. In the meantime, the plethora of brochures, manuals, and courses instructing future teachers had become so widespread that the theories had been turned into a catechism. No wonder that in all good faith one detected in these Piagetian ideas fundamental truths for a new education and conferred a halo of a great pedagogue on the image of the man.

Piaget actually in the classroom?

Publishers, for their part, were not mistaken. Denoël/Gonthier published in its series 'Médiations' – which had a large number of titles – two studies by Piaget with a 30-year interval (1935, 1965) under the title *Psychologie et éducation*. The two studies had previously appeared in the 15th volume of *Encyclopédie française*. Then, in 1976, the French translation of *Piaget in the Classroom* appeared under the title *Piaget à l'école* in the same collection. The subtitles and the cover layout are of particular interest here.

Profiles of Piaget figure on the cover; one jovial, the other lordly. The subtitles unabashedly advertise the celebrated name to attract buyers: 'The response of the great psychologist to problems in teaching' announces one jacket, and 'Liberate pedagogy' proclaims the other.

Piaget in the Classroom would let one legitimately suppose that there is a 'Piagetian pedagogy'. By 1972, though, the same Rémy Droz, along with Maryvonne Rahmy, after having expressed the usual reserve about associating images of the master with the common pedagogical norms, wrote:[21]

We have seen the importance of the subject's activity in the cognitive development of the child and it goes without saying that if we transfer this knowledge to the level of pedagogical situations and teaching, 'Piagetian pedagogy' will grant a significant space to the pupil's own activity. It is certainly by being aware of what happens – thanks to the numerous studies on the origin of the child's operational knowledge – that Piaget resolutely defended an active pedagogy.

The expectation of a great man

Alberto Munari[22] takes up this ambiguity and defends Piaget's place among true 'thinkers of education'. But the contradiction raised by Droz in his 1980 article remains a major condition in forming an accurate vision of Piaget's role in pedagogy.

The *necessity* to look at his studies of the child requires a justification of practices that are not merely a lame plea, a moral prescription, or a utilitarian device: 'the active school' is a militant slogan worthy of a Ferrière or a Binet, who were courageous pedagogues but were not scientific researchers in Piaget's sense of the term. The *impossibility* of the exploitation of Piaget's work stems from this scientific aspect because the conditions cannot be obtained within the context of the classroom. On the other hand, Piagetians were familiar with 'active children', and so the question is whether the step from active child to active pupil is impossible.

Piaget himself took an astute yet kindly distance from the matter, which Silvia Parrat-Dayan[23] shrewdly analysed:

> By keeping to the language of a specialist in the psychology of the child and without having any wish to prescribe a pedagogical attitude, Piaget held himself in a state of expectation which could be either interpreted as the best way of conceiving the educative process or seen as an invitation to pedagogues to study psychology.

Even when his former student and assistant Hans Aebli asked Piaget in 1951 to write a preface for his *Didactique psychologique* (Psychological didactics), the great man accepted. He showed no resentment towards the author who had given his book (see the subtitle) the goal of applying Piaget's theories to education. He speaks lightly of the twofold qualification of the brilliant author: experience in the best psychological milieu and pedagogical views consistent with his laboratory research. Aebli, Piaget assured the render, 'had discovered that a psychology based on the reality of operations and operative schemes bears consequence in the dialogue and the conflict of the activity and the receptivity that characterizes contemporary pedagogy'.[24]

To borrow the words of Droz,[25] one can say that 'necessity' here seems to play with 'impossible' when a pedagogue is also a trained psychologist. The latter is the very condition of the pedagogue's competence itself. This short preface goes on clearly to confirm this condition, as did the brief prologue to *Piaget in the Classroom*. Piaget commends the authors of the latter work for having avoided making 'simple deductions out of psychology'. He praises them for knowing how to transfer to the classroom the spirit of empirical research without substituting the autonomy of experimental pedagogy in favour of psychology. What he was saying was that they had not done wrong by his work, which showed how much 'Action only becomes efficient with the concrete and spontaneous participation of the child, his trials and errors, i.e., a supposed "time wasting" which is in fact necessary.'[26]

The variations of *Le Petit Larousse*

Is it surprising, then, that against the wishes of the Piagetians the image of Piaget as pedagogue emerged in the 1960s? Let us examine one such instance, namely the *Petit Larousse*. The simplifications to which its dimensions constrain it reveal only that this linguistic monument – for that is what it is – is a form of schematization of the language that finally imposes itself on thought. The *Petit Larousse*, in the 1966 edition, has an entry for Piaget between PIAF (Edith), 'French singer', and PIANA, 'capital city of a canton (Corsica)'. Piaget is defined therein as a 'Swiss psychologist and *pedagogue*, born in Neuchâtel in 1896, author of works on the development of thought in children' (emphasis added).

In his 1990 publication *Jean Piaget, biographie et parcours intellectuel* (Jean Piaget, biography and intellectual itinerary), Jean-Jacques Ducret does not give credit to the image of 'pedagogue'. He limits himself to very few words in this regard, considering it a minor aspect of Piaget's work. The late François Bresson congratulated Ducret for so containing himself: 'Ducret's work neatly separates those who present Piaget in limiting him only to a psychologist from, *worse*, those who turn him into the pédagogue of the last half-century'[27] (emphasis added).

This *worse* is amusing, for being considered in his lifetime the renovator of the pedagogy of the last half-century is, after all, no small feat. 'Liberating pedagogy' cheered Denoël/Gonthier . . . But such a performance is actually impossible because it is only a performance. In order to succeed it would have to be unscientific since the criteria for educational success have nothing to do with science. And that is certainly the 'worst' that could happen to Piaget.

In the meantime, did the authors of the *Petit Larousse* get the message? What mysterious influences manage to modify articles in this type of book? It would be interesting to know that particular archival secret. In the 1995 edition of the *Petit Larousse*, between the entries for PIAF (Edith), 'French singer', and PIALAT (Maurice), 'French filmmaker', figures 'PIAGET (Jean), Swiss psychologist (Neuchâtel 1896–Geneva 1980). He brought to light the stages of intellectual development of the child and founded genetic epistemology.'

Genetic epistemology has become part of the image, but education has disappeared!

A volatile fetish

If the great man's image as pedagogue is eclipsed or ambivalent, the construction of the image of scientist, psychologist, logician, epistemologist, and sociologist, on the other hand, is even cultivated in the course of the autobiography. This thoroughly *subjective* attitude is in contrast to Piaget's deep concern to make it known that he held an *objective* approach to the world and its creatures, and most especially to human knowledge.

Certainly, modesty is a sign of an autobiographical account seen as a tradition as much as a 'genre': the evocation of a career of research. And that is no small thing, if one wants to avoid slipping into the pitfall of reducing the account to a collection of anecdotes, colourfully filled with witnesses recounting 'Piaget-as-I-knew-him' stories.[28]

Nevertheless, anecdotal accounts are not absent from Piaget's work, as attested to by the transcriptions of his lectures, his symposia, and even his courses. Yet, in general, his biographers will tend to compliment and rarely to offer criticism of the 1952 autobiography and its subsequent completed versions.

The affair of *moineau albinos* (albino sparrow) well illustrates what one can knowingly call, while keeping the amphibology, the edification of the figure of the 'savant'. Fernando Vidal, in Chapter 7 of the present work, recalls the story of the beginnings and takes up the account he developed in his thesis in 1988.

I shall limit myself to mentioning here that the story of the sparrow shows how much the legendary characteristic of the 'precocious child' affects the image one creates. Let it be clear that we are not denying in any way this precocity, which is easily proved to have been the case.

As Paul Ricoeur[29] showed, the reader of a historical account – and autobiography is just that – distinguishes the particularity of an existence via universal and exemplary references, even if they are his own or those of the social group to which he belongs. The reader, like other members of his group, continuously attributes names to those figures.

Thus the precocity of a 'vocation' – particularly a vocation that unifies an existence – cannot help but mobilize in our cultural heritage a strongly religious imagery, taking in biblical heroes from Samuel or David to Jesus or Hellenist ones such as Dyonisus, Achilles, or Pythagoras . . .

Evoking figures from *mythos* with *logos*, legend, and history does not diminish the image of the young Piaget as a precocious savant. Nor is placing him on Olympian heights or in the ranks of the Lord an ironic excess. There is no hero figure without a legend; or, to put it another way, a place in history carries with it a place in legend. The two go hand in hand, for the good, with all honour and objectivity.

In the legendary category, the albino sparrow seems to play the role of the fabulous animal that all heroes must face. This category is passed down to us by the commentators with a rigour that is unquestionably mythic: It is the 'genius' that one celebrates as well as the precocity. In commemorative accounts the word 'celebrate' is duly deserved.

From 'fact' to legend

Piaget himself is the source of the story, told in his typically laconic style. His reference to the incident is nothing more than mentioning a 'fact' without insisting upon it. The rhetorical ploy of the autobiographer, with character-istic reserve, lends an air of genuine discretion. The effect of endearing him-self to the commentators will not be missed, whatever one may say about Piaget's text, according to what has been cited in Chapter 7 by Vidal.

The event is simply retold without any sign of vanity or of epic pretensions. The child was 11 years old. The essential for Piaget was not to make himself appear a child prodigy, but to show the precocious vocation that preceded any adolescent philosophical or social quests. Any extravagances are thus minimized.

The moderate tone of the autobiographer serves as an ellipsis, which is itself a propitious way of durably establishing the misunderstanding. The autobiography appeared in a scientific series intended for 'scientific' readers: Without doubt words like 'article', 'journal of natural history', and 'pub-lished' are reminiscent of the customs and of the images of the highly scien-tific milieu.

However, was this 'study' anything more than a short note of 100 or so words copied for circulation among amateur naturalists? None of these facts is actually concealed, after all, in the autobiographical account. Yet the image of precocity makes this summary the 'first scientific publication' of the great man.

Vidal treats with care – and a wisp of caustic humour – the career of this sparrow in the biographies of Piaget.[30] He points out how the story is insist-ently taken up by the press, in the accounts of public figures, and in the writings of 'scientists'. Vidal chooses, among the tens of possibilities, nine citations in French, German, English, Italian, Spanish, and Portuguese: each conveys the image of the precocious 'scientist' while constantly reiterating the sign of the volatile founder.[31]

The analysis of numerous biographies, beyond the story of the sparrow, shows[32] what the quasi-totality of authors confirms, simplifying, sometimes to the point of caricature, the image of the 'scientist' which the autobiogra-phy imposes. Vidal cites Caparros,[33] who summarized the repetitive embroi-dered biography as a source, not only for the scientific community but also for the cultivated public, of a triple image destined to become the Piagetian 'cliché': 'Jean Piaget, biologist by training, psychologist by profession, and epistemologist by vocation'.

Vidal comments on this set-up of the triple Piagetian image:[34] 'Biographical accounts decontextualize the (biological) interests and studies of the beginning (which were neither biological, experimental, nor specially influenced by Darwinism) and by amplification, simplification or omission, accentuate the "Piagetian" character of the original account.'

Another image of the tormented visionary

There is 'another' Piaget 'before Piaget' with whom one should be familiar if one wants to understand the scientist and the kind of ardent fervour that burned in him. Setting forth the traits of another image is not to deny the authenticity of the received image. Vidal takes several pages in *Piaget Adolescent* to analyse the attempt by Mary Van der Goot[35] in *Piaget as a Visionary Thinker*. This essayist takes the contrary position of the 'Piagetian' thesis, while nevertheless accepting the autobiography literally. What she actually does is to construct another image.

Van der Goot takes a polemical perspective with respect to *Sagesse et illusion de la philosophie*. In this work, published in 1965, Piaget – we know – returned to his past as a young philosopher. With the same sobriety he had used to write his autobiography and by glossing over certain commitments, in particular that of the highly mystical Christian, Piaget narrated his progress with regard to faith and to speculative philosophy.

With a Piagetian desire to abstain henceforth from subjective speculation in favour of objective and scientific explanation of the world, Van der Goot discloses, intact, a firm intention not to renounce categorically general ideas about man's state and that of the world. She even claims to detect the persistent religious vision of his youth.

But in so doing, she transforms the adolescent Piaget into a veritable theologian, haunted by the idea of God and the future of Christianity. Piaget's youthful speculations are more on the order of an immanent philosophy than of a believer delving into Scripture and possessed by a *timor Dei*. And, contrary to any indications or repeated witnesses, she reconstructs Piaget's entire development as a veritable, yet disguised, religious 'quest'.

The excesses of this thesis gave rise to scandalized reactions, in particular in 1986, on the part of the American David Elkind, whose review Vidal translated in part.[36] Piaget's attendance, but even more his faith in the image cast by the autobiography, led this psychologist to accuse Van der Goot of inventing improbable tales, of ignorance even, about the 'true Piaget'. In doing that, his own argument becomes in turn extremely weak, returning once again to the albino sparrow, the story of which shows the incompatibility between the leaning of the precocious scientist and the engagement of the religious visionary.

In fact, Piaget 'before Piaget' extended his questioning while developing his mature work. But he did it in a strictly secular manner and also took an intellectual approach, which aimed at demonstrating the unsound foundations of the original query.

Choosing to contribute to the objective knowledge of creatures in order to resolve the fundamental question of the origin of knowledge in humans is a philosophical position, a religious choice even. This choice of science, with all its implicit postulations, also meant casting discredit on the philosophical process.

As a human subject, Jean Piaget was equally capable, neither more nor less than any other person, of living with the contradictions that this duality engenders. It takes a philosopher to contemplate philosophy while, at the same time, denying that philosophers are legitimate.

Plurality of beliefs in the same individual

Raul Veyne,[37] in a particularly caustic work on relativism, points out that 'The plurality of ways of believing is too banal a fact to insist upon.' Such plurality, he observes, is found *in a single individual* and appears according to the moment and the circumstances. But he adds that 'It is no less banal that one believes at the same time in different truths about the same object: children know that Father Christmas brings the toys and their parents give them.'

It is striking that Veyne returns here to Piaget's work *Le jugement et le raisonnement chez l'enfant*[38] in discussing the fact that at the time of Pindar, individual adults were able to believe in the truth of the *Iliad* while at the same time acknowledging the story to be made up, putting neither their mental balance nor the status of truth at risk.

Many writers, even among Piaget's acquaintance, were eager to show – some with indulgence, others with malice – that at certain times in his life the man was the opposite of a rational scientist. Piaget himself, in his autobiography, makes mention of his restless temperament and his nearly obsessive need to reassure himself. I have repeatedly heard it told by eye-witness or hearsay how Piaget would get off a train several times to make sure – even asking other passengers – of its destination. One can be a great scientist and yet retain nervous quirks in ordinary life. As Veyne puts it: The fact is truly banal. Even Freud drew attention to his own superstitious behaviour.

But one may say that being afraid of having boarded the wrong train is not the same kind of thing as refusing to walk under a ladder on a Friday the 13th. The first case is a demonstration of a benign anxiety, and not being able to 'reason' *in situ* would not be considered excessively serious. The second case shows a belief in a system that obviously, for a rationalist, is to be contested in establishing and knowing what is true.

This, and not in the plurality of psychological attitudes, is where Veyne places the contradiction: Every human being is capable of holding many beliefs simultaneously. Scientific conviction, *which is itself a conviction*, is perfectly able to handle any sign of 'faith' in itself, even if it is a conviction about contesting belief. Piaget, moreover, said as much: 'In such a case, where each is convinced in a more or less profound manner, it is impossible to leave' the fray 'and objectivity, here again, is a necessary ideal but difficult to achieve.'[39]

The man of a single idea?

The advantage, if one can call it such, in the case of Jean Piaget is that the man himself managed both to simplify and to muddle his images. He maintained an ambiguous relationship to the labels that were attributed to him. Piaget was not a simple hero, unless that image would be to have been the 'man of a single idea'.

Piaget did not repudiate this image of a unitary person, the formula for which had come from Bergson. In his autobiography,[40] after a rhetorical precaution, he takes over the image and employs it in the process if not of persuading the reader then at least of helping the author to find himself in his own itinerary.

In his autobiography Piaget never claimed – it must be noted – that the idea had been the idea of his youth, showing him his 'mission' in 1916. Nevertheless, this is the conclusion that Ducret draws in Chapter 13 of the present work.

Ducret describes successively Piaget the biologist in the 1920s, the logician in the 1930s, the genetic 'psychologist' throughout his career, the epistemologist especially as of the 1950s, and once again the logician in the 1970s. The images of 'savant' and of 'scientist' tone down that of philosopher and, even more, that of the religious man. But without exaggeration or making Piaget a religious visionary in spite of himself, Ducret manages to recall the fine images of philosopher and religious man in a sort of *(happy?) end* that reverts to the beginning: 'The researcher and thinker of the 1970s retained the inquisitive spirit of the adolescent and young man of the 1910s.'

This quote reveals a number of images, which appear in a twofold fashion. The images show the singularity of development of Jean Piaget: The '1970s' and the '1910s' mark out the period of his own history. At the same time, they recast the figurative categories that interpret this story: 'the researcher', 'the thinker', 'the adolescent', 'the restless young man'. The successive images measure the 'type' of development achieved from childhood to old age. The entwined images go beyond yet hold on to one another: the ever-present 'adolescent' in the emerging 'thinker', when, 60 years later, he was caught up with matters far removed from the disquieting dreams of his youth. One can share Ducret's happy ending in the present work:

> Briefly, finding the 'reason of reason' with the aim of answering theoretical and practical questions was perhaps the deep-seated motive that drove Piaget, from youth to his venerable old age, to follow the path of research of which science and philosophy are, in the end, the only judges.

In order to capture Piaget in the course of his history and his legend, one need not choose between multiple images and a unique image. Plurality and unity are compatible in a destiny that has not been foreseen in the stars. *Ut initium sit, homo creatus est: l'initium* (that a beginning be made, man was created) says the *principium* and by that appears the origin, with all its founding force, from which the rest emerges like variations on a theme. The image is graded. But the *initium* is also the constant possibility of the *exagitatio*, of the renewal. Thus the image cannot be pinned down for the good of the pursuer.

Notes

1 The original title did not make reference to the word 'great'. In the original text, the author used the word 'figure', which has been translated here by the term 'image' because there was no better translation [editors' note].
2 T. Carlyle (1928). *Pages choisies* (p. 214). Paris: Colin.
3 Ibid., p. 204; and F. Vidal (1988). *Piaget adolescent, 1907–1915*, doctoral thesis submitted to the University of Geneva, manuscript, p. 1.
4 Carlyle, op. cit., p. 205.
5 Alain (1951). *Préliminaires à la mythologie*. Paris: Hartman.
6 It goes without saying that Piaget would have contested the use of 'universality' here, given that there is neither objectivity nor empirical verification. The essayist tone of the present contribution is, in fact, the type of literature Piaget opposed. He preferred contradictory accounts of experimental data as the single means of fixing a universally acclaimed truth. The rest is at best shareable 'wisdom'. On the contrary, in the wake of Montaigne and Alain, I believe that the essay tradition is an honourable and effective empirical course to pursue matters of the human condition.
7 Vidal, op. cit.; and F. Vidal (1994a). *Piaget before Piaget* (pp. 2–9). Cambridge, MA: Harvard University Press.
8 P. Domincé (1990). *L'histoire de vie comme processus de formation*. Paris: L'Harmattan Ch. Josso (1991); *Cheminer vers soi*. Lausanne: L'Age d'Homme; G. Pineau and J.-L. Le Grand (1993). *Les histoires de vie*. Paris: Presses Universitaires de France.
9 D. Hameline (1986). *Education, ses images et son propos*. Paris: ESF.
10 J. Piaget (1952). Autobiography. In E. G. Boring, H. S. Langfield, Warner, H., & Yerkes, R. M., *A history of psychology in autobiography* (Vol. 4). Worcester, MA: Clark University Press. Cited by Vidal (1994a), op. cit., p. 6.
11 Vidal, Ibid.
12 This prayer was re-edited and commented on by F. Vidal (1994b). *Revue de théologie et de philosophie, 126*, 97–118.
13 J. Piaget (1932). *Le jugement moral chez l'enfant*. Paris: Alcan. [English translation: *The moral judgement of the child*. London: Routledge & Kegan Paul, 1956.
14 Vidal (1994a), op. cit., p. 6.
15 M. Shortland (1988). Exemplary lives: A study of scientific autobiographies. *Science and Public Policy, 15*, 170–179.
16 R. I. Evans (1973). *Jean Piaget, the man and his ideas*. New York: E. P. Dutton.
17 J. Piaget (1997). *Conversations libres avec Jean Piaget/Jean-Claude Bringuier*. Paris: R. Laffont.
18 M. Schwebel and J. Raph (Eds.) (1976). *Piaget à l'école* (p. 41). Paris: Denöel/Gonthier.
19 R. Droz (1980). De la nécessité et de l'impossibilité d'exploiter les travaux de Piaget en pédagogie. *Education et recherche, 2*, 7–24.
20 J. Piaget (1969). *Psychologie et pédagogie*. Paris: Denöel/Gonthier. [English translation: *Science of education and the psychology of the child*. New York: Orion Press, 1970.]
21 R. Droz & M. Rahmy (1972). *Lire Piaget* (p. 148). Brussels, Belgium: Dessart.

22 A. Munari (1989–1990). Jean Piaget, 1896–1980. In *Les penseurs de l'éducation*, special issue of *Perspectives* (UNESCO), *XXIV*, nos. 1–2, 321–337.

23 S. Parrat-Dayan (1994). Piaget dans l'Ecole libératrice, la dialectique de l'autre et du même. *Archives de psychologie*, *62*, 171–192.

24 J. Piaget (1952). Préface. In H. Aebli, *Didactique psychologique: Application à la didactique de la psychologie de Jean Piaget* (p. vi). Neuchâtel & Paris: Delachaux & Niestlé.

25 Droz, op. cit.

26 J. Piaget, Avant-propos to Schwebel & Raph, op. cit., p. 6.

27 J.-J. Ducret (1990). *Jean Piaget, biographie et parcours intellectuel* (p. iv). Neuchâtel & Paris: Delachaux & Niestlé.

28 Anecdotes are not lacking in anniversary editions, illustrated with photographs. An important 'oral tradition' surrounds Piaget, ranging from picturesque to caustic.

29 P. Ricoeur (1985). *Temps et récit, III: Le temps raconté*. Paris: Editions du Seuil. [English translation: *Time and narrative* (3 vols.). Chicago: University Of Chicago Press, 1988.]

30 Vidal, *Piaget adolescent*, op. cit., pp. 19–20.

31 I myself took part in this 'mythification' of the image in 1969, when for the *Anthologie des psychologues français contemporains*, of which Paul Fraisse entrusted the editorship to me upon the death of my master Honoré Lesage, I wrote a biographical piece on Piaget. Evoking in 30 pages the impressive list of his 'researches and publications' up to 1966, I signalled that it began with a 'study' on *Un moineau albinos* and I praised the genial precociousness of the author, by which I reinforced, in my turn, the feeling of scientific continuity in the cause of a primary intention.

32 Vidal (1988), op. cit., pp. 22–27; and Vidal (1994a), op. cit., pp. 8–9.

33 A. Caparros (1982). Piaget y sus origenes cientificos y filosoficos. *Rivista de psicologia general y aplicada*, *37*, 285–307.

34 Vidal (1988), op. cit., p. 24.

35 M. Van der Goot (1985). *Piaget as visionary thinker*. Bristol, IN: Wyndham Hall Press.

36 Vidal (1988), op. cit., p. 37.

37 P. Veyne (1983). *Les Grecs ont-ils cru à leurs mythes?* (p. 144, note 33). Paris: Editions du Seuil.

38 J. Piaget (1924). *Le jugement et le raisonnement chez l'enfant* (p. 217). Neuchâtel & Paris: Delachaux & Niestlé. [English translation: *Judgement and reasoning in the child*. Totowa, NJ: Littlefield Adams, 1969.]

39 J. Piaget (1965). *Sagesse et illusion de la philosophie* (pp. 4–5). Paris: Gonthier. [English translation: *Insights and illusions of philosophy*. New York: The World Publishing Company, 1971.]

40 Piaget (1952), op. cit., cited in Vidal (1994), op. cit., p. 7.

Epilogue

Piaget, his elders and his peers[1]

Anne-Nelly Perret-Clermont

Is Farel the only one who came down from his hilltop to preach? Or, with Renouvier, who affected us profoundly by his mighty spirit of Protestantism, are we going to keep hoping for an alliance between the religious search and the cult of classical logic, both rational and experimental?[2]

Let us conclude . . . by an act of faith in the strength of religious philosophy in French-speaking Switzerland. . . . We should be able to reconcile moral and religious experience – have confidence in the value of the good and faith in the nature of reason which unifies reality – with the requirements of an authentic philosophical method based on a creative spirit and rational critique.[3]

Introduction

The works of the historians presented in the first part of this book allow the psychologist to see the child and the young Jean Piaget in his native cultural milieu, looking for his place and his way. This context shows him in a non-'Piagetian' way (which only becomes relevant in view of the coherent development of his point of view and his thinking) and gives a historical–cultural insight into his quest for intellectual partners and those with whom he first exchanged points of view during his time in Neuchâtel (1896–1929). Jean Piaget appears to have been a total psychological being (and not only an 'epistemological subject'), whose thinking reflects and accompanies emotional and social commitments, ideological discussions, beliefs, and aspirations. Some ideas, considered to be 'Piagetian', may lose a bit of their originality when one discovers them to have already been present in the environment in which Piaget grew up.[4] Yet it is just as interesting to see how this youth knew how to avail himself of the major scientific, religious, and philosophical discussions of the day in a small town so inaptly considered 'provincial' (but really what town would Neuchâtel be the 'centre' of?). Piaget knew how to mix with great thinkers, who were themselves in contact with all of Europe and North America. Not only did he profit from contemporary discussions, but at an early stage he also took part in them (i.e., he was stimulated to participate actively). He did so with remarkable perseverance and personal originality, the foundation of which is worth looking into.

We shall try to show here how an awareness of certain aspects of the socio-cultural and historical context in which Piaget grew up can shed light on the meaning he gave to his system by theorizing on the positions that he had adopted early in life. We hope to make evident the dimensions of his psychological theory which are often implicit premises in contemporary thought. Perhaps one will find herein the possibility of a certain critical distance that will allow some researchers of the new century to embark with like-minded audacity on confronting, as he did, the great questions of the era and to boldly go beyond the limited boundaries that senselessly segregate the humanities from the sciences, and 'humanists' (theologians included) from 'scientists'.

Jean Piaget, Sébastien, and his system

From the time of his earliest interests in philosophy, the young Jean Piaget set about conceiving a system. It was a lifelong pursuit leading to the founding of new disciplines: genetic psychology and epistemology. His system ended up being so highly developed and so widely recognized that it seems sometimes to be endowed with an existence of its own, independent of its founder and its readers. This delighted Piaget because it did not contradict his epistemology: The fact that a system could be detached from its practical context[5] was for him an ennobling sign of just how well his thoughts had developed. He considered it a necessary condition that any such system of thought be submitted to the laws of logic in order to attain the status of a universal. Piaget considered concrete situations, whether physical or historical, only as particular cases among 'possible worlds' (possible . . . in thought, to be sure). But is the real not mingled with the imaginary? And how can one reply to the epistemological question that Piaget kept coming back to, himself the heir of many philosophers, such as Kant: How can structures of intelligence correspond adequately to those of reality, as the brilliant scientific discoveries seemed to show?

For Piaget, the task as well as the force of thinking lies in being able to describe reality just as it is, thanks to a mental exteriority (conquered with difficulty during years of intellectual development!) that allows the realization of its necessity. This 'necessity', which finally imposed itself on the spirit, Piaget describes as being at once logical and biological, i.e., 'bio-logical': It is the fruit of a thinking organism, a living being, with physiological, dynamic, self-regulated sensorimotor structures, which becomes little by little, stage by stage, aware of these structures and goes beyond them by thinking. The outcome of this ability to go beyond these structures forms a system because thought retains, in its very workings, the 'motor' of its origins, i.e., the *mechanism of self-regulated adaptation*. This is a kind of keystone in the Piagetian system, which allows its author simultaneously to account for ontogenetic and phylogenetic development and to found, in biological roots, the abstraction of his model – while at the same time seeing reflected therein his belief in the individual and in reason.

Piaget's personal and intellectual path is admirably coherent. The task he set for himself in his youth, while writing his novel *Recherche*,[6] in which he identifies with his protagonist Sébastien, who is in the throes of a metaphysical crisis, became his life's work. Jean Piaget managed to his last breath to create an enormous work that reflected his desire to develop a system that could satisfy his scientific and rationalist ambitions and that could especially deal with his philosophical and metaphysical queries. He seems to have wanted to answer the latter, categorically and in the least agonizing way possible, by affirming the value of individual responsibility and autonomy and by showing that such is possible with the development of thought. In developing his theory, did Piaget not end up by reversing his terms? Do his ideas, initially 'on a divine mission' (to take up his own language of 1916[7]) in the service of personal responsibility and likewise to humanity not end up taking centre place, leaving Piaget, a relatively depersonalized individual, in the role of a servant to *thought*, itself promoted to the place of immanent reality, a unique source of justification?[8]

A rereading of Piaget's early writings allows us to see that this direction of his work is present and conscious from the beginning, with all the intellectual, philosophical, theological, affective, and social ways of thinking that it implies. Our author is avowedly constant and retains throughout his intellectual life the bases of the ideas that were there from the beginning. At an early stage he was able to explain the reason for his faith in the unprovable and personal character of the premises of all reasoning about values: They are indisputable. These premises rest on personal decision:

> Science cannot prescribe judgement of values to its premises. The premises of reasoning about value are given through awareness and cannot be demonstrated. If I set as my starting point 'I want to live and that which helps me to live is good for me', I make a judgement that is immediate and cannot be contested either by an individual or by science.[9]

'Science states, faith evaluates, and this evaluation is always in the last instance a matter of personal decision.'[10] Furthermore, we know how important coherent thinking was for Piaget. He held on to this essential value over and above contradictions in the face of reality, which only made him mindful of the need to continue seeking better explanations. In order to found a psychology of values, he said, one has to treat the premises as a given, then check the experiences that led to these value judgements, *'making sure that the individual has remained consistent with himself'*.[11]

Contextualizing the cognitive activity of the young Piaget

We shall start by examining the *original views* that Piaget, first as a youth and then as a university student, defended in his quest for meaning, and the *effect of his views in their historical contexts*. What was the choice of values made by this person who was seeking his way as the First World War raged? Our hypothesis is that the young Piaget adopted at an early stage a certain number of views – which were to become premises as such in his later theory – to which he committed himself deeply in a milieu that included discussions as well as practices and conflicts, formed by the institutions (family, school and university, churches, parties, youth clubs, scientific associations, etc.) that framed ideological discourse, the means of interpersonal relations, and the psychological and material conditions that made some projects feasible and others quite difficult.

What interests us is not so much the study, which we have left to others (in particular Ducret[12] and Vidal[13]), of the social influence as such under which Piaget found himself or the network (quite limited, as we shall see) of relations that the young man established within his milieu, but, rather, the description of the social interactions in which he fully took part. Jean grew up, mindful of the meaning of life, in a milieu equally aware of all that was at stake for society in the education of its youth.[14]

Our presentation does not concern the individual psychological approach that would explain by the single, internal dynamic of the subject, the study of a beautiful 'case' or a deterministic approach from a social point of view that would make Piaget the 'product' of social factors acting on a personality pre-disposed to scientific creativity. What is at stake here is an attempt to set the development of the young Piaget's cognitive activity in its historical, cultural, and social background.

We shall bring a contemporary view to Piaget's youth, influenced by rereading Vygotsky and shaped by the contextual approach of acts of meaning[15] and by that of the study of social interactions.[16] While psychologists speak of 'situated cognition'[17] within 'communities of practice',[18] we shall try to observe Piaget's thought in its historical place, in a world 'of many voices'.

Of course, we shall see that during the Neuchâtel period (1896–1929) that concerns us, Jean Piaget, child, pupil, student, young researcher, and then young professor, was not left alone, abandoned to an epistemological investigation of inanimate objects. On the contrary, as he noted on several occasions in his autobiographical writings, he was in regular contact with his peers and elders. Together they supported his participation in lively discussions and 'authentic' scientific activities. This kind of support at an early age could create envy in today's youth, who, at the end of the twentieth century, are held back for long periods in what Lave calls the role of 'peripheral participants'.

Rediscovering the circumstances, the people, and the institutions that shaped the social and cultural landscape in which Piaget developed his model allows us to point out, over and beyond the meaning that Piaget attributed to his scientific involvement, its wider impact. Piaget's intellectual activity is not an abstract reality divorced from time. It is, certainly, historically situated. Being aware of this context will allow us to take a critical look at the effect of the Piagetian theory of psychological development because it will put it into perspective.

Certainly our aim is rather grand for the means at our present disposal. In spite of the undertaking of the present work, much more information would doubtless be needed to truly capture the context in which Piaget grew up. Nevertheless, we hope the boldness of our endeavour (after all, Piaget himself encouraged boldness in the face of great subjects of study) will encourage others to pursue research in psychology, not only of the child but also of those who claim to practise it, as Gilliéron has done.[19] The reader must understand that our intention is not another biographical study of Piaget, nor a historical recounting of his interests but, rather, an attempt to reread a certain number of his positions and his formulations of ideas, *as practical, contextualized activities coming from a person who tried to set his individuality at the heart of the questions and demands of his social and cultural milieu.* In this perspective, Jean Piaget's thoughts seem in part to be active and intentional *responses*[20] to his milieu, i.e., to his masters and the people whom he met (including the famous child who treated him like a 'clown'![21]).

Many years later, in rereading his personal journey, Piaget declared:

> I was greatly struck after the First World War . . . by the repercussions from the flow of ideas of the social and political instability that reigned in Europe, which led me naturally to doubt the objective and universal value of philosophic positions taken under such conditions. In my small country, so calm and relatively isolated from events, many symptoms showed the dependence of ideas on these social upheavals.[22]

It is clear that one of Piaget's aims was to give value to what he often called the 'autonomy of thought', i.e., *freedom*. Our intention is certainly not to deny Piaget these liberties but, on the contrary, to make them appear as many meaningful answers amid the expectations and constraints of his original milieu.

Partners from Piaget's youth

In order to situate the development of Jean's convictions and to understand his positions, one needs to identify those with whom he was in contact, especially those who were important in forming his emotional, intellectual, and moral character. We have already met them in the preceding chapters, in the tight family circle, at primary school, at grammar school and at university, in the church, and in social life. Certain features of Piaget's relationships with his partners, and their context, can clarify the inclinations and options of this young researcher.

Naturally his family and childhood relationships come first, those who always remained close to him: a region that formed a small political entity, strongly aware of its past or in any case of its myths,[23] at the heart of which the virtues of clock-workings, of commercial export, and of the cultural and economic development of the region criss-crossed. It seems that on this level at least, Piaget was at one with the reigning spirit, for years later in the Netherlands he would claim in his acceptance speech for the Erasmus Prize:

> I am pleased to see that the distinction which I am receiving is European and comes from a country of modest size, like my own, for I am convinced of the essential role that small European countries play in contemporary culture.[24] It seems to me that researchers in all fields benefit from a rather particularly free spirit and a non-conformism that are harder to achieve in larger countries, where the weight of national traditions and especially fashions and 'schools' seem slightly more apparent.[25]

The family

Even if Piaget spoke little of his parents, we know the influence of their personalities and in particular his father's important role in the Neuchâtel intelligentsia. We remember, in effect, the polemic his father provoked that is still talked about. Growing up beside him, Jean watched for at least 20 years *the psychological weight of social constraints* that overshadowed a free spirit acting in defiance of received ideas. He also was able to measure the force, and then later to detach himself from the hold of momentary ideologies, of the method of historical critique that his father used. Was the genetic psychologist who verified the authenticity of his subjects' behaviour in relation to their stage of development remembering his father's studies of anachronisms? Jean Piaget identified himself[26] with his father, who was active, committed, rigorous on the intellectual level, and politically engaged,[27] but we do not know how Jean felt about this person who, though inspiring respect and even sometimes admiration, also left the memories of an occasionally gloomy, difficult personality. In any case, he was an authority figure whose qualities his son praised.[28] But there are no traces of cooperation between father and son in the sense of jointly pursued activities to accomplish a common project. One can imagine that they limited themselves essentially to intellectual contact, in the sense that Piaget would later apply the term 'cooperation' to his theory.

Jean Piaget spoke even less of his mother, also an active person and committed to political and religious causes. It seems that the delicate health that affected her nerves would be foremost in his memories:

> My mother was very intelligent, energetic, and, above all, truly good; but her somewhat nervous temperament made our family life

rather difficult. The consequence of this was that early on I neglected playing in favour of serious work, as much to imitate my father as to escape.[29]

Jean Piaget had several sisters, but in spite of the emotional ties that united them, he hardly mentioned his female siblings – who perhaps did not count as significant 'peers' for the intellectual life of a budding scientist who identified with his father. It could also have been a matter of reserve in talking about family relationships.

On the other hand, Piaget often spoke of his godfather, Samuel Cornut, who, it seems, made only a furtive appearance at a key moment in his adolescence.

Studies

Piaget frequently evoked his comrades, in particular his friend Gustave Juvet, who accompanied him through nearly every stage of growth: at school, in the Club of the Friends of Nature, and even in the philosophy society.[30] Many of his schoolmates had impressive careers in science, academia, etc., sometimes in fields similar to his own. For example, Jean de La Harpe succeeded Piaget at the University of Neuchâtel, where he treated subjects close to Piaget's interest (reason, the relation of dogmatism and faith, the notion of time, etc.).[31] But the traces of camaraderie in the study of these interests are weak. 'Piaget precociously ran through the marshes for his malacology, doing research that was fundamentally solitary, and when he returned, his social relations remained tense.'[32] They did not, it seems, develop further. Piaget, on the other hand, often mentioned his relations with teachers who knew how to encourage him, such as Arnold Reymond, 'who follows my juvenile attempts with an admirable patience and benevolence'.[33]

Extracurricular activities

Piaget spoke frequently of the elders whom he met outside of school and who influenced his intellectual activity: 'I began with biology, having had the chance quite young to be initiated by an elderly naturalist';[34] this was Paul Godet. One finds here Jean Piaget collaborating in *joint experiments*, fixed in a very precise scientific field. The social and affective bond with this specialist was such that it seems to have permitted the young neophyte to quickly leave behind the status of apprentice, of *peripheral participant*, for that of a fully integrated researcher. Pierre Bovet is another example of an older figure who contributed to create particularly stimulating socio-cognitive conditions for the adolescent Jean, in particular with opportunities for concrete cooperation (in the full sense of the term) between peers and with intellectual contacts, offered by the Club of the Friends of Nature which he had founded with others while still an adolescent.[35] Pierre Bovet, at the time when Jean was a highly active member, still regularly supported the activities of this club with his presence and his advice. Other intellectually and scientifically minded adults, engaged in the life of the country, took an interest in some of the club's activities. It is quite striking to see that the life of the club depended greatly on the *initiative of the young* (on this point it seems similar to scouting[36] and other youth groups started between the end of the nineteenth and the beginning of the twentieth centuries). Adults certainly had an important role but rarely directly; they approved, encouraged, suggested resources – principally intellectual, but sometimes material. They did not organize the activities but were content with watching over the 'frame' of the activities.[37]

The church

There are certainly other places where the adolescent Jean Piaget met elders and peers, in particular the official church, where he followed courses in religious instruction. In spite of his critical stance, Piaget was inspired by these lessons. The social form of the courses reminded him, undoubtedly, more of the magisterial atmosphere of school than of the intellectual discussions of the Club of the Friends of Nature. The violence of his remarks in his pamphlet *La mission de l'idée*[38] gives the impression that the catechumen found the church too authoritarian, more interested in imposing its beliefs and dogmas than in serving as a genuine foil in his quasi-mystical search for the meaning of life.

On this point, one can ask why neither Jean Piaget, the future epistemologist of international renown, nor Maurice Zundel, the future famed theologian, though schoolmates and members of the Friends of Nature, ever mentioned each other on matters of *faith*. Nevertheless, Piaget wrote extensively on the relations between science, philosophy, and faith, and Zundel put at the centre of many of his works questions that were certainly already nagging him at the time of the Friends of Nature:

> What pushes a scholar to give himself to research? Is it domination of the world, which applied science offers? Is it freedom from sustained reality? Is it the thought of an ever-imperfect truth? Is it the inspiration of the Truth? What is there of Jacob's struggle that the scholar surrenders to the real: an illusion, a possession, contemplation?
>
> (Zundel's questions as reported by Donzé[39])

Of course they were still young. Without a doubt it was a difficult time for inter-confessional discussions on religious matters: Jean Piaget was Protestant while Maurice Zundel was Catholic.

Zundel would later write:[40]

> As a child I lived in a Protestant region; I listened to the polemics and the parades of the 'anti' who would plaster the Catholics' walls. My

grandmother, who was Protestant, never failed to mistreat anyone who was Catholic. On the other hand, the surrounding Catholic environment was full of ritual, offering an easy world that required nothing; it was sufficient to have committed to memory the formulas of the service to be satisfied. A lot of opposition, of talking, very little of the Gospel, none of that makes religion. We listened to the Gospels read in a neutral tone that we often heard, and the sense completely escaped me. All of that can be reduced to a religious practice without any experience of God; the formulas were right and true, thus acceptable, but stale. Salvation conformed to well-chosen formulas. . . . An imposed family religion without resistance.[41]

Maurice Zundel became a priest and committed himself profoundly to the search for a living and well-cultivated faith. This cost him the misunderstanding of the ecclesiastical institution and exile, but he was a major influence in Catholic Action and Christian Youth movements as well as on many people who felt drawn to his meditations. The invitation of Pope Paul VI to preach a retreat at the Vatican in 1972[42] brought him out of a long isolation and sanctioned the recognition of his international reputation.

Jean Piaget would later say:[43]

Growing up Protestant between a faithful mother and agnostic father, I soon keenly felt the conflict between science and religion . . . Reading Bergson was a revelation . . . in a moment of enthusiasm close to ecstasy, I was seized with the certainty that God was life, in the form of that *élan vital* or vital force of which my interests in biology allowed me to study a small section. I thus found inner unity in the direction of immanentism, which fulfilled me for many years, though in much more rational forms. . . . I made my decision: I would give my life to philosophy with the sole aim of reconciling science and religious values.[44]

For Jean Piaget, research in the direction of immanentism was a way of fighting against the idea of a transcendent being distinct from the human spirit. His remarks on the matter reflect his polemical attitude towards the Church, particularly Catholicism. Piaget clearly made known his view of ecclesiastical tradition and authority that seemed to him to be the social constraint *par excellence*: 'No other social institution shows better than the Catholic Church the fundamental relation between the idea of transcendental being and *de facto* authority.'[45]

For Maurice Zundel, God is not an 'idea', and an encounter with Him is to be recognized in its otherness rather than seen as a constraint. At the time, Zundel was greatly influenced by mystical experiences.[46] But could these young people talk openly of such matters, given the polemical climate of the time? Maybe at meetings of the Friends of Nature. It is not certain that even in this context, exchanges of this kind went beyond the sprightly remarks of youth. One can read in the *Cahiers des présences* (attendance records) of the club[47] some ironic allusions, reflected, for instance, in the nickname Tiécelin, taken from *Roman du Renart*, which Piaget suggested for Zundel: 'Tiécelin, because the crow has an ecclesiastic exterior that well suits Zundel' (15 September 1911). Note that Piaget's nickname was Tardieu, an allusion to a snail in the same novel, and which he would occasional spell Tar-dieu. The relationship between Piaget and Zundel seems to have been one of open camaraderie and perhaps even genuine friendship, based on the comments each scribbled in the *Cahiers des présences*. Tardieu was president and Tiécelin was secretary.

Some years later, young Piaget made contact with the clergyman Paul Pettavel, a person with a socially committed vocation to Christianity. Pettavel did not skimp in his efforts or his commitment: personal support and accompaniment, publication – largely at his own expense – of the *Feuille du Dimanche* with its political analyses from a Christian perspective, and his public defence of positions in a difficult and tense socio-historical context. Let us recall in particular what was happening in La Chaux-de-Fonds between 1917 and 1918: The national councillor, Paul Graber, had been arrested, and the crowd invaded the prison to free him; the city was occupied by the army; there was a general strike, added to which was the flu epidemic that put many families in mourning.[48] Pettavel made room for Piaget at the heart of the editorial staff of the newspaper *L'Essor*. This same Paul Pettavel left lively memories among other Neuchâtel youths who numbered among Piaget's entourage, in particular Samuel Roller and Laurent Pauli, who came from La Chaux-de-Fonds and would many years later, one after the other, co-direct with him the Rousseau Institute at the University of Geneva.[49] It is somewhat surprising to see that Piaget maintained contact with people from this milieu, because he never mentioned, either in his autobiographies or in his theological writings, the historical events that significantly shaped their context and commitments. As of 1914, Jean Piaget was a member of the Swiss Students Christian Association. He actively partook in the intense discussions.[50] He took an interest in psychoanalysis when he heard Théodore Flournoy speak.[51] More and more Piaget distanced himself from theology and gave up this kind of convoluted abstract reference to experience in considering the regulation of values, the role of intellectual cooperation, and the evolution of moral judgement, all of which replaced in his theory what Bovet had called the 'awakening of a religious feeling'. But let it not be forgotten that in this field as well, Piaget once again found favour with an elder, Paul Pettavel, an expert (using contemporary psychology vocabulary) who *encouraged the young man's speaking out by introducing and including him in his own social circle.*

When one places Piaget in the context of his origins, one cannot help being struck by the remarkable vitality of Neuchâtel at this time, and the opportunity it offered its youth to actively participate in its life. Piaget certainly remembered it when he theorized on the role peers play in the structuring of thought and in the sociability of thought. Yet this insistence in the Piagetian model on the importance of horizontal relationships should not lead to overlooking the elders who cleared the way for him to take part in scientific, philosophical, religious, and political discussions of his time. Why, then, did Piaget, the epistemologist and psychologist, not give due credit to this kind of experience with experts?

Jean Piaget's relation to his socio-cultural matrix

This bountiful background of family, intellectual and social life that flowered in Neuchâtel taught Jean to take a position, to shape and to defend his thinking (he also learned greatly appreciated organizational skills such as finding venues and funding, stimulating comrades, winning over their collaboration – abilities that would later be highly useful for him for setting up a scientific laboratory[52]). It was at this time that his wish to construct a 'system' was born, and even if he would later give up this term to talk instead about a 'theory' (a 'discipline' even: genetic epistemology), one can already recognize certain attitudes and choices that became indicative of his work. We shall look at the basis of his theoretical position from four viewpoints: affective relationships, relationships with authority and opportunities offered by his elders, the respective roles of peers and experts, and finally, overstepping boundaries.

The affective dimension had extremely little place in the work and writings of Piaget. Even in his autobiographical accounts references to such matters are rare: Expressions of affection are few and reserved. He clearly spoke of his great friendship for his childhood companion Gustave Juvet; we know of the importance of his schoolmate Rolin Wavre;[53] one feels a sort of collusion between him and his master Godet; he acknowledged his appreciation for the support given by Arnold Reymond, and his admiring respect for his father; but as for his mother, he admitted to having sheltered himself from her. His memories of her later contributed to both his interest in psychopathology[54] and his wish to break off his didactic analysis:[55]

> I never felt the wish to go further in this particular direction, always preferring the study of normal cases and the functioning of intelligence to that of the abuses of the unconscious.[56]

Other than this difficult maternal presence, Piaget spoke of few women. We know nearly nothing about Cécile-Marie Berthoud (1848–1931), who was his teacher in the private school he attended at the age of eight.[57] After that, only names of schoolmasters figure in his curriculum. Of course, at the time, the education of boys and girls was not the same at the secondary level. The Friends of Nature did not have any female members until 1987. Nevertheless, female students attended the university at the same time as Piaget, and it is striking to see that the majority of them were foreigners: From 1911 to 1918, at least 110 female students came from the vast Russian Empire to study at the University of Neuchâtel.[58] It seems that Piaget mixed in an essentially masculine world, where there was only a marginal feminine presence.

Pierre Bovet[59] gave excellent descriptions of the feelings of love and fear, which are based on the experience of respect for elders, and which he believed influence the growth of a child's psyche and faith. Jean Piaget, 18 years his junior and writing at a different time, sets the problem of relationships with authority in different terms. Was it the effect of his relationship with his father and with the hierarchy of the conservative society of his native city? Was it even a reaction to the tormented atmosphere of his early years: pre-revolutionary activity in Russia, the start of the First World War, and social movements and internal tensions in his own country? It is certain that Piaget felt his milieu to be very constraining and doubted the benefits of what he would later call 'social constraints'. The heritage of his predecessors often seemed negative to him on various levels: in religion (see his tirades in *La mission de l'idée*[60]), in philosophy (he feared the notion of a transcendence beyond understanding[61]), and even in science as seen in the preface to his doctoral thesis on malacology, in which he essentially expresses his dissatisfaction with the current methods of research.[62] Several times in his psychological work he returns to the idea that intergenerational transmission can hardly be the source of understanding if it is subject to an authoritative principle that precludes the autonomy of thought.[63]

However, the elders who ranked as experts in the young Piaget's entourage were not all sententious professors or dogmatic thinkers – far from it. One sees them, on the contrary, conscientiously making room for the young, whether they were Arnold Piaget, editor of the revue *Musée neuchâtelois*;[64] Paul Pettavel, in his own publication; Arnold Reymond in dialogues with his students; or Pierre Bovet, through the Friends of Nature but also with the activities of Bovet's family at Grandchamp.[65] And let us not forget Paul Godet in his laboratory at the Natural History Museum.

Jean Piaget belonged to two types of circles: those where relations among peers were favoured, especially the Friends of Nature, and those where he had to learn to assert himself among experts: first the Jura Club, then from 1912 to 1914 the Neuchâtel Society of Life Sciences, the Swiss Zoological Society, and the Swiss Society of Life Sciences,[66] as well as those mentioned above.

Certainly, to a great extent, Jean Piaget benefited from the role of his peers: But were they truly 'peers'? Piaget probably quickly assumed the position of 'leader', doubtless with the support of his comrades, who found him both entertaining and interesting. Some of the minutes of the meetings of the Friends of Nature give this impression. He soon became its president.

Piaget speaks little of discussions between equals and does not refer, as far as we are aware, to the fruits of exchanges with those less expert than himself at the time. Did he miss out due to the erudite status already acquired in his youth? The question may be worth looking into. In fact, the first experience that he relates of the cognitive benefit gained from an unequal relationship seems to be that which he had during interviews with children in Th. Simon's laboratory in Paris.[67] One wonders if the pleasure that Piaget had in holding these interviews did not reveal a self-projection that allowed him to relive a situation that he had often experienced with success: that of the brilliant student who knows how to take part in adult talk.

During his childhood and his Neuchâtel youth, Piaget mingled in a social milieu that his parents left relatively open and that gave him the chance to overstep boundaries: straddled between two churches with parents of different religious convictions; living in Neuchâtel but with contacts in La Chaux-de-Fonds, the other metropolis of the canton that was also bourgeois but with socialist leanings; joining student societies where one discussed theological, philosophical, and scientific questions; studying at the science faculty yet regularly attending lectures in the humanities,[68] at a small university with an international student body; leaving Neuchâtel to continue his studies at Zurich (in another language), then on to Paris before returning to the Rousseau Institute in Geneva after being summoned by Claparède and Bovet.

Searching for a construction of meaning: Positions taken by Jean Piaget and their significance in their contexts

We have pointed out some of the characteristic features of the socio-cultural and intellectual world in which Jean Piaget grew up. We shall now look at the positions that this young man took and at his precocious entry into the discussions of his elders. Searching for meaning and nourished by philosophical reading, he attempted to develop a system, which he founded on a certain number of firmly held premises, as if they were fundamental to his *identity* more than his thinking. The relation between reason, society, transcendence (or, more exactly, immanence), and action were essential to him. Given his interests as a naturalist and his studies in biology, Jean Piaget discovered philosophy and theology and confronted the great questions of his day (God, war, justice, freedom, truth, the social order, evolutionary theory, etc.) by trying to respond to them with a particular vision of Man.

Piaget's leading ideal: Reason and personal thought

It is already evident in Jean Piaget's adolescent texts that he did not see the individual destined to be a disciple. Beginning as a young specialist of the snail, Piaget then awoke to philosophy and discovered another living species: *Homo sapiens*! He was captivated by the problem of access to *knowledge* to such an extent that he made it the primary characteristic of Man – that is to say, Man's 'essence' (even if he himself does not use this term). It was an era of lively discussions, for both academics and clergy, on the evolutionary theories of Darwin, Lamarck, and others. Piaget's attitude as a biologist and his focus on thinking as the source of knowledge led him to approach from a very particular angle philosophical and theological problems that his contemporaries (especially his elders) were discussing.

His inaugural lecture, delivered in 1925 when he assumed the chair of philosophy, history of science, and psychology at the University of Neuchâtel, makes his position explicit. He talks, first of all, of a return to Kant and his concept of *a priori*; then he proposes the idea, which seems to him contrary, 'of a radically contingent spiritual development, such as Brunschvicg believed to see in the history of human thought'. But Piaget does not seem to be very convinced by this alternative and opts for a third possibility: his own method – which he sees as impartial – of genetic analysis in psychology, because he feels that 'it is possible that such a method imposes the concept of a kind of *ideal that directs reason*,[69] an ideal that is at once active yet not fulfilled'.[70]

Previously, in particular in his competitive work titled 'Réalisme et nominalisme d'après les sciences de la vie' (1917, neither published nor available), Piaget had already treated this *ideal*. His philosophy professor, Arnold Reymond, who had amply read through this work, was critical of 'the equivocal character of the definition that is given of God, sometimes presented as a "mere idea"', sometimes appearing as a 'reality existing independently of our judgements. The author was constantly floating between the two value judgements and this indecision seems to come from the fact that the fields of metaphysics and that of psychology are not adequately distinguished.'[71]

Many years later, in his work *Biologie et connaissance*, under the title 'Vie et vérité', Piaget[72] makes his position clear:

> If the truth is not a copy, it is an organization of the real. But who is the organizer? . . . All the philosophers concerned with the absolute have had recourse to a transcendental being, which goes beyond man and especially 'nature' in such a way as to place the truth beyond spatial–temporal and physical contingences and makes its nature intelligible in an a-temporal or eternal perspective. . . . Before placing the absolute in the clouds, it is perhaps useful to look within things. If truth is an organization of the real, we should first try to understand how an organization is organized, and that is a biological question. . . . It is better, before positing a transcendental organization, to exhaust the resources of immanent organization . . . [and to look for] the secret of rational organization in the living organization which even includes *its development*. The method consists then in trying to understand knowledge through its own construction, which is no longer absurd because it is *essentially construction*.[73]

At this stage it is no longer a matter of essential and abstract 'reason' but a kind of 'biological reason' that Piaget tries to account for by his works on the processes of self-regulation.

This evolution towards a more and more 'biologizing' explanation of life and of thought changes neither Piaget's initial fundamental position nor his rejection of a reduction of intellectual processes to the phenomena of cultural transmission. Thought for him is first of all an *individual* affair and is socialized only gradually. 'Four- and five-year-old children . . . are still not subjugated to social habits and objective thinking.'[74] But this socialization will only lead to a personal thought if, as Piaget later wrote,[75] the child is 'reared in function with the cooperation of minds and not [in function] with the respect of the word'. Certainly society can impart opinions and beliefs, but it cannot provide the subject with understanding itself. The latter requires some kind of *personal enlightenment*, an inner conviction that gives a sense of balance. The only 'constraint' is intellectual coherence, which can be attained through a particular type of social cooperation: verification by peers free of all hierarchical pressure.

The social as constraint

Piaget always rejected any kind of constraint. His rejection of impersonal thought could on occasion be surprisingly violent – for example, in the writings of his youth,[76] or as a young professor when he refused not only dogmas and static views of knowledge but also the implicit constraint on the child by teaching him a language:

> From his first smile, and especially his first words, the baby is subjected to social influence, at first very lightly but then with more and more coercion, which begins by channelling his mind, but then goes on to shape, and maybe even alter him entirely. It is, particularly, a system of ideas, of implicit judgements. It is made up of crystallized thinking and impersonal thought inherited from preceding generations. An infinitely tyrannical thought will weigh on every state of individual conscience, however intimate it may be.[77]

We can wonder how Piaget came to reject a certain kind of heritage. His elder, the professor Arnold Reymond, in commenting on the competitive essay mentioned above, suggested an interpretation: This work is 'directly inspired by an ever present circumstance . . . the war . . . raises once again and in a painful way the old problem of the relation of the individual with the social organism of which he is a part.'[78] Jean Piaget was a young adult when the war of 1914 broke out. His generation were the heirs (and potential soldiers) of an untenable situation. Still other aspects of the socio-historical context shaped the framework in which Piaget found himself: The Russian Empire, with which Neuchâtel was closely associated through its watch industry, was in the throes of the violent repressions of the tsarist regime. Locally, the ideological ambience of the canton was coloured by the relatively recent rejection of the feudal heritage from which Neuchâtel had only a few decades earlier freed itself completely. What sense could be given, under such circumstances, to the relation between the individual and society?

In searching for the meaning of life, the young Piaget found an answer in individual free thinking, which he raised to the level of a mission of salvation. Here he allied himself with the values of the Protestant ethic that scorned social meddling and favoured the absolute responsibility of the individual as the sole judge of one's conscience. Was Piaget giving himself a sort of religious *mission* in promoting the understanding of the importance of individual thinking? For Piaget, the meaning of life was to be found in freedom of thought, in the protection of essential values, and in the struggle against ideological allegiance and involvement in war. For him, such a commitment was the same as the quest for greater social justice.

Piaget obviously took from his youthful experience the importance of peer interaction. Knowledge, including religious knowledge, grows from intellectual contacts governed by an ethic of discussion.[79] Piaget neglected the intergenerational dimension of access to knowledge. On this point he was in contradiction with his Russian contemporary, Vygotsky,[80] who based his paradigm of research on the coexistence of the elder's elevated social position and expertise.[81]

In this paradigm, the view of knowledge that results cannot be static. Knowledge cannot be pre-shaped either in the object or in the subject; it emerges from a living development, owing as much to historical evolution as to an ontogenetic development. The categories of thought are not immutable. They evolve in function with the subject's *experience*, which, containing concrete facts, is necessary for thought because it is not by pure speculation that thought is ennobled. Piaget, the biologist, concentrated on the dynamics of living beings and sought to observe the processes by which the creative spirit – he had read Bergson – allows intelligence to construct itself.

In following Piaget, one realizes that by concentrating on the dynamic of individual intelligence, he was also looking to affirm the autonomy of the person and to discuss the possible development of a person through the freedom of independent thinking in the social context and especially under the pressure of elders. But he hardly ever uses the word 'person' to designate the subjects he studied.

He courageously opposed, at different levels, anything that he felt to have an illegitimate social ascendancy, particularly institutions. This *social*, which Jean Piaget so greatly mistrusted, seems to be collective opinions (reminiscent of the 'collective representations' of Durkheim?) which lack the means to justify themselves: institutions such as the state and the churches, and all the sources of coercive ideological thought. Also included here are social practices that do not assure social justice for the deprived or for the role of women (Piaget, like his parents,[82] in a country that only relatively recently [1971] recognized the woman's right to vote and constitutional equality for men and women, was ahead of his century). Piaget refuted the value of education that constrained the intellect rather than awakening a spirit of researching and questioning. He lashed out against preceding generations, who, by exercising their authority, prevented the growth of personal judgement. Instead, he pleaded in favour of contacts between peers, who alone would be likely to respect the autonomy of thought and to enrich it by reciprocity and unconstrained agreement.

How does one account for a young Piaget, barely out of an adolescence that he himself described as a period of 'freedom, because it was a period of primacy for exchanges between peers about obedience towards adults, as well as a kind of intellectual revolt of each generation against its predecessors', as a step that allows 'an adolescent to escape, at least internally, adult authority in order to seek in his relationships with his contemporaries the living source of his future activity'?[83] How could this former adolescent be the object of the magnificent praise of his elder, Arnold Reymond, who saw in him the *'the genial continuation of his elders'*?[84] Added to this one ought not to forget the fair treatment of his masters, who seem to have been able to recognize and support the competence of their junior without holding his outbursts against him.[85]

Piaget and discussions with his elders

Was Jean Piaget moving ahead in constructing his personal theoretical thinking by essentially taking positions that broke with his background, like a game made of cognitive conflicts with his elders? Or was he, as Reymond said, a young thinker who distinguished himself in discussions with his elders by using their own critical historical methods? Our working hypothesis in this chapter will be that Piaget first absorbed, little by little, the concepts and ways of the intellectuals around him in Neuchâtel and French-speaking Switzerland before changing them to his own ways.

Owing to family ties, Jean Piaget was first exposed to the field of history. From his experience with the new science of history developing in France, his father maintained a 'constant care to go to the sources themselves' and a 'critical attitude that never accepted non-verified opinions'.[86] This critical–historical method had not been unanimously received. In particular, one wonders 'if it is judicious to give credit to all the doubts that critical history casts on documents'.[87] Châtelain[88] relates the remarks of Alexandre Daguet in the pedagogical journal *L'Educateur*:[89]

> One ought not to play with the sacred feeling [patriotism] as a great reserve is necessary in rectifying certain facts in the field of historical literature that is aimed at the youth and the wide public. Once one has destroyed the belief of the young and of the people in a few of the traditions that are dear to them and that symbolize in their eyes freedom, independence, republican virtues, one will have destroyed all historical and patriotic faith.

Châtelain remarked that in Switzerland 'The historians were running up against this obstacle: on one hand, the objectivity aimed at by the historical method, and, on the other, the need to win over the vast public to the values of the Republic.'[90] Was Piaget following the path of a critical historian as his father had? It would not seem so, and in fact he never did any work of a proper historical nature. However, it must be noted that he was keenly involved in courses in the history of science taught by his professor of philosophy, Arnold Reymond, and from which he kept the 'historical–genetic attitude';[91] like his father, Piaget cultivated a critical scientific spirit, seeking the facts even (maybe especially) if they went against accepted ideas.

Arnold Reymond also taught him to read critically. In reading Kant, for example, he showed how much this philosopher had been dependent on the state of science of his day and how much it had evolved since then. Piaget raised the question of the historical relativity of ideas, and in particular of the philosophical debate on the nature of scientific knowledge. He continued his training in this direction during his stay in Paris. Some years later, succeeding Reymond at the University of Neuchâtel, he would say:

> History has shown that the categories of the mind are not fixed and immutable, and contemporary thinkers are so convinced of this idea that, by a curious reversal of values, mobility seems to be . . . the criterion of proper work on intelligence.[92]

Did Jean Piaget borrow from his elder, Pierre Bovet, the methods of 'observation and testing by questioning',[93] which he then developed further in his work?[94] Usually the method of clinical questioning is cited as having been adapted by Piaget, who borrowed it from psychiatry.[95]

Piaget studied psychological growth in different fields, as Bovet (1912 and 1925)[96] had done in the development of religious feelings, and like Claparède (1915)[97] in his studies of the evolution of interests and the role of play for the child. But Piaget systematized these kinds of observations and theorized further than his elders the processes of the psychological genesis, historical as much as individual, of knowledge. It is interesting to see that his historical and genetic relativism caused, to some extent, the same kinds of resistance as his father's critical–historical relativism. Piaget thus recounted that his colleague P. Godet, professor of philosophy at the University of Neuchâtel, would often tell him, without beating about the bush, that his 'psycho-genetic point of view in epistemology would suit him fine if he confined himself to the intellectual aspects, but socially these views are dangerous because man needs a stable and absolute reality'.[98] Even his dear schoolmate and friend, as a student of science and philosophy, Gustave Juvet, told Piaget: 'I am ontogenetic because a permanent Order is as necessary for intelligence as for Society.' Piaget commented: 'A Maurassian [right-wing] air was disturbing the metaphysics of elite individuals in French-speaking Switzerland, who had, however, been brought up as democratic Protestants.' In spite of the reactions of his peers, Piaget stayed faithful to his father's rigorous intellectual attitude, i.e., Protestant, democratic, and critical. The genetic approach became central to his work for decades, throughout which he would try to draw parallels between the history of ideas and individual intellectual development. In his search for phylogenesis and ontogenesis we see the biologist at work.

Because of his studies in biology, Piaget was especially drawn by the important post-Darwin controversy on evolution. The question of the respective parts of the innate and the acquired in the adaptation of the individual to his milieu remained with him for ever. Piaget had been involved with malacology for a long time. He continued to experiment on the adaptation of molluscs transferred from one lake to another[99] by asking if there was a possible hereditary transmission of what is acquired. This is the same question he asked, by extension, in examining the processes of adaptation on the psychological level.

Pierre Bovet had studied the social instinct and tried to understand under what circumstances it could be taught.[100] Piaget was not particularly interested in the social instinct. He mistrusted the social and sought, in reason, its opposite. But he presented a model that ascribes to instincts the role of biological premises for the development of adaptation processes. These, according to Piaget, extend on the level of thought into a process of self-regulation and equilibration. According to him, reason does not 'educate instinct' but supplants it. The social can contribute only by learning how to regulate exchanges between peers.

One can see that while he engaged in discussions with his elders and stayed mindful of the issues discussed, Piaget was nevertheless systematically pursuing his own views. The positions he defended on the sources of knowledge and of faith gave him occasion to express his differences.

Self-autonomy in relation to his elders and the idea of transcendence

Piaget clearly took a position in discussions on the sources of knowledge and of faith in favour of immanentism, which, for him, 'in different societies supplants the notion of transcendence little by little . . . [because], in the measure to which reciprocity and mutual respect develop unilateral respect diminishes in importance and, with it, the source of belief in transcendental gods'.[101] For Piaget, knowledge is neither a revelation progressively conceded by the Creator to the mind of His creature, nor an adaptation of the creature to the Creation that would enable it to understand the latter. The source of knowledge is in the evolution and even in the dynamic of thought: 'Thought explains being but, to the degree to which we learn to know it, being explains thought.'[102] Meaning and understanding identify with each other. Like his predecessors and contemporaries, Piaget was looking for the 'meaning of life' (which is, by the way, the title of Bridel's lecture at the meeting in Sainte-Croix in 1922 attended by Piaget)[103] and, with them, he gave an eminent place to ethics in individual thinking. His religious questions were not original to him:

It is a mystery to no one that most of the French-Swiss philosophers began by doing studies in theology and, all things considered, that is an excellent beginning, *under the condition of leaving it* and being formed, as are ours, in *the spirit of free research and respectful independence*, declared Reymond in 1931.[104]

In these discussions, the place that Piaget attributed to God seems to be his own, even if he tried to show that it was not completely in opposition to that evoked by his challengers:

> The two great ideas of God the creator and God the guarantor of truth retain their importance if one translates them into immanent language. ... Neither perception, nor notion, nor judgement is possible in any of us without there being implied in those acts a supreme Ideal, a norm at once intellectual and moral that enlightens our thinking like our conscience. If God is not there, the source of intellectual light and love, then where is He? ... Limited by the given, on one hand, and by the laws of thinking, on the other, we delve thus into Being and Spirit, in the hope of seizing one day the Unity ... Where does human thinking end; where does God begin? The problem is above all moral: God steps in when we give up our self, when we renounce intellectual egocentrism as well as practical egocentrism ... Immanentism is as much entitled to the spiritual food as he who said: 'the Realm of God is inside of us'.[105]

A thought that distances itself from action

To summarize, we think it can be said that after the elders whose authority he feared, and in a social world that he found repressive and constraining, the young Piaget carried out intrepid research to discover a meaning that would make the individual the source of his own reflected action, an individual endowed with a kind of divine guarantee of a rational nature. He developed a system from that premise that, starting with the problem of meaning, ended up with a *logical, abstract model* of coherence.

We can ask *why*? Piaget, who was particularly active in those discussions, gave such priority to *thought* that he probably did not notice to what extent this underlay, at least with certain masters – Bovet, in particular – concrete and committed *actions*. Piaget spoke in terms that could lead one to believe that he was concerned only with discussion. Yet the political and educational stakes to which his elders were committed were loaded with meaning. Their epistemological models had immediate direct social and pedagogical implications. For example, the positions of the pastor Pettavel marked him politically and ecclesiastically in a very precise way in highly fraught matters. Pierre Bovet certainly set forth interesting ideas in the field of psychology and pedagogy, but they owed their meaning to the long tradition of the Bovet family, who, just a few kilometres from Neuchâtel at Grandchamp, were actively involved in social foundations.[106] Let us remember that it was this same Pierre Bovet who not only reflected on the education of youth but also created and supported the Club of the Friends of Nature where Piaget spent much valuable time. It is certain that Piaget assigns a fundamental place to *action* in his system. He presents it even as the basis of thought. But in his developmental view, he leaves action at a stage so primitive that he does not even study its adult forms. As a consequence, in his psychological study, Piaget leaves the field of action in order to concentrate principally on the study of *judgement* and *rational thought* in a movement that ends by detaching thought completely from action. Piaget explicitly favours this detachment towards abstraction, without reflecting, it seems, on the practical consequences of his position. This detachment results in favouring logic over an understanding of the problem of meaning, such as it is psychologically experienced, i.e., in direct contact with individual and collective daily life.

Where does this detachment come from in Piaget? In his novel *Recherche*, he lets Sébastien say in his mystical quest:

> If [the thinker] renounces action, it is to render a greater service, to give to those who act a purer truth. Because action necessarily distorts the ideal, mixing fact with right. It is not for thought to throw the stone, to be sure, but nor is it for thought to take part in this distortion. If not, progress is no longer possible. Progress is made by individuals strong enough to ignore action and to lean, in spite of the fact, towards the ideal of the right.[107]

Is the adolescent interpreting in his own way the traditionally Protestant mistrust of 'salvation by works'? He goes on to say a few lines later:

> It is true that the thinker must not lose sight of reality. 'They are not of this world, says Christ, but I send them into the world.' If the truth is not reality, not floating above it, then it is interior to reality, driving it. Thus the soul of the thinker must be open to all the surrounding miseries. It explains them without remedying them. This work is for others, once evil has been identified.[108]

The 'interior truth' that Piaget describes seems to appear only in the breath of inspiration, producing thought and speech but not action. Christ is evoked for his words, but they are placed neither in the context of his actions (feeding, caring, consoling, etc.) nor in the concrete contexts of his living interlocutors.

Piaget and his cultural heritage

At a time when one seeks to liken by comparison the works of Piaget and Vygotsky, it may be worthwhile to recall the specificity of their socio-cultural heritages and the historical contexts at the heart of which they forged their positions and their thoughts.

One sees that Piaget grew up at the crossroads of social influences that were very different from those of his Russian contemporary.[109] He belonged to a political entity at the heart of what one may describe as a 'confederation of minorities' (and not an empire) that offered the possibility of identifying neither with the ruling members of the nation nor with a dominant culture. The Neuchâtel citizen was not out to 'civilize the world' by his culture – but perhaps by his religious ethic. The transactions that would have been familiar to Piaget were rather commercial.[110] He was not a citizen of a colonial power but of a country of farmers, watchmakers, engineers, mercenaries, tradesmen, and bankers. Nor was he from a Catholic region that might consider instruction a good to be distributed from a central entity in the interest of the coherency of the social body. Rather, he grew up in a traditionally Protestant state where the religious atmosphere tended to emphasize the dignity of the individual (and not that of the church) in direct contact ('democratically', so to speak) with God. Personal experience – and in particular the highest part of that, religious experience – was seen as unique and intimate, like a kind of incommunicable premise.

Piaget was also the child of political, cultural, religious, and parental traditions that cultivated a critical distance from authority. His indifference to social factors in his development, apart from its roots in his biography and his personal inclinations, was perhaps also due to the ideological atmosphere of his background, where authority was generally seen as foreign, repressive, at best protective; where institutions had for a long time needed to find their place under the threat of foreign takeovers.

But Piaget would go further in his ideas of a quasi-egocentric individualism,[111] regarding the development of one's own thinking as a primary and universal task. As a result his system recognizes neither the importance of social solidarity nor the relational interdependence that makes possible not only psychological growth but also access to knowledge gathered by preceding generations. This 'egocentrism' led Piaget to underestimate the role of his elders as much as that of his peers.

Reopening the discussion from the premises of the model

Based on the present (unfortunately still limited) 'case study' of the thought of this future scholar, numerous questions can be asked or reopened. His premises are not necessarily those of today's researchers, yet should not stay implicit. The same certainly goes for the underlying postulates of the hypotheses of other 'grandfathers' of contemporary psychology, especially Vygotsky.

It is important to see the historical and social situations of today, while asking ourselves if the great theories, especially of those two predecessors, are not only for us instruments of thought, but also *distorting filters* owing to their socio-historical choices (perhaps ill-timed for our current situation), the importance of which we ignore because of our lack of appreciation. Returning to those implicit *a priori* factors can also be an occasion to work out the construction of new psychological, social, and cognitive insights by drawing on the experiences and reflections of very different schools of thought.

In particular, in the circumstances that pertained at the turn of the twentieth century, it seems important to us to reconsider the imparting of knowledge and the development of know-how by looking with new terms at the political and technological changes (which pose problems of freedom, identity, and relations between age groups) that underlie them. Entering into the mould of preceding generations can hardly suit the young confronted by considerable social and ideological upheavals. Yet denying cultural heritage leaves future generations without references, tools, acquired experience, or memory.

How should one rethink relations between adults and youth, between expert and novice, between those committed to actions based on different responsibilities? Cultural context structures in part ways of reacting and thinking, and the search for abstraction – outside of action, relations, and time – is not necessarily the most adequate norm in every circumstance. The universality of thought is perhaps not where one should seek the answer. Contemporary research has made evident the dimensions of the problems different from those Piaget treated.[112] It seems to us that the 'case' study of the adolescent Jean Piaget, of such vivacious thinking, may be used to illustrate a certain number of characteristics of cognitive activity that can be understood with the theoretical tools currently available, which we shall now briefly recall.

Cognitive activity begins in relational spaces that make it possible, while at the same time this activity contributes to structuring these spaces.[113] The epistemic quest is not motivated just by cognitive activity. The learning subject mobilizes and constructs different strategies according to what he perceives at stake in the situations that he meets. Thinking does not take place in a void, without relations or social actions.

Recent research on learning has also brought to light the importance of considering the specificities of the different domains of knowledge and the forms (conceptual or procedural) of cognition in order to improve the study of psychological development.[114] It would be interesting to look at what forms of knowledge Piaget was exposed to as a child, since the learner is not confronting merely a feeling of logical necessity and a feedback of physical reality, but also the actions and interpretations of other social actors. These take place in institutional contexts that legitimize (or not) certain approaches and certain memories. Memory and action sometimes work towards contradictory aims and in somewhat contorted organizational schemes and conscious plans. We also know better how the 'micro-history' of the subject influences how one will interpret new situations on the basis of the elaborations already made of those previously encountered. This transfer of earlier psychological experiences concerns not only the cognitive aspects but also, certainly, the emotional and affective dimensions, particularly connected to the meaning that the learner gives to events that he has experienced, in social fields marked by institutional and ideological traditions and by emotional bonds within the family. How did the personal history of Jean Piaget, something of a loner himself, create in him a need to so greatly value abstract thinking, which he placed above action and to which he entrusted a superior social role? One cannot forget here the words of Sébastien and can hardly wonder about the experiences that led him to say:

> The thinker begins with an attitude of revolt. He must be free, intensely free; he must dare to see all the turpitudes and all the cowardice. . . . It is the action of practising with the adversary for the needs of the cause: thought has nothing to do with compromises. It is independent and sufficient unto itself. This independence is only won at the cost of extreme struggle and outward revolt. . . . Revolt against his own who tried to tie him down, against orthodoxy that tried to divert his thinking, against politics that tried to nationalize him, against fellows and enemies, against those who wanted his good and those who would diminish him. And, after the revolt, solitude. . . . 'Solitude is holy', so the poet says.[115]

The *mediation* between the object of knowledge and the learner, since the invention of printing and with the growth of modern means of communication and of information, seems (rightly or wrongly?) no longer direct. It is no longer given through words, facial expressions, or hands of the elder, the master, or the expert. It appears more often indirectly, coming from a teaching 'transmitter' (and not 'creator') of knowledge or from semiotic tools that reify the word: books, audio and visual recording, computerized data, etc. What is the psychological impact, in relation to knowledge, of this symbolic mediation? This question prompts another with respect to Piaget's experience: What would happen to Jean's experiences of hearing directly the combative stories of the historian Arthur Piaget, of working at the museum with his old naturalist friend, of witnessing the action of the pastor Pettavel, of practising philosophical enquiry with his master Reymond or his godfather Samuel Cornut, and scientific research with the experts who supported the Club of the Friends of Nature? What would happen to the person-to-person contacts that served as levers in Piaget's development? Are they accessible to today's students?

Returning to the philosophical and theological discussion that was at the heart of the beginnings of Piagetian psychology, one can see – at least among many contemporary Neuchâtel adolescents – that the question of meaning is no longer asked in the same terms as at the time of Piaget's youth: These terms are no longer those of *history* (which adults perhaps fail to pass on); nor are they about *the meaning of the relation between the person and his/her*

Creator, or whether the ways of conceiving these relations are intellectually and morally adequate. Maybe the contemporary period has taken so seriously the human being as in the image of God, of which he is also the Creator, that it finds itself greatly challenged in its search for understanding of not only Creation but also the effects of its own material, relational, ecological, social, and intellectual activity. Do older generations still know how to talk to the youth and encourage them to discuss? Or are these generations no longer able to do so because they have been so affected by the war of 1940–1945, even more violent than the preceding one, by the revolutions of their colonies and other collective trials, and by 40 years of a divided Europe that they have conflicting relations with the heritage of their past that make it difficult for them, as for Piaget, to accept and transmit the memory?

Has the fall of the Iron Curtain opened for Europe, less divided, other areas of action and thought to take on these questions? And towards ends other than theological, ideological, or scientific?

Notes

1 A partly similar version of this chapter has been published under the title 'Revisiting young Jean Piaget in Neuchâtel among his partners in learning'. In L. Smith, J. Dockrell, & P. Tomlinson (Eds.), *Piaget, Vygotsky and Beyond* (pp. 91–121). London: Routledge, 1997.

2 J. Piaget (1921). L'orientation de la philosophie religieuse en Suisse romande. *La semaine littéraire, 29*, 410.

3 Ibid., p. 412.

4 We will concentrate principally here on the context of Jean Piaget's youth. For an examination of the international framework of his early scientific activities in child psychology and pedagogy, see S. Parrat-Dayan (1993). Le texte et ses voix: Piaget lu par ses pairs dans le milieu psychologique des années 1920–1930. *Archives de psychologie, 61*, 127–152; (1993) La réception de l'oeuvre de Piaget dans le milieu pédagogique des années 1920–1930. *Revue française de pédagogie, 104*, 73–83.

5 And its socio-cultural context – but it is we who are making this distinction, because Piaget hardly ever labelled these aspects except in the vague and pejorative terms of 'social constraints'.

6 J. Piaget (1918). *Recherche*. Lausanne: La Concorde.

7 J. Piaget (1916). *La mission de l'idée*. Lausanne: La Concorde.

8 Thought seems here to take the place that, in Protestant theology, is filled by a transcendental God and salvation by faith.

9 Piaget (1916), op. cit., p. 65.

10 Ibid., p. 80.

11 J. Piaget (1922). *La psychologie et les valeurs religieuses*. (Sainte-Croix: Christian Association of French-Swiss students). Lausanne: La Concorde, 1923, pp. 38–82 [emphasis added].

12 J.-J. Ducret (1984). *Jean Piaget, savant et philosophe: Les années de formation*. Geneva: Droz; Chapter 13 of the present volume.

13 F. Vidal (1994). *Piaget before Piaget*. Cambridge, MA: Harvard University Press; Chapter 7 of the present volume.

14 A. Reymond (1931). La pensée philosophique en Suisse romande de 1900 à nos jours. *Revue de théologie et de philosophie, 81*, October-December, Lausanne,

pp. 5–20. In this report on philosophical activities in French-speaking Switzerland, one can read, for example, the questions that were raised by the work of Edouard Claparède on *The right to educate*: 'In view of what or whom does one educate the child? In view of a particular society (nation)? But what right has this society to do so? In view of an ideal? But on what basis is this ideal founded and how is it justified?' (p. 7).

15 For example, J. Bruner (1990) *Acts of meaning*. Cambridge: Cambridge University Press; B. Rogoff (1990) *Apprenticeship in thinking: Cognitive development in social context*. Oxford: Oxford University Press.

16 For a discussion of these questions (among others), see A.-N. Perret-Clermont (1980) *Social interaction and cognitive development in children*. London: Academic Press; and A.-N. Perret-Clermont & M. Nicolet (Eds.) (1988) *Interagir et connaître*. Cousset, Fribourg: Delval; also C. Pontecorvo (Ed.) (1993) *La condivisione della conoscenza*. Florence: La nuova Italia.

17 See specifically L. Resnick, J. Levine, & S. Teasley (Eds.) (1991). *Socially shared cognition*. Washington, DC: American Psychological Association.

18 Also J. Lave & E. Wenger (1991). *Situated learning: Legitimate peripheral participation*. Cambridge: Cambridge University Press.

19 Ch. Gilliéron (1985). *La construction du réel chez le psychologue*. Berne: Lang.

20 Piaget had a practice of thinking as a *response*, for he would often tell his students in Geneva: 'To develop an idea always choose one or two scapegoats with whom you can imagine a response.' Following this advice, for the present article, I shall try not to lose sight of two 'scapegoats': Vygotsky for one, whom I shall reproach for a model of the development of thought that makes the cultural expert the ultimate reference, with, as a result, quite a weak account of the creative initiative and commitment of the individual as a person, and an over-estimation of the need for asymmetry in the roles of expert and novice in the construction of understandings; my other 'scapegoat' will be Piaget, whom I shall try to get to show how the model is an abstraction of the affective, relational, and cultural processes intrinsically connected to the development of the fruits of thought, including Piaget's own.

21 J. Piaget (1972). Discours de Jean Piaget. *Stichting Praemium Erasmianum*, Amsterdam, pp. 27–32.

22 J. Piaget (1965). *Sagesse et illusions de la philosophie* (p. 22). Paris: Presses Universitaires de France. [English translation: *Insights and illusions of philosophy*. New York: The World Publishing Company, 1971.]

23 J.-M. Liengme (1994). Le sens de la mesure. L'émergence d'un discours historique centré sur l'industrie horlogère neuchâteloise. *Cahiers de l'Institut d'histoire*, no. 2.

24 Notice how Piaget's emphasis here is not unlike that of another Neuchâtel personality who also reflected on the areas of Europe, Denis de Rougemont. He was among Piaget's first students at the University of Neuchâtel in 1925: see B. Ackermann (1996). *Denis de Rougemont: une biographie intellectuelle* (2 vols.), Geneva: Labor & Fides.

25 Piaget (1972), op. cit., p. 27. This reading of social reality by Piaget is not without humour and says more about the role of certain identity myths ... when one knows the importance of the *school* of psychology that Piaget himself founded in this small country.

26 J. Piaget (1976). Autobiographie. *Cahiers Vilfredo Pareto – Revue européenne des sciences sociales*, *14*, 1–43, p. 2.

27 He was director of the State Archives, the first rector of the university, an influential member on the commission for the grammar school, etc.

28 Ducret, op. cit.; Vidal, op. cit.

29 Piaget (1976), op. cit., p. 2.

30 See Reymond, op. cit.

31 P. Muller (1976). *Approches de l'homme contemporain* (pp. 23–28). Neuchâtel: Messeiller.
32 Philippe Muller, personal communication.
33 Piaget (1965), op. cit., p. 14.
34 Piaget (1972), op. cit., p. 27.
35 See Vidal, op. cit., and Chapter 17 of the present volume.
36 Pierre Bovet had translated into French Robert Baden-Powell, the founder of scouting.
37 N. Guinand & R. Lüscher (1993). *Amici Naturae: un siècle, une histoire*. Neuchâtel: Club des Amis de la Nature. Published in 70 examples for the 100th anniversary of the Club of the Friends of Nature.
38 Piaget, op. cit., 1916.
39 M. Donzé (1980). *La pensée théologique de Maurice Zundel* (p. 62). Geneva & Paris: Editions du Tricorne & Editions du Cerf.
40 M. Zundel (1976). La clé du royaume. *Choisir, 200/201*, 3–7. We are grateful to Rev. René Castella, former chaplain of the University of Neuchâtel, for this reference.
41 But if the inter-confessional relations were stagnant and the formulas stale, there remained interpersonal contacts. Zundel in effect continues his remarks by adding: 'In the second class, I met a comrade who was not Catholic. He approached the Gospel in a new way; intelligent and passionate, he took to the Gospel and to the thinking of Pascal. He was that admirable instrument who made me feel that the Gospel was not a collection of speeches and formulas, but a presence that I perceived by the way he read the Sermon on the Mount.'
42 Published subsequently: M. Zundel (1976). *Quel homme et quel Dieu, Retraite au Vatican*, Paris, 1976.
43 Piaget (1965), op. cit., p. 12.
44 Ibid.
45 J. Piaget (1930a). *Immanentisme et foi religieuse* (pp. 8–54). Geneva: Swiss-French Group of former members of the Christian Association for Students, cited by L. Barbey (1982). La pensée religieuse de Jean Piaget. *Nova et vetera, 4*, 261–314. We are indebted to Georges Panchaud, honorary professor at the University of Lausanne, for this reference. While Professor Panchaud was visiting professor at the University of Neuchâtel, he drew our attention to the theological stakes in Piagetian positions.
46 Donzé (1980), op. cit., p. 21.
47 We would like to thank our colleagues Jacques Méry and Luc-Olivier Pochon, mathematicians, alias Synopipe and Bromure, honorary members of the Amici Naturae, for information about the life and spirit of this still active club. We are indebted to Jacques Méry for reading these attendance records.
48 But Piaget does not refer to these political and social events.
49 Samuel Roller, personal communication; Laurent Pauli, personal communication.
50 See Chapter 8 of this volume. Piaget (1922), op. cit.
51 F. Vidal (1995). Sabrina Spielrein, Jean Piaget – chacun pour soi. *L'évolution psychiatrique, 60*, 100.
52 Attendance records of the Amici Naturae.
53 Philippe Muller, personal communication.
54 Piaget (1976), op. cit., p. 2.
55 L. Appignanesi & J. Forrester (1992). *Freud's Women*. London: Virago Press. Cited by A. J. Soyland (1993). Sabina Spielrein and the hidden psychoanalysis of psychologists. *Newsletter of the History and Philosophy Section of the British Psychological Society, 17*, 5–12. We are grateful to Irena Sirotkina for having brought to our attention this interesting study of the psychoanalysis of Jean Piaget.
56 For the relation of Jean Piaget to psychoanalysis during his stay in Paris

(1919–1921), see P. Harris (1997). Piaget in Paris: from 'autism' to logic. *Human Development*, *40*, 109–123.

57 See Chapter 4 of the present work.

58 These students, perhaps frequently (but not always) enrolled in the Department of Modern French at the Faculty of Arts, were doubtless drawn to Neuchâtel by the reputation this region had for speaking 'good French' (i.e., without much trace of regionalisms) and by the reputation of the emigrant tutors and governesses to Russia (Maeder, 1993). The Russian students were also numerous in other Swiss universities at the time, finding in that country a freedom of expression and study that was lacking in their tormented native cities owing to pre-revolutionary events (D. Neumann (1987). *Studentinnen aus der Russichen Reich in des Schweiz (1867–1917)*. Zurich: Rohr.) We are grateful to Professor Rémy Scheurer of the University of Neuchâtel for those remarks and references.

59 P. Bovet (1925). *Le sentiment religieux et la psychologie de l'enfant.* Neuchâtel: Delachaux & Niestlé.

60 Ibid., 1916.

61 Ibid.; and P. Bovet (1929). Pour l'immanence. Réponse à M.J.D. Burger. *Revue de théologie et de philosophie*, *17*, 146–152.

62 J. Piaget (1971). *Introduction à la malacologie valaisanne.* Thesis submitted to the Faculty of Science at the University of Neuchâtel with a view towards obtaining the degree of Doctor of Science, Sion, Aymon, pp. 1–3.

63 See for example, J. Piaget (1958–60). Problèmes de la psycho-sociologie de l'enfance. In G. Gurvitch (Ed.) (1958–1960). *Traité de sociologie* (Vol. II, pp. 229–254). Paris: Presses Universitaires de France.

64 See Chapter 3 of the present volume.

65 The Bovet family had been active there for several generations. Pierre Bovet was familiar with the hospital, school, evangelical teachers' college, and spiritual retreats that gave birth to the Protestant congregation, the Evangelical Community of the Sisters of Grandchamp.

66 See Chapter 7 of the present volume.

67 J. Piaget (1972), op. cit.

68 See Chapter 6 of the present volume.

69 Emphasis added.

70 J. Piaget (1925). Psychologie et critique de la connaissance. *Archives de psychologie*, *29*, 210. (Inaugural lecture delivered 1 May 1925 for the chair of philosophy of science and psychology at the University of Neuchâtel.)

71 A. Reymond (1917). Rapport du jury sur le prix de la société académique. *Département de l'Instruction Publique, Première partie: Enseignement supérieur*, pp. 53–63, cited in Chapter 6 of the present volume.

72 J. Piaget (1967). *Biologie et connaissance.* Paris: Gallimard. [English translation: *Biology and knowledge: An essay on the relations between organic regulations and cognitive processes.* Chicago: University of Chicago Press, 1971.]

73 Piaget (1967), op. cit., pp. 414–415; emphasis in original.

74 Piaget (1925), op. cit., p. 207.

75 J. Piaget (1931). 'L'individualité en histoire', L'Individualité: 3ème semaine internationale de synthèse (Individuality: 3rd International Week of Synthesis, organized by the Centre International de Synthèse), Paris, 15–23 May, p. 115.

76 Piaget (1916), op. cit.; Piaget (1918), op. cit.

77 Piaget (1925), op. cit., pp. 204–205.

78 Reymond (1917), op. cit., p. 53. From the same perspective and in circumstances a little different, some 30 years later, Piaget would take on teaching at the Collège de France, in 1942, which he spoke about in these terms: 'The hour when academics feel the need to show their solidarity in face of violence, and their fidelity to permanent values': J. Piaget (1947). *La psychologie de l'intelligence* (p. 5). Paris:

Armon & Colin. [English translation: *The psychology of intelligence*. Totowa, NJ: Littlefield Adams, 1972.]

79 See in particular Piaget (1922), op. cit., p. 82.

80 R. van der Veer (1996). Vygotsky and Piaget: A collective monologue. *Human Development*, *39*, 237–242. Van der Veer shows that Piaget had known since the 1920s how critical Vygotsky was of his theory but he did not want to take up the matter. Did he feel personally vulnerable on this point? Did he fear recognizing a formidable adversary? Or did he hold back because of his own political and ideological stance in the difficult post-war period?

81 For a discussion of this question that fundamentally divided Piaget and Vygotsky, see A.-N. Perret-Clermont (1995). Les partenaires de l'intelligence. *Vous avez dit pédagogie*, *40*, 10–17.

82 See Chapter 3 of the present volume.

83 Piaget (1931), op. cit., pp. 96, 99.

84 Reymond, op. cit., p. 13.

85 In 1925, in the preface of his work *Le sentiment religieux et la psychologie de l'enfant*, Pierre Bovet wrote: 'The research undertaken in a completely independent manner by Mr Jean Piaget, and continued by him since 1922, at the Rousseau Institute, on the reasoning of the child, has opened new avenues in thinking.' Bovet took the precaution here of emphasizing the autonomy of the one whom he had just named head of his institute. Why would Bovet have taken this unusual precaution? Was it a respectful and laudatory attitude (protective, even) or prudence in handling a vengeful attitude of the junior who allowed himself to be called 'boss' by his collaborators a few years later at the same institute?

86 See Chapter 3 of the present volume.

87 Ibid.

88 P.-Y. Châtelain (1994). Les manuels d'histoire Suisse dans l'école primaire neuchâteloise (1850–1900). *Musée neuchâtelois*, *3*, 238.

89 A. Daguet (1872). *L'Educateur*, pp. 211–212.

90 Châtelain, op. cit., p. 139.

91 J. Piaget (1931). Post-scriptum à la 'Pensée philosophique en Suisse romande de 1900 à nos jours' par A. Reymond. *Revue de théologie et de philosophie*, *81*, October–December, 20.

92 J. Piaget (1925). Psychologie et critique de la connaissance. *Archives de psychologie*, *19*, 196.

93 Piaget often acknowledged that the *results* of Pierre Bovet had inspired him, particularly in his work on moral judgement. See J. Piaget (1930b) Les procédés de l'education morale Rapport. *Cinquième congrès international d'éducation morale* (pp. 182–219). Paris: Alcan; (1932) *Le jugement moral chez l'enfant*. Paris: Alcan; p. 301 of 1957 edition. The question that we are asking here is relevant to the *methods* of investigation.

94 See Reymond (1931), op. cit., p. 13.

95 For example: Vinh Bang (1966/1988). *Textes choisis* (p. 39). Geneva: Faculty of Psychology and of Science of Education, Geneva University.

96 P. Bovet (1922). L'éducation de l'instinct social. *L'Educateur*, *48*, 145–150; Bovet (1925), op. cit.

97 E. Claparède (1946). *Psychologie de l'enfant et pédagogie expérimentale*. I: *Le développement mental* (re-edition). Neuchâtel: Delachaux & Niestlé.

98 Piaget (1965), op. cit., pp. 23–24.

99 This is not a matter of Piaget going from the banks of Lake Neuchâtel to those of Lake Geneva! In fact, Piaget sought to observe the processes of adaptation of molluscs from Neuchâtel thrown into the waters of Geneva: would they pass on to their descendants new characteristics that they had acquired as a result of this uprooting?

100 See especially P. Bovet (1922). L'éducation de l'instinct social. *L'Educateur*, *48*, 145–150.

101 Piaget (1929), op. cit., 17, p. 149.

102 Ibid., p. 150.

103 P. Bridel (1923). Le sens de la vie. Christian Association of Students in French-Switzerland, *Sainte-Croix 1922*, Lausanne, pp. 16–37.

104 Reymond (1931), op. cit., pp. 14–14 [emphasis in original].

105 Piaget (1929), op. cit., pp. 151–152.

106 See Note 65; and P. Bovet (1965) *Un siècle de l'histoire de Grandchamp: entre la fabrique d'indiennes et la communauté spirituelle*. Citta di Castello, Italy: Tiferno; J.-P. Mouchet (1967) *L'école secondaire de Boudry-Cortaillod. Grandchamp, 1876–1967*. Boudry, Neuchâtel: La baconnière. We are grateful to Sister Irmtraud of the Evangelical Community of Grandchamp for this reference. See also G. de Rougemont & G. Bovet with the participation of M. Bovet (1992) *La geste des Bovet de Grandchamp*. Boudry, Neuchâtel: Baillod.

107 Piaget (1918), op. cit., p. 116.

108 Ibid., p. 117.

109 But this fact should not make us forget the contacts between the two milieux. Claparède's wife was Russian, and she may have contributed to Vygotsky's awareness of Piaget's early works, which were quickly translated into Russian.

110 Does one not find traces of intellectual transactions that manifested the Piagetian model? 'Give me your point of view and I will give you mine; we will judge the respective values and reach an agreement', one could say.

111 Certainly Piaget recognized the importance of the socialization of individual thought through interaction with peers. But it is always the subject's own initial thought that evolves and is not a matter of 'collective interventions' or resolving 'socio-cognitive conflicts'. It is for this reason that we think the Piagetian model remains centred on the *ego*.

112 A.-N. Perret-Clermont et al. (2005). *Thinking time: A multidisciplinary perspective on time*. Paris: L'Harmattan.

113 R. Hinde, A.-N. Perret-Clermont, & J. Stevenson-Hinde (Eds.) (1985) *Social relationships and cognitive development*. Oxford: Oxford University Press; M. Grossen & A.-N. Perret-Clermont (Eds.) (1992) *L'espace thérapeutique: Cadres et contextes*. Neuchâtel & Paris: Delachaux & Niestlé.

114 C. Hoyles & E. Forman (Eds.) (1995). Processes and products of collaborative problem solving. *Cognition and Instruction*, special issue, *13*, 479–587.

115 Piaget (1918), op. cit., pp. 117–118.

Index